Mashups

Mashups

Strategies for the Modern Enterprise

J. Jeffrey Hanson

✦Addison-Wesley

Upper Saddle River, NJ • Boston • Indianapolis • San Francisco
New York • Toronto • Montreal • London • Munich • Paris • Madrid
Capetown • Sydney • Tokyo • Singapore • Mexico City

Many of the designations used by manufacturers and sellers to distinguish their products are claimed as trademarks. Where those designations appear in this book, and the publisher was aware of a trademark claim, the designations have been printed with initial capital letters or in all capitals.

The author and publisher have taken care in the preparation of this book, but make no expressed or implied warranty of any kind and assume no responsibility for errors or omissions. No liability is assumed for incidental or consequential damages in connection with or arising out of the use of the information or programs contained herein.

The publisher offers excellent discounts on this book when ordered in quantity for bulk purchases or special sales, which may include electronic versions and/or custom covers and content particular to your business, training goals, marketing focus, and branding interests. For more information, please contact:

U.S. Corporate and Government Sales
(800) 382-3419
corpsales@pearsontechgroup.com

For sales outside the United States please contact:

International Sales
international@pearson.com

Visit us on the Web: informit.com/aw

Library of Congress Cataloging-in-Publication Data

Hanson, J. Jeffrey.
   Mashups : strategies for the modern enterprise / J. Jeffrey Hanson.
      p.   cm.
   Includes index.
   ISBN 978-0-321-59181-4 (pbk. : alk. paper) 1. Software engineering. 2. Mashups (World Wide Web) 3. Web site development. I. Title.

   QA76.758.H363 2009
   006.7—dc22

2009004655

ISBN-13: 978-0-321-59181-4
ISBN-10:   0-321-59181-X
Text printed in the United States on recycled paper at RR Donnelley in Crawfordsville, Indiana.
First printing, May 2009

Editor-in-Chief
Mark L. Taub

Acquisitions Editor
Trina MacDonald

Editorial Assistant
Olivia Basegio

Development Editor
Michael Thurston

Managing Editor
John Fuller

Full-Service Production Manager
Julie B. Nahil

Copy Editor
Geneil Breeze

Indexer
Michael Loo

Proofreader
Linda Begley

Cover Designer
Chuti Prasertsith

Compositor
Rob Mauhar

I want to dedicate this book to my children and grandchildren, and to Sandy, for being there when I needed you.

Contents

Preface

In this book I introduce you to a trend in software engineering that will permeate several areas of software development for many years to come. This trend is referred to as "mashups," and in this book I discuss the concepts of mashup implementations as they affect the enterprise.

The discussions and projects started while writing this book will continue to be a work in progress as the mashup landscape evolves.

I chose the topic of mashups for this book because I am excited to see the things that are being done with mashup development and to see this excitement starting to crop up in the enterprise as organizations begin to adopt a mashup development mindset. Companies such as JackBe, IBM, Microsoft, Yahoo!, and others have developed powerful mashup tools and environments that are beginning to show the power mashups can offer to an enterprise.

I have been privileged for a couple of decades to see many attempts to create an environment in which existing UI artifacts and processes can be reused with little or no programming intervention. Mashup development using semantic technologies, reusable markup-based UI artifacts, and metadata-enabled data formats has reached the point at which powerful applications and services can be constructed with existing code, data, and UI components using very little programming intervention.

Overview of This Book

This book discusses implementation strategies, frameworks, and code samples for enterprise mashups. The term "mashup" originated from the music industry to define the technique of producing a new song by mixing together two or more existing songs. The term has been adopted by the software development industry to define applications created by mixing user-interface artifacts, processes, and/or content from multiple sources, typically using high-level web programming languages such as HTML, JavaScript, and others.

A mashup infrastructure enables a development model that can produce new pages, applications, and services rapidly with very little additional work. The use and reuse of semantic web technologies, user interface artifacts, and loosely coupled services provide a powerful domain for mashup application development.

Mashups are being created at an almost unprecedented rate for different consumer and social environments. This trend is starting to spill over into the enterprise domain due to the power and speed with which development teams can create new services, applications, and data transformations by exploiting the agile and dynamic environment of mashup infrastructures. Some of the more popular, publicly accessible mashups include HousingMaps, TwitterVision, Big Contacts, Weather Bank, and others.

As mashups begin to migrate to the enterprise, more sophisticated programming languages and constructs become involved. Lower-level concepts also become involved including data mediation and transformations, interprocess communications, single sign-on, governance, and compliance to name a few.

This book discusses how developers can create new user interfaces by reusing existing UI artifacts using high-level web page markup and scripting languages such as HTML and JavaScript. Also discussed is the ability that a mashup infrastructure gives to developers to integrate disparate data using semantically rich data formats.

The ideas presented in this book are focused on implementation strategies using such technologies as XML, Java, JavaScript, JSON, RDF, HTML, RSS, and others. The discussions presented in this book look at programming and scripting languages in a generic sense—that is, I do not attempt to address mashup implementations across all popular frameworks. For example, I do not delve into how mashups can be implemented using Spring, JSF, Struts, and so on. However, whenever possible, I do mention some of the more prevalent frameworks that can be used to address a specific need.

It is my hope that a reader of this book will gain a good understanding of the main concepts of mashup development, particularly as applied to the enterprise. I present code examples and actual working mashups. I seek to provide a reader with a running start into mashup development for the enterprise.

Target Audience for This Book

This book is intended for use by software/web developers as well as by managers, executives, and others seriously interested in concepts and strategies surrounding mashups and enterprise mashups. The book strives to serve as an instructive, reliable introduction to the enterprise mashup arena. I hope that the book will answer many of the questions that might be asked by those seeking to gain a good foundation for discovering the world of mashup development. This book also describes solid business reasons for choosing enterprise mashups: speed of implementation, quick results, and rapid value-add.

To get the most use of this book, it is advisable that you briefly introduce yourself to HTML, JavaScript, XML, Java, and the basics of the HTTP protocol. However, many of the abstract concepts of mashups and mashup development can be garnered from this book without the need of programming skills.

About JSF, Spring, Hibernate, and Other Java Frameworks

The goal of this book is to present the concepts and techniques for designing and building enterprise mashups and enterprise mashup infrastructures. Concepts and techniques for mashups and mashup infrastructures are topics broad enough to discuss without attempting to weave in the specifics of multiple frameworks such as Spring, JSF, Hibernate, and Struts. Also, many of the concepts and techniques for mashups are currently realized using web page markup and scripting languages such as HTML and JavaScript. However, where warranted, I highlighted some frameworks that fill a specific niche for tasks such as transforming data, authentication, manipulating XML, and providing kernel functionality.

Frameworks such as Spring, JSF, Hibernate, Struts, EJB3, JPA, and others are very powerful. For example:

- Spring provides libraries and frameworks for building rich web applications, integrating with BlazeDS, building document-driven web services, securing enterprise applications, supporting Java modularity, integrating with external systems, building model-view-controller (MVC) applications, and others. Spring also includes a popular MVC framework.

- JavaServer Faces (JSF) is a set of APIs and a custom JSP tag library for building user interfaces for web applications, managing UI-component state, handling UI events, validating input parameters, defining page navigation, and other tasks.

- Struts is an MVC framework that extends the Java servlet API to allow developers to build sophisticated web flows using the Java programming language.

- Hibernate is an object-relational mapping (ORM) framework that allows developers to map a Java-based object model to relational database tables.

These frameworks are ubiquitous and, of course, useful, and one might expect to find a discussion of each of them in a book such as this. However, they are not mashup-oriented in nature at this point and would, therefore, require the reader to have an in-depth knowledge of each framework to engage the reader in a coherent discussion as they relate to mashups. With this in mind, I have chosen to keep my discussions of mashups and the Java programming language as generic as possible. A detailed discussion of building enterprise mashups using frameworks such as these deserves a complete book for each. Some enterprises purposely disallow JavaScript in user interfaces. It is a good idea to explore JSF tools, such as JBoss Rich Faces, which includes artifacts that intelligently manage JavaScript availability.

Acknowledgments

During the course of writing this book I have received good advice and ideas on how to improve it. I thank the many editors and reviewers for that as it has directed my efforts towards a more relevant and effective result.

About the Author

J. Jeffrey Hanson has more than twenty-two years of experience in the software industry, including work as senior engineer for the Microsoft Windows port of the OpenDoc project and lead architect for the Route 66 framework at Novell. Jeff was an original member of the expert group for JSR 160: Java Management Extensions (JMX) Remote API. He is currently the CTO for Max International, LLC, where he directs efforts in building mashup infrastructures to support service-oriented and resource-oriented systems within the retail/wholesale industry. Jeff is the author of numerous articles and books, including *.NET versus J2EE Web Services: A Comparison of Approaches* and *Pro JMX: Java Management Extensions*, and is coauthor of *Web Services Business Strategies and Architectures*. Jeff's software engineering experience spans many different industries, including mortgage lending, newspaper publishing, word processing, networking infrastructures, retail banking, developer tools, reinsurance, IP filtering, and retail marketing.

Introduction

The term "mashup" originated with the technique of producing a new song by mixing together two or more existing songs. This was most notably referred to in the context of hip-hop music. Mashup applications are composed of multiple user interface components or artifacts and/or content from multiple data sources. In the context of software engineering, the term "mashup" defines the result of combining existing user interface artifacts, processes, services, and/or data to create new web pages, applications, processes, and data sets.

Very rapid implementations of new functionality are afforded by mashups via the use of semantic web technologies, reusable user interface artifacts, and loosely coupled services. Many different consumer and social spaces use mashups. However, enterprises are beginning to reap the benefits afforded by a mashup environment. Mashups create an extremely agile and dynamic design and implementation environment within the enterprise realm allowing users with limited technical skills to develop powerful and useful applications and services.

In a mashup environment, users can create new user interfaces by reusing existing UI artifacts using high-level scripting languages such as HTML and JavaScript. Mashups also enable users to integrate disparate data very quickly and easily using semantically rich data formats that don't require complex programming and middleware technologies. Services and processes are beginning to be integrated with similar speed and ease using loosely coupled techniques inherited from the lessons learned from service-oriented architecture (SOA) solutions.

Web 1.0 to Web 2.0 to Web 3.0

Technologies surrounding the presence of an organization or user have taken two significant steps over time, transitioning from what is sometimes referred to as "Web 1.0" to what has become known as "Web 2.0." Web 1.0 began with the first HTML-based browsers and, even though it still lingers in many web sites, the Web 1.0 model has evolved rapidly towards a Web 2.0 model.

1

Web 1.0 delivered content in a static manner using HTML markup and simple HTML forms. Applications written to a Web 1.0 model typically responded to HTTP requests with entire web page updates created from data pulled from relational tables and content management systems using standard web application programming languages such as Perl, C, C++, Java, and others.

Web 2.0, fueled by ubiquitous access to broadband, originated soon after the turn of the century and is in some form in most up-to-date web sites and web applications today. Web 2.0 moves the online experience away from static content delivery towards a model based on interactive participation, blogging and RSS feeds, search and tagging, AJAX and partial-page updates, collaboration and social networking, wikis, online bookmarking and content sharing, and so on. Web 2.0 turned the Internet into a true application platform. Technologies surrounding Web 2.0 have led to the enablement of shareable and embeddable UI artifacts such as widgets, dynamic JavaScript, videos, and HTML snippets.

Web 3.0 is a term that describes the next online evolutionary trend following the Web 2.0 model. The model for Web 3.0 is emerging as a transformation to a decentralized and adaptable framework across virtually any type of connected entity including web browsers, desktops, handheld devices, and proprietary firmware. Content and functionality are delivered in the Web 3.0 model via on-demand software as a service (SaaS), cloud computing, open APIs, standard web-based protocols, and semantically rich data formats. Content is secured using open, decentralized, security protocols and standards. Web 3.0 is moving organizations away from proprietary, closed systems to a model that encourages sharing, collaboration, and reuse.

To many, mashups are becoming synonymous with Web 3.0. Mashups are the embodiment of true open, reusable, web-based components and data. This concept will certainly change the way organizations do business and yield a flood of activity towards enterprise mashups.

Overview of Mashup Technologies

Technologies used today to produce a mashup application include HTML snippets, widgets, dynamic JavaScript, AJAX, and semantic-web formats. Content for a mashup is retrieved from internal systems as well as third-party web sites. Protocols and data formats include HTTP, HTTPS, XML, SOAP, RDF, JSON, and others.

Mashups are created ad hoc most of the time. However, in the enterprise realm, mashup applications must take into consideration such things as privacy, authentication, governance, compliance, and other business-related constraints.

Mashups can combine data from disparate data sources, existing UI artifacts, and/or existing software processes or services. The specific design for a mashup depends on whether the mashup will be visual or nonvisual. In many cases an enterprise mashup solution will be a combination of data, UI artifacts, and software processes. The solution might be a combination of nonvisual and visual efforts.

Ultimately, a mashup application exploits existing data, UI artifacts, and software processes to create new applications and services that might also be exploited as components for other mashup efforts. This propagation of reusable components or modules is creating a revolutionary atmosphere where underlying programming frameworks and languages are irrelevant and higher-level scripting languages, semantics, and UI components are emerging as the primary application enablers.

Figure I.1 illustrates a shopping-specific mashup application that combines data gathered from a geocoding site, a wholesaler site, a local database, and a social networking site. The data is then mashed together inside a browser web page to form the new application.

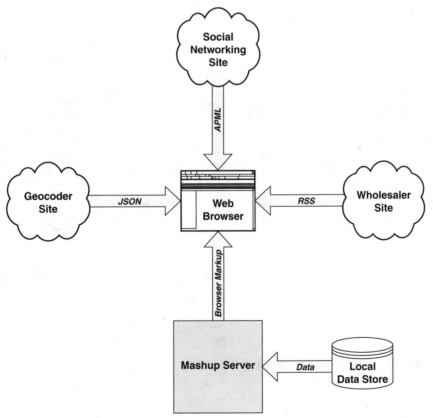

Figure I.1   *A shopping-specific mashup application combining data within a browser web page*

As shown in Figure I.1 data for a mashup can be retrieved from a number of different locations and combined within a browser web page to create a new application or interface. Building a mashup in this scenario typically uses Java-Script processing and DOM manipulation within the browser page to create the user interface for the new application.

Mashups can be created using traditional programming languages outside the browser. Figure I.2 illustrates a shopping-specific mashup application that combines data gathered from a geocoding site, a wholesaler site, a local database, and a social networking site. The data is then mashed together inside a mashup server to create the new application.

As shown in Figure I.2 data for a mashup can be retrieved from a number of different locations and combined within a mashup server to create a new application or interface. Building a mashup in this scenario typically uses traditional programming languages such as Java, PHP, Python, C#, Perl, Ruby, and C++ to integrate the data. The user interface for the new application is created using traditional web frameworks such as JSP, ASP, Struts, and others.

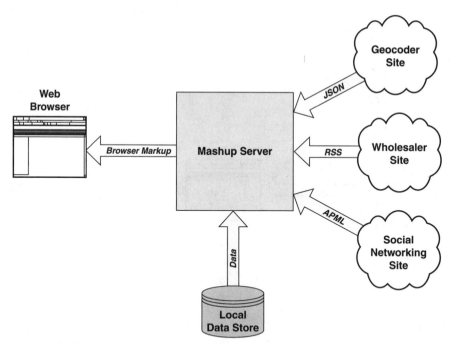

Figure I.2   *A shopping-specific mashup application combining data within a mashup server*

Enterprise Mashup Technological Domains

Mashup domains depend on what is to be "mashed" together. Generally, three high-level categories of items can be mashed together—user interface artifacts (presentation), data, and/or application functionality (processes). This might include HTML snippets, on-demand JavaScript to access an external API, web service APIs from one of your corporate servers, RSS feeds, and/or other data to be mixed and mashed within the application or pages. The implementation style, techniques, and technologies used for a given mashup depend on this determination. Once the items are determined, a development team can proceed with applying languages, processes, and methodologies to the application at hand.

Technologies used to create a mashup also depend on the sources from which the mashup items will be accessed, the talents a development staff needs to build the mashup, and the services that need to be created or accessed to retrieve the necessary artifacts for the mashup.

Mashups rely on the ability to mix loosely coupled artifacts within a given technological domain. The requirements of the application determine what artifacts (UI, data, and/or functionality) are needed to build the mashup.

From a high-level perspective, the technological domain as applied to mashups can be viewed as presentation-oriented, data-oriented, and process-oriented. Different languages, methodologies, and programming techniques apply to each technological domain.

As shown in Figure I.3, mashup categories can be divided according to presentation artifacts, data, and application functionality/processes.

Certain preparations must be made to design and implement a mashup that is ready for the enterprise. Primary areas of concern are requirements and constraints, security, governance, stability, performance, data, implementation, and testing. Certain aspects of each area of concern are unique to the environment of enterprise mashups in respect to other enterprise software disciplines.

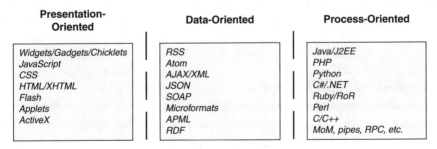

Presentation-Oriented	Data-Oriented	Process-Oriented
Widgets/Gadgets/Chicklets	RSS	Java/J2EE
JavaScript	Atom	PHP
CSS	AJAX/XML	Python
HTML/XHTML	JSON	C#/.NET
Flash	SOAP	Ruby/RoR
Applets	Microformats	Perl
ActiveX	APML	C/C++
	RDF	MoM, pipes, RPC, etc.

Figure I.3 *Three primary mashup technological domains*

The requirements and constraints for an enterprise mashup must integrate with the existing policies and practices of the environment for a company or enterprise. Identifying the requirements and constraints for a mashup is an evolutionary process, since the environment is bound to be affected by the mashup community with which it will interact. However, there are some basic requirements and constraints of a mashup that can be identified and addressed. As the mashup evolves these items will evolve or be replaced.

Preparing for enterprise mashup implementations involves a thorough understanding of the processes and IT landscape unique to a given company and/or industry. Techniques and technologies used for one company or industry are generally transferable to another; however, some aspects are unique and must not be overlooked. In fact, these very points of uniqueness typically create the most value for an enterprise mashup. Effectively exposing the distinctive facets of an organization is a primary goal of any online endeavor. Achieving this goal with a mashup infrastructure can add value in ways that are not even apparent until a given mashup community is exposed to the resources and artifacts you present. Once a community becomes actively involved with your mashup infrastructure, the infrastructure itself evolves as a result of the community's unified creativity. Therefore, it is very important for an organization to make sure it has certain foundational preparations in place in anticipation of this creative evolution.

Considerations Unique to the Enterprise Mashup Domain

An enterprise mashup must heed a more restrictive set of considerations such as compliance, standards, and security that public domain mashups are often free to ignore. In addition, a company or enterprise mashup must not expose certain types of intellectual property and/or protected information. This is similar to the issues that service-oriented organizations face when exposing service APIs to the web community. Enterprise mashups face the same issues as well as new issues related to data and UI artifacts that may be used by the mashup community.

If the promise of mashups is realized and a company or enterprise does experience a viral wave of activity and popularity due to its mashup environment, the company or enterprise must be ready to handle the surge of online activity. This is why preparatory efforts relating to security, performance, and scalability must be taken to ensure that your infrastructure will handle the surge. Every aspect of an IT infrastructure should be optimized and modularized to enable as much flexibility and, therefore, creativity as possible. The atmosphere of a community-based creative mind can be created; not only in the presentation domain, but in the data domain and process domain as well if you take the proper steps to create an infrastructure that supports loosely coupled interactions throughout.

Implicit to a loosely coupled infrastructure hoping to benefit from a viral community is the importance of the ability of a company or enterprise to monitor and manage the infrastructure effectively. As viral effects take place, it is inevitable that bottlenecks in the infrastructure will be encountered even after painstaking efforts are taken in the design and implementation of the infrastructure. Therefore, it is vital that a potent monitoring and management framework be in place to identify bottlenecks quickly so that they might be rectified immediately.

As shown in Figure I.4, a typical loosely coupled enterprise architecture embodies a number of different frameworks from which data, services, processes, and user interface components emerge.

The need for an agile security model for an enterprise mashup cannot be emphasized enough. Since the mashup infrastructure will need to handle requests and invocations from a vast array of clients and environments, the mashup infrastructure must be ready to handle many types of identity management and access controls. Since it is impossible to know beforehand just how

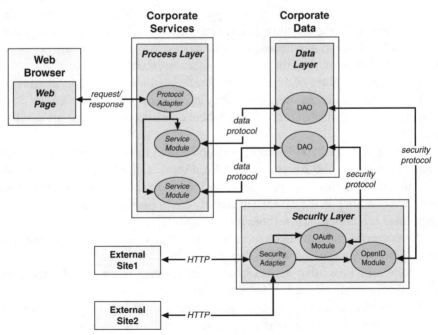

Figure I.4 *Typical loosely coupled enterprise architecture*

data modules, UI artifacts, and services will be used by the mashup community, an organization must have an infrastructure in place that allows it to control how its information is used without inhibiting creativity.

Being able to support an agile and viral environment is also very important when it comes to deploying enterprise mashups and the components of the mashups. Flexible deployment techniques and technologies must be used throughout the scope of the infrastructure to allow updates and enhancements to be deployed without affecting the mashup community's interactions with the mashup infrastructure. This includes activities related to editing and/or execution of the mashup artifacts.

Finally, the enterprise mashup and its artifacts must be tested. Testing enterprise mashups and mashup artifacts is one of the most important tasks a company or enterprise must address since the infrastructure and artifacts will be exposed to such a dynamic and vast community. Methods and techniques for testing mashups and mashup artifacts must be as agile and dynamic as the environment in which they will operate.

Solving Technological Problems

An enterprise mashup infrastructure must present solutions for a very agile and evolutionary environment. Data sources can change rapidly, services are added and changed at any given time, presentation technologies are constantly being integrated with the system, marketing and sales departments are eager to apply the potential facilitated by the easy UI generation model, and so on.

The dynamic nature of an enterprise mashup environment must be flexible and powerful enough to handle existing business operations as well as many new operations that arise out of the dynamic nature of the mashup development model.

An enterprise mashup infrastructure can be used to update, access, and integrate unstructured and structured data from sources of all kinds. An enterprise mashup infrastructure can apply structure to extracted data that was previously unstructured. Such is the case when structure is applied to an ordinary HTML page using screen-scraping techniques.

An enterprise mashup infrastructure presents views of existing resources and data to other applications where they are restructured and aggregated to form new composite views that may even create new semantic meaning for the composite data and, therefore, for the enterprise itself.

As shown in Figure I.5, an enterprise mashup infrastructure provides a number of different frameworks and layers from which data, services, processes, and user interface components are integrated.

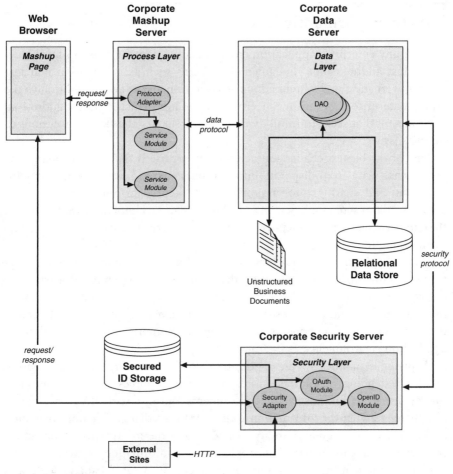

Figure I.5 *High-level view of an enterprise mashup infrastructure*

An enterprise mashup infrastructure helps to solve nonvisual integration problems as well as visually related problems. Nonvisual integration solutions enabled using the resource-oriented and semantic nature of an enterprise mashup infrastructure can be applied directly to specific business problems or indirectly through the orchestration and aggregation of the reusable components presented by the infrastructure.

Addressing mashups in a nonvisual sense relies on accurate and comprehensive organization and structure of information using semantically rich data formats to create an environment where content and data are easily discovered and reused.

Structuring Semantic Data

As with any enterprise application environment, enterprise mashup infrastructures must address some fundamental concerns such as information management, governance, and system administration to name a few. In addition to the typical enterprise application concerns, mashup infrastructures must address an environment that seeks to fulfill dynamic requirements and flexible solutions to business issues.

One of the biggest challenges facing an enterprise is that issue of managing and sharing data from disparate information sources. Legacy mechanisms for managing and sharing information typically kept data and metadata (data about the data) separated. Semantic techniques and technologies seek to bridge the gap between data and metadata to present a more effective means for applying meaning to information.

Choosing the fundamental format for data within your mashup infrastructure should be one of the first areas that you address. Mashup infrastructures derive much of their benefit from being able to apply and present semantic meaning to data and content. This enables consumers of the data and content to create aggregate components and content much more easily than traditional application environments.

Applying semantics to an aggregate repository of corporate information involves extending typical data stores and content sources to enable the information stored within unstructured documents and files with structured meaning, thereby giving the information sources features that enable both machines and humans with a greater ability to understand the information. Once effective semantic meaning has been applied to an information source, the data stored within can be discovered, aggregated, automated, augmented, and reused more effectively.

As shown in Figure I.6, an enterprise mashup infrastructure can provide components, modules, and frameworks to transform and enable data with semantic richness.

Figure I.6 illustrates some of the disparate sources from which corporate information is stored and how a mashup infrastructure might provide a solution for structuring the data from these sources with semantic meaning.

When determining a solution for building a semantic foundation, an organization should turn to formal specifications. These specifications currently include XML, the Resource Description Framework (RDF), the Web Ontology Language (OWL), RDF Schema (RDFS), microformats, and others.

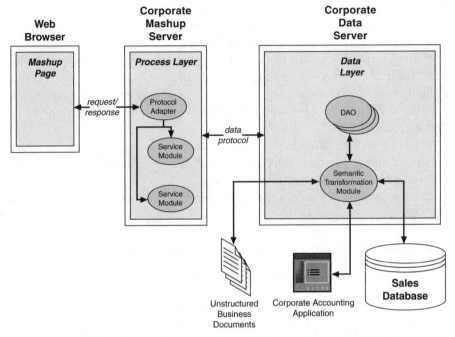

Figure I.6 *High-level view of semantically enabled enterprise mashup infrastructure*

Effective Design Patterns

Software design patterns present tested and proven blueprints for addressing recurring problems or situations that arise in many different design and development scenarios. By defining a design/development solution in terms of a pattern, problems can be solved without the need to rehash the same problem over and over in an attempt to provide a custom solution each time.

Using design patterns for software development is a concept that was borrowed from architecture as it applied to building homes, workplaces, and cities. The idea revolved around the concept that looking at problems abstractly presented common solutions to different architectural problems. The same concept was applied to software engineering and proved to work equally as well.

Design and implementation efforts of a mashup share many of the same development issues as traditional software engineering. Therefore, many of the same techniques and methodologies that provide successful results to traditional software paradigms work equally as well with mashup development. Software patterns are one of the most widely used methodologies in traditional software engineering and are also strongly suggested as a mechanism for addressing mashup design and development scenarios.

Since mashups address many different, dynamic scenarios and technologies, finding any sort of common ground on which to base design and implementation decisions can be a great help to software practitioners.

Mashups are very data-intensive. Therefore patterns that define common solutions to the conversion or adaptation of different data formats offer a substantial benefit to developers. A pattern defining a common solution for enriching data as the data is transferred from one module to another offers significant benefits, as well.

Mashups seek to provide rich experiences for client-side users. Therefore, patterns defining common solutions applied to AJAX, JavaScript, XML, and CSS can provide benefits to UI developers.

The following is a list of some of the mashup activities for which patterns can offer useful design help:

- Semantic formats and patterns for data access and extraction

- Semantic formats and patterns for data transfer and reuse

- Patterns and methods for data presentation

- Patterns and methods for scheduling and observation

- Content reuse with clipping

- Data/content augmentation patterns for normalizing content

- Patterns and purposes for notifications and alerts

With many of the processes in a mashup running externally in the Internet cloud, it is extremely desirable to find common patterns that address issues such as scalability, security, and manageability within this nebulous environment.

Unique Security Constraints

A mashup development model is very open by definition. This openness introduces many new security risks; therefore, security must be a primary concern when developing a mashup infrastructure.

Traditional mechanisms such as firewalls and DMZs are not sufficient for the granularity of access that mashups require for UI artifacts and data. The mashup infrastructure itself must be prepared to deal with issues such as cross-site request forgery (CSRF), AJAX security weaknesses, cross-site scripting, and secure sign-on across multiple domains.

The fact that a mashup is a page or application built typically using data combined from more than one site, illustrates the manner in which security vulnerabilities can multiply quickly. As new invocations are added to access resources or to call service API, new security vulnerabilities become possible. In addition, external mashups can embed your components and UI artifacts, thereby combining your functionality and data with components and UI artifacts of unknown origin. These wide-open integration possibilities make it imperative to ensure that your data and functionality are not open to hacker attempts and other forms of intrusion.

The most common attack scenarios within a mashup environment are cross-site scripting, JSON hijacking, denial of service attacks, and cross-site request forgeries.

The intrinsic openness of a mashup environment and the inability to predict exactly how components of a mashup infrastructure will be used in the future implies the need to address security at every aspect of the development lifecycle. Therefore, security must be a primary part of a development team's code review and testing processes.

A mashup environment most likely uses components and UI artifacts developed externally. This means that testing external components must be included in a development team's testing process right alongside an organization's own components. External components should be tested individually and in aggregate with other components of a given mashup.

One of the most important steps for any organization is to institute best practices and mashup security policies based on standards established by industry, government, and compliance groups.

When instituting a security policy, an organization should note the following guidelines:

- Create a thorough security policy.

- Establish a proper authentication and authorization plan.

- Allow for flexibility.

- Employ message-level and transport-level security.

- Implement corporate standards for secure usage patterns.

- Support industry security standards.

Conceptual Layers of an Enterprise Mashup

A mashup infrastructure must expose and support programming entities that can be combined in a mashup. The infrastructure must also address the corresponding issues and solutions for each type of entity. This is modeled as three high-level categories of items: user interface artifacts (presentation), data (resources), and/or application functionality (processes). UI artifacts include such entities as HTML snippets, on-demand JavaScript, web service APIs, RSS feeds, and/or other sundry pieces of data. The implementation style, techniques, and technologies used for each category of mashup items present certain constraints and subtleties.

Content and UI artifacts used to build a mashup are gathered from a number of different sources including third-party sites exposing web service APIs, widgets, and on-demand JavaScript. RSS and Atom feeds are also common places from which mashup content is retrieved. Some tools are now exposing services that will glean content and information from any existing site using screen-scraping techniques.

The three-category architecture of mashup web applications is discussed next.

Presentation Layer

The presentation layer for a mashup can pull from a local service platform, publicly available APIs, RSS data feeds, dynamic JavaScript snippets, widgets, badges, and so on. The presentation layer uses technologies and techniques for viewing disparate data in a unified manner. This unified view integrates UI artifacts representing business documents, geocoded maps, RSS feeds, calendar gadgets, and others.

The presentation layer for an agile and powerful enterprise mashup application depends on a modular and flexible infrastructure. The foundation for an effective enterprise mashup infrastructure is typically structured around a multilayered platform. The layers for the mashup infrastructure can be implemented as interconnected modules that manage service registrations, service unregistrations, and service lifecycles.

Since mashups are based on principles of modularity and service-oriented concepts, a modular technology is warranted that combines aspects of these principles to define a dynamic service deployment framework facilitating remote management.

Data Layer

UI artifacts and processes for a mashup infrastructure rely on content and data from multiple sources. Content and data are modeled as resources. Resources can be retrieved using a REST (Representational State Transfer)-based invocation model. In other words, resources are created, retrieved, updated, and deleted using a simple syntax that relies on URIs to define the location of each resource.

A mashup infrastructure should provide a mashup data layer that can access data from multiple sources perhaps using a REST-based invocation model. The resources can then be serialized to a mashup application or page in different semantic formats.

The data layer for a mashup infrastructure combines data in one of two ways: client-side data integration or server-side data integration, as discussed next.

Client-Side Data Integration

In client-side data integration, data is retrieved from multiple sites and mixed together in a client-side application pane or web page typically using scripting techniques and languages such as JavaScript, AJAX, and DOM manipulation. In this type of mashup, data is returned from a site or server in the form of XML, RSS, JSON, Atom, and so on. Much of the data returned originates from data-oriented services sometimes referred to as Data-as-a-Service (DaaS). DaaS describes a data-oriented service API that can be called without relying on third-party processes or components between the service provider and the service consumer.

Figure I.7 illustrates data being integrated on the client in a mashup infrastructure.

Server-Side Data Integration

In server-side data integration, data is retrieved and mixed at the server using technologies such as Java, Python, Perl, and C++, among others. In this style, mashup data is retrieved from one or more sites/servers and used as values or configuration settings to create new data models within a server-side process.

Figure I.8 illustrates data being integrated on the server in a mashup infrastructure.

Process Layer

Processes in the mashup infrastructure can be encapsulated as independent services. Each service can be defined and deployed within the context of a module

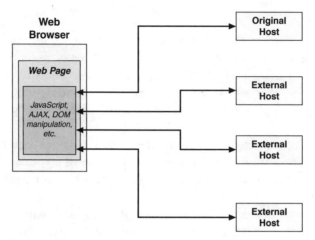

Figure I.7 *Client-side data integration*

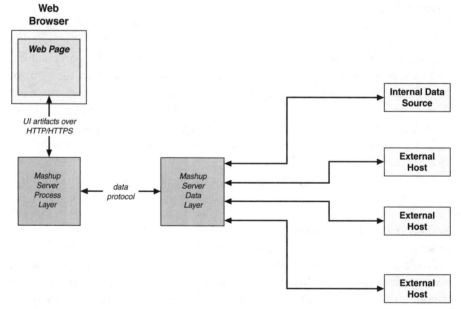

Figure I.8 *Server-side data integration*

managed by a service container. Service modules might consist of one or more services that are deployed automatically to the service container.

The process layer will combine functionality together in one or more aggregate processes using programming languages such as Java, PHP, Python, C++, and so on. Mashups built for enterprise applications or web applications can involve frameworks such as JEE, .NET, and Ruby on Rails.

In the process layer, functionality is combined using interprocess/interthread communication techniques such as shared memory, message queues/buses, and remote procedure calls (RPC), to name a few. The aggregate result of the process layer differs from the data layer in that the data layer derives new data models, whereas the process layer derives new processes and/or services.

Due to the number of disparate sources from which functionality and data are typically retrieved for an enterprise mashup, enterprises often employ a hybrid approach when building a mashup infrastructure.

Using REST Principles for Enterprise Mashups

Interactions within an enterprise mashup often involve the exchange of data from one or more hosts. Data is often referred to as a resource. Therefore, it is important to provide coherent interfaces for resources exposed by an enterprise mashup infrastructure. The resource-oriented architecture defined by Roy Thomas Fielding in his Representational State Transfer (REST) dissertation is a model used by many mashup frameworks and platforms.

REST is a model for interacting with resources using a common, finite set of methods. For the HTTP protocol, this is embodied in the standard methods GET, POST, PUT, DELETE, and sometimes HEAD. In a REST-based application or interaction, resources are identified by a URI. The response for REST-based invocation is referred to as a representation of the resource.

To help define interfaces for accessing resources in a mashup infrastructure, an understanding of how the interfaces will be accessed is needed. An examination of REST-based interactions across the HTTP request/response space can help to understand the interactions for services and resources in an enterprise mashup.

- **HTTP GET**—Retrieves resources identified by URIs (Universal Resource Identifiers), named in a consistent manner for an organization.

- **HTTP POST**—Creates a resource identified by the data contained in the request body. Therefore, to create the resource named myfeed.rss, the URI shown for the HTTP GET request would be used in an HTTP POST request along with the additional POST data needed to create the resource.

- **HTTP PUT**—Updates the resource identified by the request URI using the data contained in the request body.

- **HTTP DELETE**—Deletes the resource that is identified by the request URI.

In a REST model, content and data are modeled as resources. Resources are retrieved using a REST-based invocation model—that is, resources are created, retrieved, updated, and deleted using a simple syntax that relies on URIs to define the location of each resource.

The significance of REST is being made apparent by the vast number of web service API providers promoting REST as the invocation model for their APIs. Many of these same service providers are using semantically rich data formats such as RDF, RSS, and Atom as responses to service invocations.

With REST being supported by so many API providers, mashup infrastructures supporting REST-based invocations and semantic data formats will be highly adaptable to interactions with external hosts and service providers.

Emerging Mashup Standards

Standards for mashup development are just beginning to emerge. In the meantime, standards based on open data exchange, semantically rich content, and open security models are driving mashup implementations.

The following list shows some of the more prominent standards influencing mashup application development:

- **XML (eXtensible Markup Language)**—A general-purpose markup language for representing data that is easy for humans to read and understand. Data formatted as XML is easy to transform into other formats using tools that are available in nearly every programming language. XML supports schema-based validation and is supported by many formal enterprise data-format standards. XML supports internationalization explicitly and is platform and language independent and extensible.

- **XHTML (eXtensible HyperText Markup Language)**—A standard introduced in 2000 to form an integration of XML and HTML. XHTML embodies a web development language with a stricter set of constraints than traditional HTML.

- **OpenSocial API**—A unified API for building social applications with services and artifacts served from multiple sites. The OpenSocial API relies on standard JavaScript and HTML as the platform languages developers can use to create applications and services that interconnect common social connections. OpenSocial is being developed by an extensive community of development partners. This community partnership is leading to a platform that exposes a common framework by which sites can become socially enabled. Some of the sites currently supporting OpenSocial include iGoogle, Friendster, LinkedIn, MySpace, Ning, Plaxo, Salesforce.com, and others.

- **The Portable Contacts specification**—Targeted at creating a standard, secure way to access address books and contact lists using web technologies. It seeks to do this by specifying an API defining authentication and access rules, along with a schema, and a common access model that a compliant site provides to contact list consumers. The Portable Contacts specification defines a language neutral and platform neutral protocol whereby contact list consumers can query contact lists, address books, profiles, and so on from providers. The protocol defined by the specification outlines constraints and requirements for consumers and providers of the specification. The specification enables a model that can be used to create an abstraction of almost any group of online friends or user profiles that can then be presented to consumers as a contact list formatted as XML or JSON data.

- **OpenSAM (Open Simple Application Mashups)**—A set of open, best practices and techniques for integrating software as a service (SaaS) applications into applications to enable simple connectivity between platforms and applications. OpenSAM is supported by a number of high-profile web application leaders such as EditGrid, Preezo, Jotlet, Caspio, and others.

- **Microformats**—An approach to formatting snippets of HTML and XHTML data to create standards for representing artifacts such as calendar events, tags, and people semantically in browser pages.

- **Data portability**—Introduced in 2007 by a concerted group of engineers and vendors to promote and enable the ability to share and manipulate data between heterogeneous systems. Data in this context refers to videos, photos, identity documents, and other forms of personal data.

- **RSS and Atom**—XML-based data formats for representing web feeds such as blogs and podcasts. RSS and Atom are ideally suited for representing data that can be categorized and described using channels, titles, items, and resource links. An RSS or Atom document contains descriptive information about a feed such as a summary, description, author, published date, and other items.

- **OPML (Outline Processor Markup Language)**—An XML dialect for semantically defining generic outlines. The most common use for OPML at this time is for exchanging lists of web feeds between feed-aggregator services and applications. OPML defines an outline as a simple, hierarchical list of elements.

- **APML (Attention Profiling Markup Language)**—Seeks to facilitate the ability to share personal attention profiles so that interests might be easily shared between users. An Attention Profile is a type of inventory list of the topics and sources in which a user is interested. Each topic and/or source in the profile contains a value representing the user's level of interest. APML is represented as an XML document containing implicit interests, explicit interests, source rankings, and author rankings.

- **RDF (Resource Description Framework)**—A standard built on the notion that all resources are to be referenced using URIs. RDF also attempts to promote semantic meaning to data. This idea is central to the mashup environment, where data is a collection of loosely coupled resources. With respect to this knowledge, RDF makes a great fit as a universal data model for the data layer of your mashup infrastructure. RDF describes data as a graph of semantically related sets of resources. RDF describes data as subject-predicate-object triples, where a resource is the subject and the object shares some relation to the subject. The predicate uses properties in the form of links to describe the relationship between the subject and object. This interconnecting network of resources and links forms the graph of data that RDF seeks to define.

- **JSON (JavaScript Object Notation)**—A JavaScript data format that offers the advantage of easy accessibility and parsing from within a JavaScript environment. JSON supports a limited number of simple primitive types allowing complex data structures to be represented and consumed easily from standard programming languages.

- **OpenID**—A free service that allows users to access multiple secured sites with a single identity. Sites enabled to use OpenID present a form to a user where the user can enter a previously registered OpenID identifier such as jdoe.ids.example.com. The login form information is passed on to an OpenID client library where it is used to access the web page designated by the OpenID identifier—in this case, http://jdoe.ids.example.com. An HTML link tag containing a URL to the OpenID provider service is read from the web page. The site hosting the client library then establishes a shared secret with the OpenID provider service. The user is then prompted to enter a password or other credentials. The client library site then validates the credentials with the OpenID provider service using the shared secret.

- **OAuth**—A protocol for handling secure API authentication by invoking service invocations on behalf of users. OAuth-enabled sites direct users and associated OAuth request tokens to authorization URLs where the users log in and approve requests from the OAuth-enabled sites. OAuth uses a key, such as an OpenID identifier to enable authentication without passing around usernames and passwords.

- **WS-Security**—Specifies extensions to SOAP messaging to ensure message content integrity and message confidentiality using a variety of security models such as PKI, SSL, and Kerberos. The WS-Security specification is the result of work by the WSS Technical Committee to standardize the Web Service Security (WS-Security) Version 1.0 recommendation. The WS-Security specification defines message integrity, message confidentiality, and the ability to send security tokens as part of a message. These definitions are to be in combination with other web service standards, specifications, and protocols to support a variety of security models and technologies.

Solving Business Problems

Mashups are beginning to play a big role in the business domain. Some of the most prominent uses for mashups within the context of a business are emerging in the space of business process management and IT asset management. The reason for this lies in the ease in which mashups can be created along with the reduced investment needed to adopt the technology.

The nature of mashup development is to use existing technologies such as JavaScript, HTML, XML, and others. This reduces or eliminates the need for large investments in IT retooling and makes a significant difference on the bottom line of organizational staffing, especially in terms of the money saved on integration projects.

Since mashups can retrieve data and UI artifacts from multiple sources, they help to reduce the workload shouldered by a single organization. Mashups promote reuse by definition; therefore, they also reduce the workload for an organization by enforcing reuse within the organization.

Mashup efforts across the enterprise are creating applications and services that complement existing business activities such as business process management (BPM), IT asset management, enterprise information services (EIS), and software as a service (SaaS). How mashups complement business activities can be seen in the following trends:

- **BPM**—Mashups enable business experts to organize workflow and process management activities without relying on highly skilled IT resources, thereby allowing workflows to be modified as needed to meet business requirements.

- **EIS**—Properly architected mashup infrastructures provide semantically rich data layers that allow disparate data to be integrated from multiple sources with little or no help from skilled IT staff. In addition, intuitive user interfaces can be provided using mashup technologies to further simplify the complexities of data integration.

- **IT asset management**—Mashups enable business users with the power to wire UI artifacts, processes, and data together in a graphical manner. Furthermore, mashups allow the creation of applications using components linked to low-level IT functionality. IT asset management is exploiting this model to provide IT asset management components exposing such functionality as time-series data, resource monitoring, and device deployment, to name a few.

- **SaaS**—Mashups flourish in service-oriented and resource-oriented environments. As more businesses move towards a mashup model, on-demand services will become second nature and ubiquitous across the enterprise. This will lead tool vendors to drive SaaS as a prominent model for distributing value.

A mashup environment promotes reuse of existing data, UI artifacts, and software processes to create new applications and services, which might also be reused as components for other mashups. This model is creating a revolutionary atmosphere where underlying programming frameworks and languages are irrelevant, and higher-level scripting languages, semantics, and UI components are emerging as drivers for creating new application functionality.

Enterprises are exploiting the mashup revolution in many different ways to drive down the cost of IT resources and to increase the time-to-market for new business services.

Summary

Mashups allow rapid implementations of new functionality via the use of semantic web technologies, reusable user interface artifacts, and loosely coupled services. Mashups are used in many different consumer and social spaces.

However, enterprises are beginning to reap the benefits afforded by a mashup environment. Mashups are creating an extremely agile and dynamic design and implementation environment within the enterprise realm allowing users with limited technical skills to develop powerful and useful applications and services.

Mashups enable users to create new user interfaces by reusing existing UI artifacts using high-level scripting languages such as HTML and JavaScript. Mashups also enable users to integrate disparate data very quickly and easily using semantically rich data formats that don't require complex programming and middleware technologies. Services and processes are beginning to be integrated with similar speed and ease using loosely coupled techniques inherited from the lessons learned from service-oriented architecture (SOA) solutions.

This introduction discussed some of the high-level concepts surrounding enterprise mashups. In the following chapters I expand on these concepts to guide you through the design and implementation of mashups and mashup infrastructures.

Chapter 1

Mashup Styles, Techniques, and Technologies

To begin design work on a mashup, you must determine what is to be "mashed" together. Three high-level categories of items can be mashed together—user interface artifacts (presentation), data, and/or application functionality (processes). This might include HTML snippets, on-demand JavaScript to access an external API, web service APIs from one of your corporate servers, RSS feeds, and/or other data to be mixed and mashed within the application or pages. The implementation style, techniques, and technologies used for a given mashup depend on this determination. Once the items are determined, your development team can proceed with applying languages, processes, and methodologies to the application at hand.

In this chapter, I point out some of the most widely used styles, techniques, and technologies to build mashups for each of the three primary categories or items.

Determining the Technological Domain for a Mashup

Along with determining what is to be mashed, you must also determine the sources from which the mashup items will be accessed; the style, technologies, and techniques your staff needs to build the mashup; and what services you need to build or access to retrieve the necessary artifacts for your mashup.

Mashups rely on the ability to mix loosely coupled artifacts within a given technological domain. The requirements of the application determine what artifacts (UI, data, and/or functionality) will be needed to build the mashup.

From a high-level perspective, the technological domain as applied to mashups can be viewed as presentation-oriented, data-oriented, and process-oriented. Different languages, methodologies, and programming techniques apply to each technological domain.

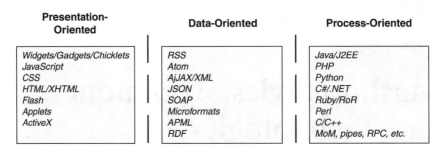

Figure 1.1 *Three primary mashup technological domains*

As shown in Figure 1.1, mashup categories can be divided according to presentation artifacts, data, and application functionality/processes. Each of these categories requires specific skills and programming technologies, as discussed next.

Presentation-Oriented

A presentation-oriented mashup mixes different user interface (UI) artifacts together to create a new application or page. Typically, this type of mashup aims to create an application or page displaying UI artifacts in a manner similar to a conventional portal. That is, each artifact is to be displayed in a separate small area on an application pane or page in a segregated manner in relation to the other artifacts. Very little or no interaction takes place between the UI artifacts in a presentation-oriented mashup.

Technologies used in a presentation-oriented mashup can include

- **Gadgets and widgets**—User interface components that can be placed on an application pane or page independent of other items on the application pane or page. Legacy definitions of widgets referred to them in a more fine-grained manner as applied to desktop components, for example, buttons, scrollbars, sliders, and toolbars. The definition has been expanded in relation to web pages and mashups to include components comprised of more complex and self-contained functionality such as a clock, calculator, weather information, and so on. Gadgets and widgets may or may not retrieve data from an external site.

- **On-demand JavaScript, JavaScript snippets, and badges**—Small sections of JavaScript code that can be inserted within an application pane or page to create user interface components. Typically, the JavaScript relies on interaction with a web service API that returns data and functionality used to build the user interface artifact.

- **CSS/HTML/XHTML**—Snippets that can be inserted to create segregated user interface components that can be reused without regard to the application domain.

- **Flash components/Java applets/ActiveX controls**—Self-contained user interface components that rely on proprietary container technologies such as a virtual machine or runtime that is embedded within the application pane or browser page.

A presentation-oriented mashup is usually the easiest and quickest type of mashup to build. Since there is little or no interaction between the mashed items, the mashup developer can simply worry about placing the items on the application pane or page in the desired location with the desired UI theme.

Data-Oriented

Data-oriented mashups (in-process or out-of-process) involve combining data from one or more externally hosted sites together in an application pane or web page typically using scripting techniques and languages such as JavaScript, JScript, and others. In this type of mashup, data is returned from a site or server in the form of XML, RSS, JSON, Atom, and so on. Much of the data returned originates from data-oriented services sometimes referred to as Data-as-a-Service (DaaS). DaaS describes a data-oriented service API that can be called without relying on third-party processes or components between the service provider and the service consumer.

In-Process Data-Oriented Mashups

In-process data-oriented mashups rely on data being mixed together using application or browser technologies such as JavaScript, AJAX, or the Document Object Model (DOM). In this style of mashup data is retrieved from one or more sites/servers and used as values or configuration settings to build user interface artifacts within an application process or browser page.

Out-of-Process Data-Oriented Mashups

Out-of-process data-oriented mashups rely on data being mixed together using technologies such as Java, Python, Perl, C++, XML, and XSLT, to name a few. In this style of mashup data is retrieved from one or more sites/servers and used as values or configuration settings to create new data models within a server-side process or separate client-side process.

Process-Oriented

Process-oriented mashups (out-of-process) involve combining functionality together in one or more external processes using programming languages such as Java, PHP, Python, and C++. Mashups built for enterprise applications or web applications can involve frameworks such as JEE, .NET, and Ruby on Rails.

In a process-oriented mashup, functionality is combined using interprocess/ interthread communication techniques such as shared memory, message queues/ buses, remote procedure calls (RPC), and so on. Even though data is exchanged between processes and threads in a process-oriented mashup, the end result differs from a data-oriented mashup in that the data-oriented mashup seeks to derive new data models, whereas a process-oriented mashup seeks to derive new processes and/or services.

More often than not, enterprises require a hybrid approach when building a mashup. This is due to the number of disparate sources from which functionality and data are retrieved such as geocoding sites, RSS feeds, and corporate data stores.

So, when preparing to build a mashup you must first determine what is to be mashed, the technological domain in which to build the mashup, and the sources from which the mashup artifacts will be accessed. With this information in hand you can then determine whether your development staff possess the skills to employ the techniques and technologies needed to build the mashup. The skills of your staff have a big impact on the decision of which mashup style you choose. The following section discusses the reasons for choosing different mashup styles and/or domains.

Choosing a Mashup Style

There are some clear reasons for picking one mashup style/domain over another. Depending on the goal of the mashup, you should weigh the pros and cons of each mashup style before beginning work.

Pros and Cons of Presentation-Oriented Mashups

Presentation-oriented mashups are popular because they are quick and easy to build. They rely primarily on data and UI artifacts retrieved from sites using service APIs, data feeds, and so on. This model is often referred to as a Software-as-a-Service (SaaS) model, although many of the artifacts used in this model are not technically services. Presentation-oriented mashups often require no preauthorization, no installation steps, and no other technologies than those found within any standard web browser.

It is easy to implement presentation-oriented mashups because you can usually use services, components, and script libraries that are publicly accessible without requiring you to install application platforms or tools. In this model, you can simply embed or include the scripting code or service call right in an HTML page as needed. Many publicly available scripting components today allow you to customize the look-and-feel of the UI artifacts that they generate.

Presentation-oriented mashups typically don't require any service coding or deployment; all service coding is provided by external processes/sites to be used by service consumers at will.

Performance is typically quite responsive with presentation-oriented mashups, since all requests are made directly to a service provider or script provider. This direct-access model eliminates any interactions with an intermediary process through which data is retrieved or functionality is derived. However, this also creates a direct coupling to the service or services that can eventually turn into broken links, partially drawn pages, and/or slowly drawn pages if one or more of the services fail or become nonperforming.

Relying on presentation-oriented techniques and technologies, enterprise mashups can reduce the load that might otherwise be shouldered by one or more corporate servers. Since requests are made directly between a service or data consumer and the provider, the use of presentation-oriented techniques and technologies in at least part of a mashup places the processing burden outside the corporate development domain.

One of the biggest challenges with presentation-oriented mashups is attempting to access services hosted on a site other than the site from which the original page was retrieved. Most standard web browsers enforce a sandbox security model in which a given web page is not allowed to access a site/service located external to the host in which the page originated. This is referred to by a number of names including the server-of-origin policy, the browser security sandbox, the same-origin policy, and the same-domain policy.

The browser security sandbox is in place as an attempt to secure sensitive information and ward off attacks from rogue scripts and components attempting to violate privacy and security. Figure 1.2 illustrates the browser security sandbox.

Many mashups employ the use of AJAX to communicate with a server and retrieve data. AJAX is a technology that uses a standard JavaScript object—XMLHttpRequest—to pass data from the JavaScript container (browser) to a web host. AJAX enables web pages to perform in a manner more similar to desktop applications, for example, less page refreshing and use of dynamic data updating. However, this dynamic communication model opens the door to malicious scripts; hence the need for the browser security sandbox. The browser security

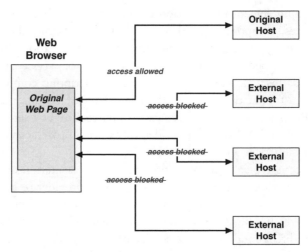

Figure 1.2   *The browser security sandbox*

sandbox only allows JavaScript code to use the XMLHttpRequest object to communicate with the host or domain from which the containing page originated. This restriction is a major constraint for building mashups. Therefore, alternative mechanisms are needed if a presentation-oriented mashup is to incorporate data and services from multiple sites. Alternatives have been developed, specifically the use of a technique known as "on-demand scripting" or "dynamic scripting." This technique, which I talk about in detail later, exploits the inclination of a browser to execute JavaScript as it is encountered in the process of interpreting an HTML page.

Pros and Cons of Data-Oriented Mashups

Data-oriented mashups present their own set of challenges and benefits. Primarily, a data-oriented mashup must deal with the intrinsic requirement to act as the data mediator and/or broker. The mashup in this model must take data from multiple sites and mix it together in a form that will be useful to the mashup application or page. As a data broker/integrator, the mashup must deal with multiple data formats and, possibly, communication protocols, such as office document formats, message queue exchange protocols, and HTTP.

In-Process

Mashing data together within a web browser can be a formidable task. Depending on the type of data, browser-based scripts and technologies are not particularly suited for data integration. Most data-mashing techniques performed within a browser involve manipulating XML-based or JSON-based

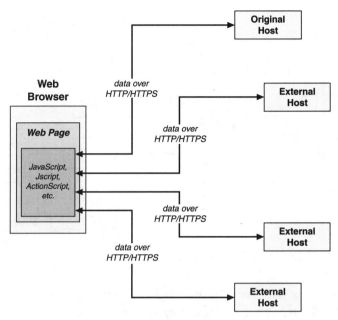

Figure 1.3 *Flow of data in an in-process mashup*

(http://json.org/) data using various JavaScript techniques and applying the results to the web page using DOM manipulation.

Figure 1.3 illustrates the flow of data in an in-process mashup. As illustrated, data is received from multiple sites/hosts and is processed using scripting technologies within a browser page.

Out-of-Process

Mashing data together outside a web browser is nothing new. Any web application or desktop application framework will provide some form of time-tested data integration technology. Frameworks for processing plain text, comma-separated text, XML, relational data, and so forth have been around for decades and optimized to process heterogeneous data very efficiently. New technologies built specifically for disparate data integration, such as enterprise service buses, are also available in this mashup model.

Figure 1.4 illustrates the flow of data in an out-of-process mashup. As illustrated in the figure, a mashup server receives data from multiple sites/hosts and integrates the data using languages, libraries, and frameworks well-suited for data parsing, assembly, mediation, and so on.

Mashing data out-of-process can typically handle many more data formats and apply more robust transformations and data-augmentation techniques than an in-process model.

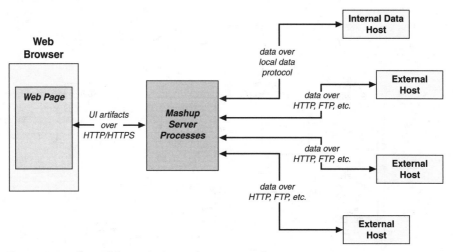

Figure 1.4   *Flow of data in an out-of-process mashup*

Out-of-process data mashing offers the advantage of evaluating the data payload before returning the result to the mashup client. In this model a mashup server can monitor a data feed for just the data updates and return the updates to the client rather than the entire payload.

Data caching at the mashup server and returning results directly to the client rather than invoking the data request on a remote host is also a benefit of mashing data out-of-process.

Pros and Cons of Process-Oriented Mashups

In a process-oriented mashup, service requests are transmitted from a mashup client to the mashup server in the same fashion as an out-of-process data-oriented mashup. So, from the perspective of the mashup client, the process is the same. However, from the perspective of the mashup server, things change.

A process-oriented mashup server deals with integration of data as well as integration of services and processes. Just as data can be retrieved from multiple different internal and external sources in a data-oriented mashup, services and processes can be invoked on multiple different internal and external service hosts and/or processes.

As illustrated in Figure 1.5, a process-oriented mashup server deals with integration of processes and services from many different internal and external processes and hosts. Since this situation exists in most standard web application or server-oriented environments, it is inevitably encountered in most mashup environments where any form of processing takes place outside the mashup client (browser). The pros and cons of this model are also shared with standard ser-

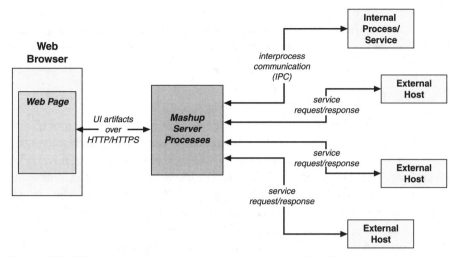

Figure 1.5 *Flow of services and processes in a process-oriented mashup*

vice-oriented server environments, including the intricacies of IPC, transaction management, and service availability.

Process-oriented mashups and out-of-process data-oriented mashups allow you to deal with shared security keys, tokens, credentials, and so on using many currently available technologies and frameworks such as SAML, OpenID, and OAuth. Shared security mechanisms are becoming available more and more from an in-process mashup domain, but server technologies still dominate. Handling data security at the server level also allows you to incorporate data-retrieval and security in the same step resulting in fewer hops from client to server.

Out-of-process, data-oriented mashups and process-oriented mashups allow data and services to be processed asynchronously, often resulting in a more efficient use of processing power and time. Browser-based concurrency is usually limited to far fewer calls than server-based concurrency.

Presentation-Oriented Mashup Techniques

When you work with a mashup in the presentation domain, you are constrained to an environment that has evolved in a hodge-podge way from processing simple text and graphics pages to one that is on the verge of offering as many or more features as a complex desktop application framework. This messy evolution has suffered because of the mismatch between the free-natured needs of the web environment and the restricted nature of the few primary browser vendors. Nevertheless, standards and best practices are emerging that offer sanity to the mess. The following sections discuss some of the popular techniques and technologies being used to produce mashups in the presentation domain.

Mashing Presentation Artifacts

The easiest form of presentation-oriented mashup involves aggregation of UI artifacts within a web page in a portal-like manner—that is, completely segregated from each other using discrete areas within a single HTML page. In this model, UI artifacts such as gadgets, widgets, HTML snippets, JavaScript includes, and on-demand JavaScript are embedded within an HTML document using layout elements and techniques such as HTML tables and CSS positioning.

When mashing together UI artifacts in a web page using browser layout techniques, each artifact typically resides in its own separate area, as illustrated in Figure 1.6

As illustrated in Figure 1.6, a mashup using aggregated UI artifacts references one or more web sites from a web page and retrieves UI code that builds each artifact as a separate component in a separate area on the browser page.

Mashing Presentation Data

A browser page can also build and modify UI artifacts using data retrieved from multiple sources using such data formats as XML, RSS, Atom, and JSON. In this model, the data is retrieved from one or more sites and parsed by the

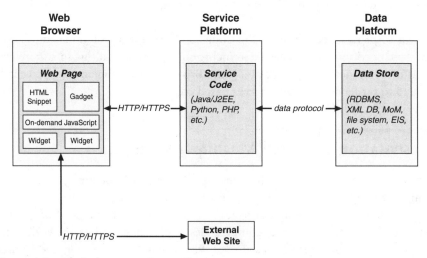

Figure 1.6 *Mashed presentation artifacts*

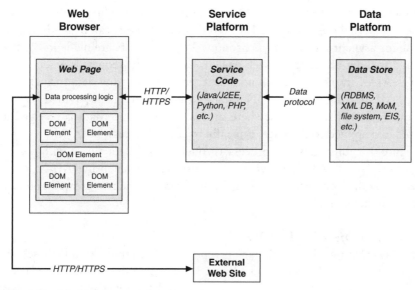

Figure 1.7 *Mashed presentation data*

browser, and UI artifacts are created or updated using scripting techniques such as DOM manipulation to alter the resulting HTML document.

Figure 1.7 illustrates the flow of data from service hosts and external sites to a mashup created by aggregation of data in the presentation domain (browser page).

This model is more complex than mashing together UI artifacts. In this model, the scripting code that processes the data must be robust enough to handle multiple data formats or restrict the page to accessing services that only support the formats supported by the page. However, since the scripting code will be parsing the data to a fine-grained level, the UI can be created and updated to create a more sophisticated user experience. This model offers more flexibility at the cost of additional complexity.

Using AJAX and the XMLHttpRequest Object

Asynchronous JavaScript and XML (AJAX) is a set of technologies and techniques used for handling data feeds using JavaScript and for creating dynamic web pages with a sophisticated look and feel. One feature of AJAX is the use of JavaScript and CSS techniques to update a UI artifact on a web page without refreshing the entire page. AJAX also features a JavaScript-based HTTP request/response framework that can be used within a web page.

The HTTP request/response framework provided by AJAX is enabled by a component known as the XMLHttpRequest object. This object is supported by most browsers and offers the ability to pass data to an external host and receive data from an external host using the HTTP protocol. Requests can be made synchronously or asynchronously. Asynchronous AJAX requests are made in the background without affecting the web page from which the request is made.

The AJAX framework can send and receive virtually any data format. However, XML-based data and JSON data are the most frequent payloads used for various reasons discussed elsewhere in this chapter. Once data is received it is parsed and applied to the page, typically by manipulating the DOM.

Figure 1.8 illustrates the process through which data flows within a web page using the AJAX framework. As illustrated, when using AJAX, data is received by the XMLHttpRequest object. UI artifacts can then be created and modified using the data.

Document Object Model (DOM)

Every JavaScript-enabled web page is represented internally to a browser as an instance of the W3C Document Object Model (DOM). DOM is a platform-independent and language-neutral object model for representing XML-based documents that allows programs and scripts to dynamically access and update the content, structure, and style of a document.

The HTML DOM is part of the official DOM specification that defines a standard model for HTML documents. The HTML DOM facilitates accessing and manipulating HTML elements in a given web page. The HTML DOM presents web page as a node-based tree structure containing elements, attributes,

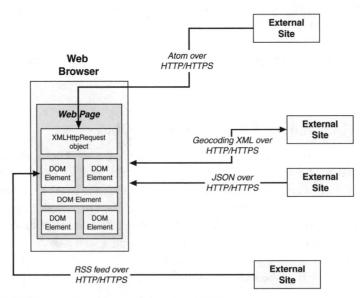

Figure 1.8   *Presentation data mashup using AJAX*

and text. Every element on a web page (for example, div, table, image, or paragraph) is accessible as a DOM node. JavaScript allows the manipulation of any DOM element on a page dynamically. This allows you to perform such operations as hiding elements, adding or removing elements, and altering their attributes (color, size, position, and so on).

Listing 1.1 presents a simple HTML document.

Listing 1.1 *Simple HTML Document*
```
<html>
<head>
<title>A simple HTML doc</title>
</head>
<body>
    <p>
    This is a simple HTML document.
    </p>

    <img id="image1"
        src="http://example.com/image1.png"
        width="250"
        height="350"/>
</body>
</html>
```

Listing 1.2 is an example of a JavaScript function that changes the width and height of the image (`<img>`) element with an id of `image1` in the preceding example:

Listing 1.2 *JavaScript Manipulation of DOM*
```
function changeImageSize()
{
    var anIMGElement = document.getElementById("image1");
    anIMGElement.width = "400";
    anIMGElement.height = "300";
}
```

As shown in Listing 1.2, the DOM can be accessed by the global "document" variable. With a reference to the document variable, you can traverse the nodes of the DOM to find any element by name or id.

Extensible Markup Language (XML)

XML (eXtensible Markup Language) is a specification and standard for creating self-describing markup languages. It is extensible in that it allows you to define your own elements. It is used extensively in data transformation and integration frameworks to facilitate the transfer and integration of structured data across disparate systems and applications. XML is used in many web-enabled environments as a document annotation standard and as a data serialization format.

Listing 1.3 is an example of a simple XML document.

Listing 1.3 *Simple XML Document*

```
<?xml version="1.0" encoding="UTF-8"?>
<contacts>
    <contact>
        <name>John Doe</name>
        <address1>123 anywhere st.</address1>
        <address2>Apt 456</address2>
        <city>Yourtown</city>
        <state>CA</state>
        <zip>12345</zip>
        <country>USA</country>
    </contact>
    <contact>
        <name>Jane Doe</name>
        <address1>456 S 789 W</address1>
        <address2>Suite 987</address2>
        <city>Mytown</city>
        <state>NY</state>
        <zip>54321</zip>
        <country>USA</country>
    </contact>
</contacts>
```

Presentation-oriented mashups consume XML and XML derivatives returned from service hosts and web sites. Once XML is received, it is parsed and applied to a given web page. As XML is parsed, DOM manipulation techniques are usually applied to update UI artifacts.

JavaScript Object Notation (JSON)

JSON (JavaScript Object Notation) is a simple, string-based, data-interchange format derived from JavaScript object literals. JSON is very easy for users to read and write and for JavaScript engines to parse. Strings, numbers, Booleans, arrays, and objects can all be represented using string literals in a JSON object.

Listing 1.4 is an example of a simple JSON object:

Listing 1.4 *JavaScript Object Notation (JSON) Object*

```
{
  'contacts':
  [{
    'name':'John Doe',
    'address1':'123 anywhere st.',
    'address2':'Apt 456',
    'city':'Yourtown',
    'state':'CA',
```

```
      'zip':'12345',
      'country':'USA'
   },
   {
      'name':'Jane Doe',
      'address1':'456 S 789 W',
      'address2':'Suite 987',
      'city':'Mytown',
      'state':'NY',
      'zip':'54321',
      'country':'USA'
   }]
}
```

Presentation-oriented mashups also consume JSON objects returned from service hosts and web sites. Once a JSON object is received, it must be parsed in order to apply to a given web page. Since JSON is pure JavaScript, it is easily parsed using standard JavaScript utilities. As with XML, DOM manipulation techniques are usually applied to update UI artifacts once a JSON object is parsed.

Sidestepping the Browser Security Sandbox

Perhaps the biggest challenge in doing a presentation-oriented mashup is contending with the browser security sandbox, which is in place to keep sensitive information secure. To protect against malicious scripts, most browsers only allow JavaScript to communicate with the host/server from which the page was loaded. If a mashup requires access to a service from an external host, there is no easy way to access it using the XMLHttpRequest object.

When an attempt is made to access a host/server external to the host/server from which a web page was loaded, an error similar to the following will be encountered:

`Error: uncaught exception: Permission denied to call method XMLHttpRequest.open.`

Therefore, a mechanism is needed through which services can be accessed without violating the browser security sandbox. JSONP provides one solution.

JSON with padding (JSONP) or remote JSON is an extension of JSON where the name of a JavaScript callback function is specified as an input parameter of a service call. JSONP allows for retrieving data from external hosts/servers. The technique used by JSONP is referred to as dynamic or on-demand scripting. Using this technique, you can communicate with any domain and in this way avoid the constraints of the browser security sandbox.

Listing 1.5 is an example of using on-demand JavaScript to retrieve data from an external site.

Listing 1.5   *On-Demand JavaScript*

```
function retrieveExternalData()
{
  var script = document.createElement("script");
  script.src =
    'http://www.example.com/aservice?output=json&
    callback=aJSFunction';
  script.type = 'text/javascript';
  document.body.appendChild(script);
}
```

Listing 1.5 illustrates how to dynamically add a <script> tag into a page by manipulating the DOM so that the page can load and call another web site. The <script> tag executes on-demand and makes the service request to the site specified. If the service response is in JSONP format the JavaScript interpreter converts the response object into a JavaScript object. When a script element is inserted into the DOM the JavaScript interpreter automatically evaluates the script. JSONP responses wrap JSON data in a JavaScript function call using the name of the callback parameter. The JavaScript function is then called and any objects defined in the JSONP response are passed.

The following is an example of an evaluated JSONP response:

```
aJSFunction({ "item 1":"value 1", "item 2":"value 2" });
```

As shown in the preceding line of code, the response returned from the service is formatted as a JSON object wrapped in a JavaScript function call with the callback parameter name. The script is evaluated and the JavaScript function is called, completing the service request/response interaction.

Data-Oriented Mashup Techniques

Data can be mashed together in-process or out-of-process. These two domains typically equate with a web browser and a remote server application, respectively. Many times data will be mashed in a hybrid approach using both in-process and out-of-process techniques.

This section discusses in depth some of the techniques used for both in-process and out-of-process data mashups.

Mashing Data In-Process

Mashing data in-process involves applying data integration techniques in the same process as the mashup page. This is typically accomplished with scripting code such as JavaScript and JScript. However, proprietary component technologies such as Java applets and ActionScript can be used.

During the process of mashing data in this model, a request is made to a service and data is returned in the service response. The data is then parsed, processed, and applied to UI artifacts in the page. DOM manipulation is typically used to apply the processed data.

Mashing XML Data In-Process

All standard web browsers expose an XML-parser object to JavaScript that can be used to load and parse XML data. Each parser reads XML data from a string; therefore, a string response returned from a service call can be passed to the XML parser and processed as needed.

In Listing 1.6, an XML parser is created and used to parse the XML document string defined previously in Listing 1.3. As each contact item is encountered, a new paragraph element is created using DOM manipulation, and the element is added to the web page.

Listing 1.6 *Parsing XML Using JavaScript*

```
<script>
function parseXMLData(xmlString)
{
  var xmlDoc;

  if (document.implementation.createDocument)
  {
    // Create the Mozilla DOM parser
    var domParser = new DOMParser();
    // Create the XML document object
    xmlDoc = domParser.parseFromString(xmlString, "text/xml");
  }
  else if (window.ActiveXObject)
  {
    // Create the Microsoft DOM parser
    xmlDoc = new ActiveXObject("Microsoft.XMLDOM");
    xmlDoc.async = "false";
    // Create the XML document object
    xmlDoc.loadXML(xmlString);
  }

  // get root node
  var contactsNode = xmlDoc.getElementsByTagName('contacts')[0];

  // traverse the tree
  for (var i = 0; i < contactsNode.childNodes.length; i++)
```

```
{
  var contactNode = contactsNode.childNodes.item(i);
  for (j = 0; j < contactNode.childNodes.length; j++)
  {
    var itemNode = contactNode.childNodes.item(j);
    if (itemNode.childNodes.length > 0)
    {
      var itemTextNode = itemNode.childNodes.item(0);
      var paraEl = document.createElement("p");
      var textEl =
        document.createTextNode(itemNode.nodeName + ":"
                                  + itemTextNode.data);
      paraEl.appendChild(textEl);
      var bodyEl =
        document.getElementsByTagName("body").item(0);
      bodyEl.appendChild(paraEl);
    }
  }
}
}
</script>
```

In the preceding listing a DOM parser is instantiated and is accessed to get the root node. Each node is then traversed via its child nodes until the desired text data node is found. Note that there is a different parser used for Microsoft Internet Explorer and Mozilla.

Mashing JSON Data In-Process

Since JSON is pure JavaScript, a string containing JSON data can simply be evaluated to create a JavaScript object. Then the JavaScript object can be accessed using normal JavaScript. For example, suppose that you are working with a string containing the JSON data shown previously in Listing 1.4. You can pass that string to the JavaScript eval function as follows:

```
var jsonObj = eval("(" + jsonString + ")");
```

This creates a JavaScript object on which we can operate using standard JavaScript techniques. For example, you can access the name field for the first contact using the following snippet:

```
jsonObj.contacts[0].name
```

Typically, you know the structure of the data beforehand. However, you might not know the length of array data within the structure. In that case, the JSON object must be traverse and array data parsed dynamically.

In Listing 1.7, a string containing JSON data, as defined previously in Listing 1.4, is evaluated and parsed. As each array element is encountered, a new paragraph element is created using DOM manipulation and the element is added to the web page:

Listing 1.7 *Processing JSON Using JavaScript*

```
function parseJSONData(jsonString)
{
  var jsonObj = eval("(" + jsonString + ")");

  for (var x in jsonObj)
  {
    // ignore properties  inherited from object
    if (jsonObj.hasOwnProperty(x))
    {
      if (jsonObj[x] instanceof Array)
      {
        // handle arrays
        for (var i = 0; i < jsonObj[x].length; i++)
        {
          var bodyEl =
            document.getElementsByTagName("body").item(0);

          // create name element
          var paraEl = document.createElement("p");
          var textEl = document.createTextNode("Name: "
                                    + jsonObj[x][i].name);
          paraEl.appendChild(textEl);
          bodyEl.appendChild(paraEl);

          // create address 1 element
          paraEl = document.createElement("p");
          textEl = document.createTextNode("Address 1: "
                                    + jsonObj[x][i].address1);
          paraEl.appendChild(textEl);
          bodyEl.appendChild(paraEl);

          // create address 2 element
          paraEl = document.createElement("p");
          textEl = document.createTextNode("Address 2: "
                                    + jsonObj[x][i].address2);
          paraEl.appendChild(textEl);
          bodyEl.appendChild(paraEl);

          // create city element
          paraEl = document.createElement("p");
          textEl = document.createTextNode("City: "
                                    + jsonObj[x][i].city);
          paraEl.appendChild(textEl);
          bodyEl.appendChild(paraEl);
```

```
      // create state element
      paraEl = document.createElement("p");
      textEl = document.createTextNode("State: "
                            + jsonObj[x][i].state);
      paraEl.appendChild(textEl);
      bodyEl.appendChild(paraEl);

      // create zip element
      paraEl = document.createElement("p");
      textEl = document.createTextNode("Zip: "
                            + jsonObj[x][i].zip);
      paraEl.appendChild(textEl);
      bodyEl.appendChild(paraEl);

      // create country element
      paraEl = document.createElement("p");
      textEl = document.createTextNode("Country: "
                            + jsonObj[x][i].country);
      paraEl.appendChild(textEl);
      bodyEl.appendChild(paraEl);
    }
   }
  }
 }
}
```

With the ability to parse data returned from a service and to manipulate elements of the HTML DOM with the parsed data, you can dynamically create and modify UI artifacts to fit the needs of your mashup.

Mashing Data Out-of-Process

Mashing data out-of process involves applying data integration techniques in a separate process, typically on a remote host/server. In this mashup model, a remote software module receives requests from a client and takes the necessary steps to gather and transform the data needed to formulate a response.

Technologies and techniques in this approach overlap with enterprise data integration technologies and techniques, the scope of which is beyond this discussion. However, the following presents a high-level view of some of the more common approaches to enterprise data transformation and integration currently in use:

- **Brute-force data conversion**—This technique involves converting one data format to another using proprietary conversion tools or a custom byte-for-byte conversion program. Proprietary applications often offer an extension framework allowing third parties to build components or plug-ins that will convert one data format to another.

- **Data mapping**—Data mapping involves the creation and application of a map of data elements between two disparate data models—source and destination. The map is used by conversion programs to determine how an element from the source dataset applies to the destination dataset. Extensible Stylesheet Language Transformations (XSLT) is often used in this approach to convert XML data from one form to another.

- **Semantic mapping**—This approach uses a metadata registry containing synonyms for data elements that can be queried by conversion tools that use the synonyms as a guide for converting one data element to another.

Process-Oriented Mashup Techniques

A process-oriented mashup involves mashing together services and/or processes. Techniques used for this model range from simply combining method calls in an object to a complex, structured workflow system.

In Figure 1.9, object2 is interacting with a number of different services and processes. It is interacting with object1 using a standard method call and an external site using a service call over a web protocol. object2 is also interacting with an internal workflow system using asynchronous messaging. The results from these calls are then mashed together to formulate the response that will ultimately be returned to the mashup client (web page).

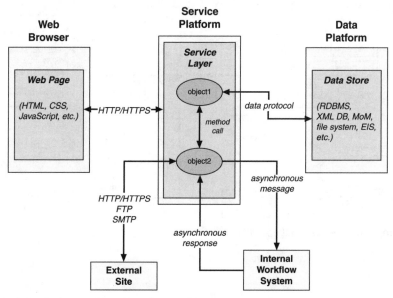

Figure 1.9 *Process-oriented mashup architecture*

Hybrid Mashups

In actuality, enterprise mashups usually involve techniques and technologies for each of the three mashup domains. Widgets, gadgets, or dynamic scripts will be retrieved using presentation-oriented techniques. Data will be retrieved using in-process data-oriented techniques. More data will be retrieved on the server using out-of-process techniques. Services and processes will be aggregated to formulate responses on the server that will be returned to the mashup client results from service API requests.

Figure 1.10 illustrates a typical enterprise mashup environment where data and services are accessed from a web page (in-process) and from the service platform (on the server, out-of-process). Presentation-oriented techniques, data-oriented techniques, and process-oriented techniques must all be employed to handle the needs for this environment.

The techniques and mashup domains discussed in this chapter are discussed further in subsequent chapters. For now, I demonstrate some of the easier techniques of a presentation-oriented mashup in a small example in the next section.

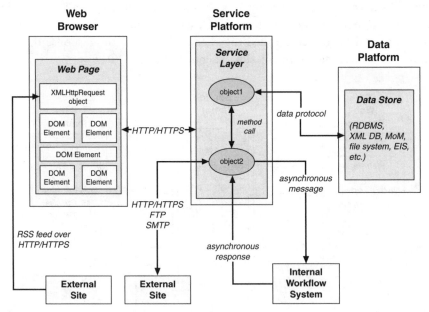

Figure 1.10 *Hybrid mashup architecture*

Implementing a Simple Mashup

This section demonstrates the application of concepts discussed in this chapter to create a simple presentation-oriented mashup. Apart from a local service platform, the sources used for the mashup are publicly available and provide either a service API, an RSS data feed, or a dynamic script feed. This section does not discuss issues such as application keys, security, and governance for this mashup; these topics are discussed in depth in later chapters.

For the sake of complete coverage of the mashup domains discussed, the mashup will make service calls and retrieve data from external sites as well as a local service platform that operates around the model illustrated in Figure 1.11.

Figure 1.11 illustrates a service platform that uses only a small number of primary components to process service and resource requests. The platform uses the Representational State Transfer (REST) approach (to be discussed later) for service and resource request/responses. The service platform provides access to services and uses a simple resource framework to create, retrieve, update, and delete resources.

The application (shown in Listing 1.8 and in Figure 1.12) allows users to view disparate data that might be available in a typical enterprise. The data is presented in a portal-like manner to simplify the layout and UI-management code. The application integrates a list of corporate documents, a map feed, an RSS

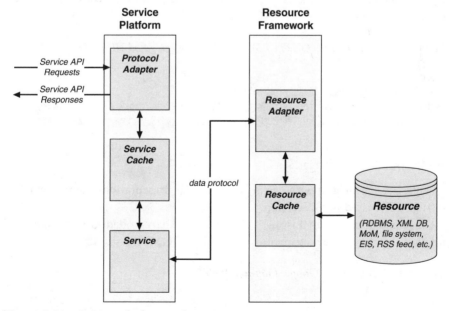

Figure 1.11 *Services platform architecture*

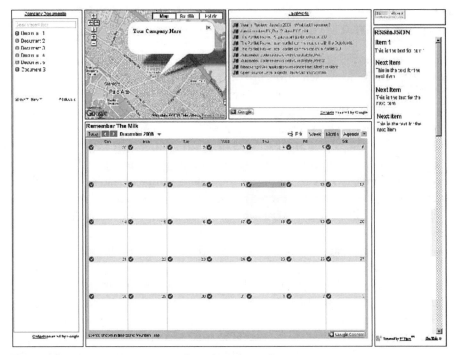

Figure 1.12   *Presentation-oriented mashup example*

feed, a calendar gadget, a Twitter counter chicklet, and a Twitter archive list delivered as RSS.

Listing 1.8   *Presentation-Oriented Mashup Using Aggregated UI Artifacts*
```
<html>
<head>
<!-- Include Google Maps Javascript Library -->
<script type="text/javascript" src="http://maps.google.com/maps?file=api&v=1& key=
ABQIAAAA01HpWF7mf2aW91RNaGDc7xTfGML3OZxtDDthfq-aZ1uFtrk9MRS_VWEizymnfki_h89lqU7A0ts2PA">
</script>

<script type="text/javascript">
```

Figure 1.12 illustrates the final result of the presentation-oriented mashup example discussed in this section.

The load function in Listing 1.9 retrieves a hard-coded Google map and applies it to the map div element in the HTML DOM.

Listing 1.9   *Applying a Google Map to a Web Page*
```
function load()
{
  if (GBrowserIsCompatible())
  {
```

```
      // create map component in div with the id = "map"
      var map = new GMap2(document.getElementById("map"));
      // create map components components
      map.addControl(new GSmallMapControl());
      map.addControl(new GMapTypeControl());
      // create center point when map is displayed
      map.setCenter(new GLatLng(37.4419, -122.1419), 13);
      map.openInfoWindow(map.getCenter(),
                         "<b>Your Company Here</b>");
      // re-open the info balloon if they close it
      var point = new GLatLng(37.395746, -121.952234);
      map.addOverlay(createMarker(point, 1));
   }
}

function createMarker(point, number)
{
   var marker = new GMarker(point);
   // create clickable point with title for address
   GEvent.addListener(marker, "click", function()
   {
      marker.openInfoWindowHtml("<b>Your Company Here</b>");
   });
   return marker;
}

function retrieveExternalData()
{
    var script = document.createElement("script");
    script.src =
      'http://www.example.com/mashups/someservice';
    script.type = 'text/javascript';
    document.body.appendChild(script);
}

</script>
</head>
<body onload="load()">
```

In the example shown in Listing 1.10 a div element is added to contain a list of corporate documents retrieved from a Google Docs account using dynamic script.

Listing 1.10 *Dynamic Script to Show a List of Documents*

```
<!-- div to hold documents -->
<div id="docs"
     style="border-style:ridge; position: absolute;
        left: 10px; top: 10px; width:200px; height:930px">
<script src="http://gmodules.com/ig/ifr?
        url=http://www.google.com/ig/modules/docs.xml
```

```
&amp;up_numDocuments=9&amp;up_showLastEdit=1
&amp;synd=open&amp;w=180&amp;h=860
&amp;title=Company+Documents
&amp;lang=en&amp;country=ALL
&amp;border=%23ffffff%7C3px%2C1px+solid+%23999999
&amp;output=js"></script>
  </div>
```

Listing 1.11 illustrates a `div` element that will hold the results from the Google map retrieval.

Listing 1.11   *Element to Contain a Google Map*
```
<div id="map"
    style="border-style:ridge; position: absolute;
    left: 220px; top: 10px; width:400px; height:300px">
</div>
```

In Listing 1.12 a `div` element is added to contain an RSS feed using dynamic script.

Listing 1.12   *Element to Contain an RSS Feed*
```
<!-- div to hold RSS feed -->
<div id="feed"
    style="border-style:ridge; position: absolute;
    left: 630px; top: 10px; width:400px; height:300px">
<script src="http://gmodules.com/ig/ifr?
  url=http://customrss.googlepages.com/customrss.xml
  &amp;up_rssurl=http%3A%2F%2Fwww.javaworld.com%2Findex.xml
  &amp;up_title=CustomRSS
  &amp;up_titleurl=http%3A%2F%2Fcustomrss.googlepages.com
  &amp;up_num_entries=10&amp;up_linkaction=showdescription
  &amp;up_background=E1E9C3&amp;up_border=CFC58E
  &amp;up_round=1&amp;up_fontfamily=Arial
  &amp;up_fontsize=8pt&amp;up_openfontsize=9pt
  &amp;up_itempadding=3px&amp;up_bullet=icon
  &amp;up_custicon=Overrides%20favicon.ico
  &amp;up_boxicon=1&amp;up_opacity=20
  &amp;up_itemlinkcolor=596F3E&amp;up_itemlinkweight=Normal
  &amp;up_itemlinkdecoration=None&amp;up_vlinkcolor=C7CFA8
  &amp;up_vlinkweight=Normal&amp;up_vlinkdecoration=None
  &amp;up_showdate=1&amp;up_datecolor=9F9F9F
  &amp;up_tcolor=1C57A9&amp;up_thighlight=FFF19D
  &amp;up_desclinkcolor=1B5790&amp;up_color=000000
  &amp;up_dback=FFFFFF&amp;up_dborder=DFCE6F
  &amp;up_desclinkweight=Bold&amp;up_desclinkdecoration=None
  &amp;synd=open&amp;w=380&amp;h=240&amp;title=JavaWorld
  &amp;border=%23ffffff%7C3px%2C1px+solid+%23999999
  &amp;output=js"></script>
</div>
```

Listing 1.13 shows a `div` element to contain a Google calendar retrieved using a JavaScript badge.

Listing 1.13 *Google Calendar Element*
```
<!-- div to hold calendar -->
<div id="calendar"
     style="border-style:ridge; position: absolute;
     left: 220px; top: 320px; width:810px; height:620px">
<iframe src="http://www.google.com/calendar/embed?
            src=o78s3eqe3ov403cpuav2bje5ja9j1tp2%40
            import.calendar.google.com&ctz=America/Denver"
  style="border: 0"
  width="800" height="600" frameborder="0" scrolling="no">
  </iframe>
</div>
```

Shown in Listing 1.14 is a `div` element to contain the Twitter counter chicklet.

Listing 1.14 *A div Element to Contain a Twitter Chicklet*
```
<!-- div to hold the Twitter counter chicklet -->
<div id="chicklet"
     style="border-style:ridge; position: absolute;
     left: 1040px; top: 10px; width:200px; height:40px">
<a href="http://twittercounter.com/?username=jhanson583"
   title="TwitterCounter for @jhanson583"><img src="http://twittercounter.com/
counter/?username=jhanson583"
                                    width="88"
                                    height="26"
                                    style="border:none;"
                                    alt="TwitterCounter
for @jhanson583" /></a>
</div>
```

Listing 1.15 illustrates the `div` element to contain the Twitter RSS feed using dynamic script.

Listing 1.15 *Twitter RSS Feed div Element*
```
<!-- div to hold twitter feed -->
<div id="ufbadge"
     style="border-style:ridge; position: absolute;
     left: 1040px; top: 60px; width:200px; height:880px">
  <script src="http://pipes.yahoo.com/js/listbadge.js">
        {"pipe_id":"dq0Qhuqp3BG1psChjtzu1g",
         "_btype":"list",
         "pipe_params":{
            "urlRSS":"http:\/\/twitter.com
            \/statuses\/user_timeline\/10852552.rss"},
         "width":"190",
         "height":"870"}
```

```
    </script>
    </div>
```

In Listing 1.16 I add the div element to contain the local RSS feed using dynamic script.

Listing 1.16   *RSS Feed Element*

```
    <!-- div to hold local RSS feed -->
    <div id="localfeed"
        style="border-style:ridge; position: absolute;
        left: 10px; top: 950px; width:1210px; height:200px">
      <script src="http://localhost:8080/mashups/js/rssbadge.js">
            {"urlRSS":"http:\/\/localhost:8080
            \/mashups\/services\/feeds\/zurn.rss"}
</script>
    </div>
</body>
</html>
```

The mashup in the preceding example illustrates many different techniques and technologies as applied to a simple presentation-oriented mashup. In the next chapter I discuss the preparations that need to be made before building an enterprise mashup.

Summary

In this chapter, I discussed some of the styles, techniques, and technologies that are used to build mashups for each of the three primary mashup domains—presentation, data, and process.

I discuss how to determine the domain for your mashup by analyzing the artifacts and data that are to be mashed. The domain is determined by analyzing user interface artifacts (presentation), data, and/or application functionality (processes).

The implementation style, techniques, and technologies used for a given mashup depend on the domain of the mashup determined by the analysis of artifacts and data. The techniques and technologies also depend on where processing will occur—in-process or out-of-process.

Once the domain is determined and the sources for the artifacts and data are established, you can proceed to apply languages, processes, and methodologies to the task of designing and building the mashup.

Chapter 2

Preparing for a Mashup Implementation

Before you design and build your mashup, certain preparations must be made. Primary areas of concern are requirements and constraints, security, governance, stability, data, implementation, testing, and performance. Certain aspects of each area of concern are unique to the environment of enterprise mashups in respect to other enterprise software disciplines, since the development model of mashups relies on a high degree of internal and external community involvement.

Preparing for enterprise mashup implementations involves a thorough understanding of the processes and IT landscape unique to a given company and/or industry. Techniques and technologies used for one company or industry are generally transferable to another; however, some aspects are unique and must not be overlooked. In fact, it is this uniqueness that typically creates the most value for your enterprise mashup. Effectively exposing the distinctive facets of your company or enterprise is a primary goal of any online endeavor. Achieving this goal with a mashup infrastructure can add value in ways that are not even apparent until a given mashup community is exposed to the resources and artifacts you present. Once a community becomes actively involved with your mashup infrastructure, the infrastructure itself evolves as a result of the community's unified creativity. Therefore, it is very important to make sure you have certain foundational preparations in place in anticipation of this creative evolution.

Unique Considerations for Mashups

An enterprise mashup must heed a more restrictive set of considerations such as compliance, standards, and security that public domain mashups are often free to ignore. In addition, a company or enterprise mashup must not expose certain types of intellectual property and/or protected information. This is similar to the issues that service-oriented organizations face when exposing service APIs to the web community. Enterprise mashups face the same issues as well as new issues related to data and UI artifacts that may be used by the mashup community, since an enterprise mashup can be available outside a corporate firewall, inside a corporate firewall, or a combination of both.

If the benefits of mashups are realized and a company or enterprise experiences a viral wave of activity and popularity due to its mashup environment, the company or enterprise must be ready to handle the surge of online activity. This is why preparatory efforts relating to security, performance, and scalability are taken to ensure that your infrastructure will handle the surge.

Every aspect of your IT infrastructure should be optimized and modularized to enable as much flexibility and, therefore, creativity as possible. The atmosphere of a community-based creative mind can be created; not only in the presentation domain, but in the data domain and process domain as well if you take the proper steps to create an infrastructure that supports loosely coupled interactions throughout.

Implicit to a loosely coupled infrastructure hoping to benefit from a viral community is the importance of the ability of a company or enterprise to monitor and manage the infrastructure effectively. As viral effects take place, bottlenecks in the infrastructure inevitably will be encountered even after painstaking efforts are taken in the design and implementation of the infrastructure. Therefore, it is vital that a potent monitoring and management framework is in place to identify bottlenecks quickly so that they might be rectified immediately.

The need for an agile security model for an enterprise mashup cannot be emphasized enough. Since the mashup infrastructure will need to handle requests and invocations from a vast array of clients and environments, the mashup infrastructure must be ready to handle many types of identity management and access controls. Since it is impossible to know beforehand just how your data modules, UI artifacts, and services will be used by the mashup community, you must have an infrastructure in place that allows you to control how your information is used without inhibiting access and creativity.

Being able to support an agile and viral environment is also important when it comes to deploying enterprise mashups and the components of the mashups. Flexible deployment techniques and technologies must be used throughout the scope of the infrastructure to allow updates and enhancements to be deployed without affecting other users' interactions with the mashup infrastructure. This includes activities related to editing and/or execution of the mashup artifacts.

Finally, the enterprise mashup and its artifacts must be tested. Testing enterprise mashups and mashup artifacts is one of the most important tasks a company or enterprise must address since the infrastructure and artifacts will be exposed to such a dynamic and vast community. Methods and techniques for testing mashups and mashup artifacts must be as agile and dynamic as the environment in which they will operate.

In this chapter I discuss the preparations that must be made to create an infrastructure that is ready to handle the dynamic and viral nature of enterprise mashups.

Determining Requirements and Constraints

The requirements and constraints for your enterprise mashup must integrate with the existing policies and practices of the environment for your company or enterprise. Identifying the requirements and constraints for your mashup is an evolutionary process, since the environment is bound to be affected by the mashup community with which it will interact. However, there are some basic requirements and constraints of your mashup that you can identify and address. As the mashup evolves these items will evolve or be replaced.

The following sections discuss the issues you must address when determining the requirements and constraints for your enterprise mashup.

Presentation Layer

Among items to address in the presentation layer are the API/content providers, the client execution environments, and the types of UI artifacts to be used in the mashup.

Service API Providers and Content Providers

One of the first items you must address is the source from which content/data will be accessed or retrieved. The type of content or data determines which sources will be used. Sources outside your internal environment will be retrieved from API and content providers that fit the needs of your mashup and the characteristic of your business. Often the API and content providers are chosen from a global pool of candidates without a format partnership being formed. Since one of the driving principles behind the success of mashups is the ability to provide value without incurring bureaucratic overhead, much of your content and/or data will be retrieved without any type of contractual arrangements or licensing formalities. This creates a very agile environment, but can pose risks to your business if you are not careful.

Some API/content providers such as Amazon.com and Google require licensing and/or the use of an application or development key before you can access their service APIs or content sites. Therefore, it is important to identify the API/ content providers well in advance and acquire the necessary keys or licensing clearance.

Many content sources do not expose formal APIs or resource URLs to access their content or data. In many cases you are forced to extract the data or content for your mashup using manual processes such as screen scraping. This is most common when using public domain sites that have not created formal procedures for accessing their content or data.

Screen Scraping

"Screen scraping" is the process of manually parsing the content of a site page, extracting the desired data from the page, and applying the data to your page or process. Once the data has been parsed and extracted, it is refactored into data structures that fit the semantics of your business and development environment. An example would be a mashup that uses publicly available data from government sites in concert with geographical or geopolitical data to create a site exposing high crime areas or to show trends in housing prices.

Screen scraping is usually used on a temporary basis, since there is no contract relating to programmatic access in place to ensure the prolonged consistency of the site and since some organizations frown on unauthorized scraping of their content. As a result, it is a fragile mechanism and must be constantly monitored to address changes that are bound to occur in the structure and/or availability of the page or site.

In Figure 2.1, the screen-scraping logic for both external sites is tightly coupled with the components using the scraped data. If either site alters the content or structure on which the scraping logic relies, the mashup page will be directly affected.

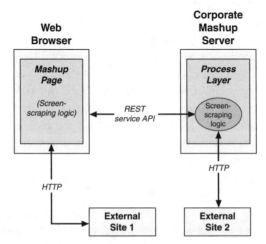

Figure 2.1 *Tightly coupled screen scraping*

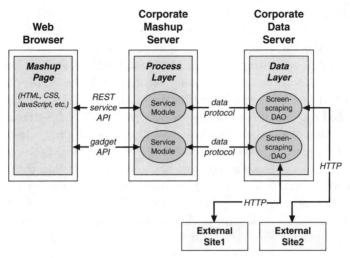

Figure 2.2 *Loosely coupled screen scraping*

To address the fragile nature of screen scraping, you should create an abstraction layer between your screen-scraping consumer component and the site or page from which the data will be scraped. With this abstraction layer in place, you can easily replace the site or page with another site if needs be or if a more preferable provider is found.

In Figure 2.2, an abstraction layer (data access objects [DAOs]) has been inserted between the screen-scraping consumer component (service modules) and the site or page from which the data is to be scraped. With this abstraction layer in place, if the external sites change, the references to the external sites can be replaced without affecting the service modules or the mashup page.

Mashup Client Execution Environments

A mashup client can be part of one of a number of different execution environments including a web browser, PDA, smart phone, and so on.

A mashup client execution environment typically interacts with a mashup server or content provider over an HTTP connection but is not necessarily restricted to this protocol. Therefore, mashup providers should be flexible enough to support different protocols and client execution environments.

Making a mashup infrastructure protocol-agnostic and capable of supporting many different clients is a process of building a modular platform with many layers of abstractions and facades. Logical layers hiding the physical details of specific pieces of logic and/or execution environments protect the mashup infrastructure from tight couplings and physical dependencies.

Part of the process of protecting your mashup infrastructure from dependencies and couplings involves hiding the details of specific locations for content providers and/or data sources.

In Figure 2.3, an abstraction layer (Protocol Adapter) is placed between the service modules and the service mashup clients to hide the details of the client protocols and locations. An abstraction layer is also placed between the service modules and the external content sites (External Site1 and External Site2) to hide the details of the data protocols and locations for these sites. With this framework in place, the service modules are shielded from protocol changes, location changes, data-source replacements, and other such events.

It is worth noting that since each client execution environment has a unique performance footprint, assumptions cannot be made about the ability of a client environment to handle large payloads or repeated request/response interactions. A pessimistic approach to client-environment capabilities will help to keep your infrastructure lean and responsive.

User Interface Artifacts

A widget, gadget, badge, or flake (among other names) is a small snippet of modular UI code that can be embedded within any distinct HTML-based page

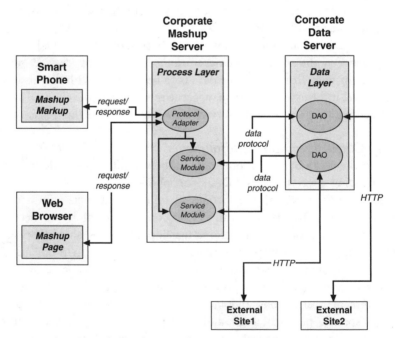

Figure 2.3 *Abstraction layers for a mashup infrastructure*

and used immediately without additional compilation or deployment. These reusable pieces of UI functionality are typically constructed from ordinary HTML, JavaScript, and/or other web markup languages.

UI artifacts such as widgets, allow high-level web developers to quickly and easily add value to a given HTML page just by embedding a small snippet of HTML or script code. The appeal of this type of UI enhancement is that it takes very little programming skill to implement, and many reputable sites are offering their services via this mechanism. Widgets, gadgets, badges, and/or flakes are being offered by companies such as Google and Yahoo! to allow functionality such as instant messaging, games, maps, and videos. The downside to using these types of UI artifacts is that they offer little or no ability to assimilate with the rest of the page. Therefore, these items are usually used in a portal-like fashion, occupying a distinct piece of real estate on a page, segregated from other items.

Very little preparation is needed to use a widget, gadget, badge, or flake. However, make sure that the snippet of code that is to be embedded in your mashup pages is from a reputable source and can be relied on to respond as you need. Also, you might be required to obtain a license to redistribute the content.

You should also screen any advertising content that is displayed in the widget, gadget, badge, or flake to be sure that it is in line with the values and style of your company or enterprise.

AJAX

As discussed in Chapter 1, Asynchronous JavaScript and XML (AJAX) is a set of technologies and techniques that enable two primary web-development functions: handling client/server requests and responses from within a browser page and manipulating the browser DOM to create dynamic user interfaces with a responsive look and feel, such as updating a UI artifact on a web page without refreshing the entire page.

AJAX techniques enable a UI experience that can be much more responsive than typical HTML. However, AJAX presents a number of advantages and disadvantages for which you must be prepared.

Following are some advantages of using AJAX:

- A communication model with a server using XML as the primary payload can be enabled.

- A more responsive UI can result due to processing small units of data at a time.

- Content can be retrieved via multiple connections, thereby possibly speeding up the retrieval process.

- Parts of a page can be updated in isolation to other parts, thereby reducing entire page problems due to an error in one section of the page.

- Bandwidth usage can be decreased since only small chunks of data from specific parts of a page can be transferred at any given time.

Following are some disadvantages of using AJAX:

- AJAX technologies and techniques are not as mature as traditional methods.

- Browser support for AJAX is not quite as secure as traditional methods.

- AJAX frameworks are not yet as mature as traditional methods.

- AJAX requires a more technical programming mindset than traditional methods, thereby raising personnel costs and reducing the size of the possible talent pool.

- Since AJAX depends on dynamic data retrieval and UI construction, search engines cannot process the content as effectively.

- The XMLHttpRequest object that AJAX depends on for its browser-to-server communication is subject to the browser security sandbox. Therefore, communication to a host other than the originating host is restricted, unless specific techniques are used to overcome the browser security sandbox.

- AJAX typically uses DOM-manipulation techniques to create dynamic UI effects. Although DOM-manipulation is becoming more consistent across browsers, there are still inconsistencies. You must be sure that the techniques you use in your mashup are consistent across all of your targeted client execution environments.

- The XMLHttpRequest object used by AJAX to handle request and response messages passing between client and server is obtained using different JavaScript methods depending on whether the browser is Microsoft-based (Internet Explorer). Most AJAX libraries address this difference already.

- The use of the XMLHttpRequest object implies the need for JavaScript being enabled by the client execution environment. While this is generally the case, some execution environments and/or companies do not or will not allow JavaScript. Also, some search-engine technologies will not pick up content semantics effectively if they are embedded within JavaScript code.

- The dynamic UI effects created by the use of DOM manipulation techniques can also play havoc on bookmarking and use of the "back" or "forward" button in a web browser and lead to a confused user experience. One of the effects enjoyed by the use of AJAX is a more desktop-like look-and-feel. However, the fundamental paradigm of the web browser is to allow unstructured browsing with the ability to go forward and backward with regards to your browsing history. Browsing history and AJAX execution history are usually unsynchronized leading to confused users if not handled effectively.

- Since AJAX can execute requests asynchronously in the background, it is important to keep the user engaged and updated as background processes execute. This typically involves the use of UI controls such as progress bars, status dialogs, and so on to inform the user of the progress of these processes.

Data Layer

When preparing your data layer, you must address things in terms of protocols and data formats. Since the environment for mashups is best addressed using a resource-oriented or REST-based architecture, you should prepare your data layer to work effectively within one or both of these environments.

Data protocols that lend themselves well to a mashup environment currently include JSON, XML, RSS and Atom, and SOAP. A careful analysis of your business model and technical climate can help to determine which are the most advantageous to the requirements of your mashup and, therefore, help you decide on the necessary steps to take from your data infrastructure.

Some of the advantages of each protocol and/or data format are

- **JSON**—A JavaScript data format that offers the advantage of easy accessibility and parsing from within a JavaScript environment. JSON supports a limited number of simple primitive types allowing complex data structures to be represented and consumed easily from standard programming languages.

- **XML**—A general-purpose markup language for representing data. XML data is easy for humans to read and understand. It is easy to transform into other formats using tools available in nearly every programming language. XML supports schema-based validation. It is supported by many formal enterprise data format standards. It supports internationalization explicitly. XML is platform and language independent and extensible.

- **RSS and Atom**—XML-based data formats for representing web feeds such as blogs and podcasts. RSS and Atom are ideally suited for representing data that can be categorized and described using channels, titles, items, and resource links.

- **SOAP**—An XML-based data format and protocol designed as a mechanism and messaging protocol to use for web services in which messages are exchanged within a payload known as an "envelope." Like XML, SOAP is platform and language independent and extensible. SOAP is a specific incarnation of XML that is supported and sometimes mandated for many formal enterprise data format standards.

Some of the disadvantages of each protocol or data format are

- **JSON**—Does not support namespaces or schema-based validation and is not accepted by nearly as many formal enterprise data format standards as XML. However, popularity and support for JSON is increasing rapidly. JSON does not support internationalization explicitly.

- **XML**—Is verbose and is strictly a data markup specification. It does not intrinsically support language-level primitives, arrays, objects, and so on. Therefore, a distinctly separate process typically occurs between serializing XML data to and from the programming language.

- **RSS and Atom**—Share the same disadvantages as XML and are primarily focused on representing resources and feed data. However, both formats are being adopted for more general purpose needs.

- **SOAP**—Shares the same disadvantages as XML as well as having the additional overhead of the SOAP envelope.

Other concerns that you should address in preparation for a mashup environment include defining your logical datasets as resources along with corresponding MIME types to facilitate a robust resource-oriented infrastructure. Also, transformation frameworks should be put in place to support such functions as data integration, sorting, and security augmentation.

Process Layer

Supporting a mashup infrastructure from the process layer involves creating a modular environment using loose-coupling techniques especially combined with service-oriented and resource-oriented techniques and REST interactions.

To effectively support a modular infrastructure, it is essential that you take steps to define semantically correct interfaces for your enterprise and that these interfaces clearly identify the resources and services you want to expose to mashup clients and resource consumers.

To help define your interfaces, try to gain an understanding of how the interfaces will be accessed. An examination of REST-based interactions across the

HTTP request/response space can help to understand the interactions for your services and resources.

- **HTTP** GET—Retrieves resources identified by URIs (Universal Resource Identifiers), named in a consistent manner for your enterprise. Name your URIs with resources and HTTP request verbs in mind and not actions. For example, rather than retrieving a resource named myfeed.rss with a URI such as the following:

  `http://example.com/resources?resource=myfeed.rss&action=get`

  Name it something like this:

  `http://example.com/feeds/123456`

  With this URI in place the resource client can use the HTTP GET command to retrieve the resource referenced with the identifier "123456", which in this case should map to myfeed.rss.

- **HTTP** POST—Creates a resource identified by the data contained in the request body. Therefore, to create the resource named myfeed.rss, the URI shown for the HTTP GET request would be used in an HTTP POST request along with the additional POST data needed to create the resource.

- **HTTP** PUT—Updates the resource identified by the request URI using the data contained in the request body.

- **HTTP** DELETE—Deletes the resource identified by the request URI.

For situations where REST-based resource URI access simply will not fit, a well-defined service API is warranted. In this case, make the semantics and purpose of the service very clear in the API. For example, a service API that instigates a process to create a bar chart from data passed to the API, you might define something like the following:

```
http://api.example.com/chartservice/v2/
bar?key=sdf97s7sf97we97wewe323?style=stacked&colorscheme=blue&data=...
```

In the preceding example, the URI clearly defines an API that calls version 2 of the chart service to create a bar chart with a style of "stacked" and a color scheme of "blue." Other necessary information such as the application key and data for the chart are also clearly indicated.

REST offers many benefits as long as necessary security preparations are made to address retrievals of resources and data over HTTP.

Preparing Your Security Infrastructure

Security for mashups is critical, since mashups include content and code from many different sources and sites, some of which you have very little control over. Care must be taken to ensure that your sensitive data is not passed along to external sites where it will be exploited by the competition, spammers, or worse. Therefore a well-designed security framework is a necessity to protect the data exposed by your mashup infrastructure.

One of the most effective means for monitoring and securing the flow of data that travels throughout your mashup environment is to send all requests through a centralized point of control.

For example, in Figure 2.4, the mashup page shown in the web browser makes requests to the corporate server and two external sites. In this scenario, data is transmitted from the corporate site to the mashup page where it is vulnerable as requests are made arbitrarily to the external sites.

A more secure mechanism would be to route all requests through a central security layer prior to transmitting to external sites. Responses received from external sites can then be monitored and managed effectively from a security standpoint.

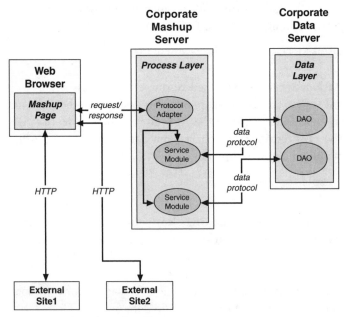

Figure 2.4 *Unsecured mashup data flow*

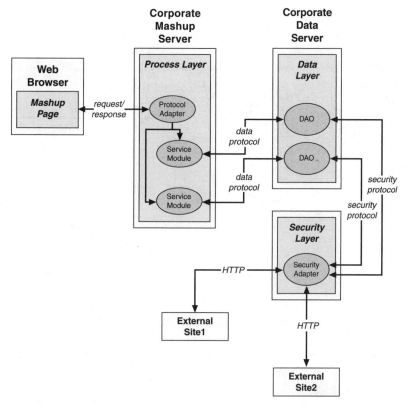

Figure 2.5 *Secured mashup data flow*

In Figure 2.5, all requests and responses are routed through the corporate mashup server and ultimately through the security layer of the mashup infrastructure. In this scenario, requests and responses to and from external sites can be regulated by the security adapter where business security rules can be applied.

By moving the build of the retrieval onto the server, you are moving more in the direction of JSF and its associated technologies, for example, Spring Acegi.

As additional data sources become involved with the mashup, new security protocols and providers are bound to become involved. With a centralized security layer in place, each new provider requiring support for technologies such as OAuth or OpenID can be addressed without involvement from the process layer or the mashup page.

In Figure 2.6, the security layer is enabled with support for different protocols and technologies by routing requests from the security adapter to the module configured to handle each specific type of security technology.

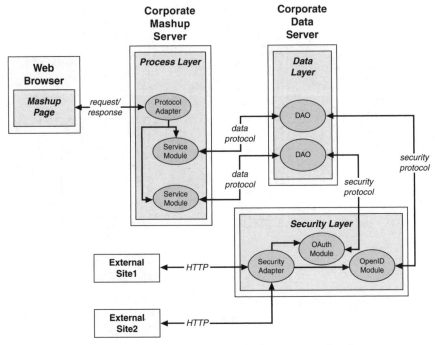

Figure 2.6 *Secured mashup data flow with multiple security technologies*

Presentation Layer

Interactions within the presentation layer for mashups are by definition community gathering events. Data is presented by providers with the very intention of being shared. As such, precautions must be taken from UI artifacts and presentation code to keep sensitive data where it belongs.

Steps can be taken to secure interactions within the presentation layer for a mashup. Some of these steps are discussed in the following sections.

Same-Origin Policy

Standard browsers are enabled with a mechanism known as the same-origin policy, the browser security sandbox, the same-domain policy, and other names. This mechanism specifies that HTML pages are prevented from making requests and receiving data and resources from sites other than the site that originated the HTML page. This is intended to prevent malicious scripts from compromising sensitive information shown on the page.

No preparations are needed to take advantage of the browser security sandbox. However, techniques are showing up that attempt to circumvent this mechanism. You need to be vigilant to watch for these and avoid their use.

DOM *Tree Access*

In a web browser, scripting code such as JavaScript can access the DOM of a page and access or make modifications to most of the elements on the page. This capability can be exploited to access sensitive data. For example, consider an HTML page with two iframes containing content from the same domain as the HTML page. In that scenario, the JavaScript snippet shown in Listing 2.1 executed in the parent HTML page within Internet Explorer can be used to swap the text for paragraph elements in the two iframes:

Listing 2.1 *Example of an iframe Swap*

```
var p1text =
  window.frames['iframe1'].document.
    getElementById('p1').innerHTML;
window.frames['iframe1'].document.
  getElementById('p1').innerHTML =
    window.frames['iframe2'].document.
      getElementById('p3').innerHTML;
window.frames['iframe2'].document.
  getElementById('p3').innerHTML = p1text;
```

If the content from one or the other iframes does not originate from the same host as the parent HTML page, the script in Listing 2.1 will be forbidden by the browser from accessing the DOM in another iframe and from swapping the text.

Access Control and Identity Management

The first step in controlling access to protected resources and managing identity is to validate all content and information received by the mashup page from any external sites or user input.

Next, recognize that at some point, your mashup will need to integrate with service APIs in proxy for a user. The goal is to do this without sharing the user's credentials across domains or sites. This problem is currently trying to be solved by open standards that specify techniques for using a common service to act on behalf of a user who has previously authenticated with the service without passing the user's credentials back and forth.

A few of these standards are

- **BBAuth**—Browser-based authentication from Yahoo! offers a single sign-on (SSO) mechanism to existing Yahoo! users, allowing them to use your services as long as you trust and accept their Yahoo! credentials.

  BBAuth requires you to register your application with Yahoo! along with a description of the application, contact information, application endpoint URL, and Yahoo! services your application will access. When registration is complete, an application ID and shared secret are provided to be used for making authenticated Yahoo! service API invocations.

Your application may not access a user's credentials until permission is granted by the user. To obtain permission, your application must direct the user to a Yahoo! login page, where the user enters his/her Yahoo! ID and password. If permission is granted at this point, Yahoo! redirects the request to your site along with a token to use to retrieve the user's credentials, represented as an auth cookie and a WSSID. The credentials last for one hour and must be supplied for every authenticated service API invocation.

- **OpenID**—A free service that allows users to access multiple secured sites with a single identity.

  Sites enabled to use OpenID present a form to a user where the user can enter a previously registered OpenID identifier such as jdoe.ids.example.com. The login form information is passed on to an OpenID client library where it is used to access the web page designated by the OpenID identifier—in this case, http://jdoe.ids.example.com. An HTML link tag containing a URL to the OpenID provider service is read from the web page. The site hosting the client library then establishes a shared secret with the OpenID provider service. The user is then prompted to enter a password or other credentials. The client library site then validates the credentials with the OpenID provider service using the shared secret.

- **OAuth**—A protocol for handling secure API authentication by invoking service invocations on behalf of users. OAuth-enabled sites direct users and associated OAuth request tokens to authorization URLs where the users log in and approve requests from the OAuth-enabled sites. OAuth uses a key, such as an OpenID identifier to enable authentication without passing around usernames and passwords.

Data Layer

As with the presentation layer, the data layer must be vigilant in controlling access to protected resources and managing identity by validating all data received from the presentation layer or from the process layer.

To facilitate secure interactions with multiple third-party security providers, ID keys and tokens should be stored securely by centralized repositories according to standard data security best practices.

In Figure 2.7, a secure repository is used to store application keys, ID keys, tokens, and so on needed by third-party security providers such as OAuth, OpenID, and others.

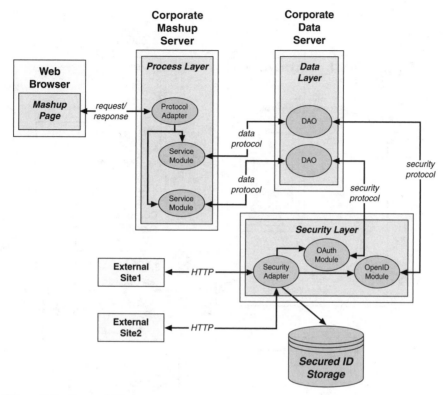

Figure 2.7 *Secured ID storage*

Process Layer

The process layer is often the first line of defense when validating and processing data received from a mashup page. Therefore, rules and processes must be in place to facilitate accurate and precise control over data as it is received.

To handle security issues such as access control, identity management, and credential propagation, the process layer may involve a separate server that can also be used by the mashup server.

In the scenario illustrated in Figure 2.8, a request requiring authentication or authorization is first handled by the corporate security server, outside any interaction with the mashup server. Once authentication and/or authorization is successfully established, the mashup server can be engaged using tokens, cookies, and so on that can be passed from the mashup page to the mashup server and ultimately to the security server.

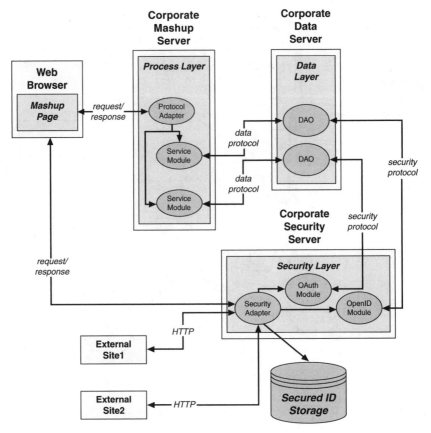

Figure 2.8 *Separate security server*

Preparing Your Governance Infrastructure

Mashup governance deals with the processes, policies, laws, and other issues that drive the way companies or enterprises conduct affairs within a mashup environment. This discipline is structured around the IT systems and technologies that personify the entire mashup infrastructure. Some areas of mashup governance overlap with standard IT governance and are not addressed here, but other areas of governance are unique to the mashup environment. These issues are the focus of this section.

Mashup governance is concerned with the manner in which the components (services, data, UI artifacts, and so on) that embody a mashup infrastructure are managed. Governance of mashup components must address the mashup lifecycle in its entirety including requirements gathering, design, implementation, testing and debugging, and deployment. Therefore, it is essential that policies and processes are put into place for each phase of the mashup lifecycle. Policies must be recorded and enforced to enable effective accountability and improvement.

Some of the other issues that a mashup organization often overlooks, but must address, include

- An accounting and logging of the software components (services, UI artifacts, and other software modules) and hardware components currently owned by the organization

- Implementation of development processes to ensure the most efficient use and reuse of these components

- Sufficient documentation and training to promote use of these components

- Strict record keeping to enable process improvements

To support governance across the lifecycle of building a mashup infrastructure, a company or enterprise should implement the use of automated toolsets to monitor, log, enforce, control, and archive the deliverables and processes for each lifecycle step. Some of the tools that fulfill these requirements include

- Project management software such as Basecamp, Microsoft Project, Open-Proj, and GanttProject

- Version-control tools such as CVS, Subversion, Git, and others

- System and software modeling tools such as UML modelers, CAD tools, and data modeling tools

- Build tools

- Testing tools and frameworks such as JUnit

- Issue tracking tools such as Bugzilla, Mantis, and Trac

- Deployment tools and frameworks

Presentation Layer

Some typical issues that you must address when managing governance of your mashup's presentation layer are

- Delivering the intended value UI artifacts

- Complying with the look-and-feel of your organization

- Effective maintenance of UI artifacts

- Monitoring performance of UI to meet service level agreement (SLA) requirements

- Managing deployment of UI artifacts to ensure an uninterrupted user experience

These issues are discussed in the following sections.

Data Layer

Mashup data governance involves the processes and technologies required to manage the views of data and resources for a company or enterprise. Goals for data governance are to ensure consistency, mitigate risk of noncompliance, monitor and improve data security, exploit the reuse potential of data via transformations and mediations, and manage the quality of data to address data integrity.

One of the most important goals in mashup data governance for most companies or enterprises is to ensure that data can be easily shared across departments, applications, and mashups. This goal is often met most effectively when a formal data authority group is established with this as its primary objective. A data authority officer or leader is often created to manage this process to ensure the success of the data authority group. This helps to establish a process that will be followed, and the benefits of proper governance, including compliance, security, among other things, will be realized.

Process Layer

Mashup governance for the process layer shares many of the same goals of a service-oriented infrastructure. A primary objective is to leverage components such as services, processes, and software modules, to deliver the most value for a company or enterprise. Governance for a mashup infrastructure seeks to comply with standards, laws, policies, SLAs, and other guides.

A mashup infrastructure should enable a company or enterprise to use services, processes, and software modules, for example, to enhance the speed and effectiveness of an organization to meet the demands of a dynamic market. This requires modular software architectures in which the semantics of software components, especially service APIs, match the business model very closely.

Change management enters a new dimension for enterprise mashups since the ultimate landscape for mashup components is dynamic and wide-reaching. The slightest change of a service API or resource URI can have extensive ramifications, both negative and positive, due to network effects of mashup component reuse. Therefore QA efforts must be diligent to ensure proper software quality for mashup components and subsystems.

Regression testing, load testing, and performance monitoring are areas that need special attention for a mashup infrastructure to ensure effective management of network effects.

Preparing for Stability and Reliability

Mashups create a dynamic environment where the potential for change is vast. Therefore, it is essential that you prepare your infrastructure to handle such issues as the potential load, error conditions, and data refactoring to name a few. This section discusses the issues and solutions to address when preparing your infrastructure to handle the evolution and stresses of a mashup environment, with attention paid to each specific mashup development type.

Presentation Layer

In the presentation layer of a mashup infrastructure, you must consider how accessing resource URIs and invoking service APIs on external sites can affect your mashup pages. The following are steps you can take to avoid errors and/or lapses from the perspective of the presentation layer:

- Be sure you rely on the results returned from external resource URIs or external service APIs. Establish a solid working relationship with external site vendors or use reliable sources. Test results thoroughly on a regular basis.

- Make sure external resource URIs and service APIs are reliable and will not change without warning. Consider protecting your pages from unanticipated changes in a UI artifact by placing a layer of abstraction between them and the external site using service APIs or resource URIs hosted on a site you control, such as your service platform or mashup server.

- Distribute local copies of third-party JavaScript libraries. Third-party JavaScript library references placed in HTML pages require a separate hop to the site where the libraries are hosted. If there is a problem with the site or the hop to the site, it is manifested in your page. Care must be taken to ensure that third-party libraries do not pose security risks. If possible, distribute copies of the libraries from a trusted source that you control.

- Observe strict management of the lifecycle for UI artifacts. Be sure to establish sound practices for handling the lifecycle for widgets, scripts, snippets, and so on. Use reliable change-management, testing, and issue-management techniques, methodologies, and tools.

Data Layer

In the data layer of a mashup infrastructure, you must consider how data returned from your own resource URIs and service APIs can affect your mashup pages and processes. The following are steps you can take to avoid trouble from the perspective of the data layer:

- **Choose the appropriate transaction isolation level**—Isolate transactions from each other using the level most effective for a given situation with special care taken to avoid unreleased locks in the event of transaction failure.

- **Use smaller datasets**—Smaller data sets reduce the potential for timeouts, interruptions, and other problems associated with larger payloads.

- **Rely on data snapshots whenever possible**—Cache data when possible and return snapshots, if a situation allows. REST-based invocations are understood to return a snapshot of a given resource; therefore, exploit this semantic to reduce overhead and unnecessary interactions with your data stores.

- **Use common/normalized schemas across data sources**—Common or normalized schemas across different data sources leads to a consistent view of the data no matter how it is accessed. Adhering to formal standards and specifications can play an important part in normalizing schemas. Some commonly used standards are the business transactions suite of schemas from the Open Applications Group, SOAP, vCard, and FIXML

Process Layer

Stability in the process layer of a mashup infrastructure involves adhering to common software-engineering and service-oriented principles, methodology, and patterns, which address modular frameworks and platforms. The following are steps you can take to ensure stability from the perspective of the process layer:

- **Modular service design**—Insulate client code from couplings defined by the process layer using patterns and techniques that allow finer-grained services to be aggregated into more general services that promote proper semantics for the business model.

- **Configuration management**—Adopt effective configuration management to deal with dependencies across multiple services, UI artifacts, and software modules, which may span multiple internal and external sites.

- **Change management**—Formulate change management methodologies in terms of entire business processes rather than just transactions. This may require a shift in employee responsibilities and roles.

- **Issue management**—Issue management tools and processes must be flexible and adaptable and able to support teams and products across a wide range of technological and business concepts.

- **Release management**—Adopt release management tools that are extremely flexible with a high-degree of communication and collaboration between affected business units and development teams. Automated processes and tools are important to reduce errors caused by manual intervention.

- **Testing and debugging**—Establish strict testing processes to support the entire mashup domain. Pay particular attention to unit testing and regression testing.

Preparing for Performance

Mashups are dynamic, heterogeneous environments where resource usage, load, and capacity requirements can be hard to predict. If network effects occur, system performance can be drastically affected. Therefore, it is essential to prepare for the potential impact that your system might encounter if such a condition is experienced. This section discusses some of the problems for which to prepare your mashup infrastructure as well as some of the solutions.

Presentation Layer

In the presentation layer of a mashup infrastructure, proper steps must be taken to keep the initial interface with your infrastructure optimized for bandwidth and network speed. The following are steps you can take to optimize the performance of the presentation layer of your mashup infrastructure:

- **Serve static when possible**—Dynamic service responses are usually slower than static data. Therefore, serve static data as service responses when it makes sense.

- **Load test UI artifacts**—Perform complete load testing on UI artifacts using isolated manual techniques or automated tools.

- **Optimize scripting libraries**—Be sure to identify script code that makes too many trips to the server for resources and service API invocations. This is especially important if the service provider monitors the number of times a request is made on a given service.

- **Compress JavaScript**—JavaScript can be compressed and used almost as easily and transportable as uncompressed JavaScript, so look into techniques and tools that can help to support this, if needed.

- **Cache and serve**—When possible, cache widgets, badges, and so on. and serve them from your site instead of an external site.

Data Layer

Mashups are typically resource/data intensive. Therefore, steps should be taken to optimize the data layer of a mashup infrastructure. The following are steps you can take to create an optimized data layer framework:

- **Cache**—If data can be used by multiple consumers and can bear being slightly stale, cache it.

- **Data snapshots**—REST-based resource URIs should return snapshots of data by design, so exploit this by providing snapshots of data. Refresh the snapshots between requests.

- **Intelligent data normalization**—Be smart about your data normalization. Instead of normalizing for the sake of normalization, normalize to the point where performance is not degraded to a large degree due to larger numbers of joins and other problems.

- **Reduce payload size**—If you find payload sizes creeping up, consider refactoring the resource-URI or service-API semantics to serve finer-grained results.

Process Layer

In addition to normal enterprise performance tactics such as load-balancing, caching, clustering, and so on, the process layer for a mashup infrastructure should be concerned with performance issues at the service and software module level, specifically addressing the following:

- **Optimize pools**—Impact on overall system performance can occur in thread pools, database connection pools, object pools, and so on. Perform thorough load tests on all pool structures and optimize accordingly.

- **Instrument effectively**—Intelligent instrumentation of services and software modules helps monitoring services and tools to identify problems earlier.

- **Exploit asynchronous interactions**—Asynchronous interactions with event-throwing services and software modules can help to build more flexible systems allowing better design decisions to be made and, therefore, leading to optimization by design. Asynchronous messaging is a natural communication model for loosely coupled infrastructures.

- **Enable hot deployment of services and software modules**—The ability to dynamically switch from one service or software module to another can eliminate downtime and lags. Service patches and updates can be applied when needed.

- **Control service and software component lifecycle**—The ability to automatically restart stalled or stopped services and/or software modules leads to a smoother-running system and an enhanced user experience.

- **Use stateless services**—Stateless services scale more easily than stateful services and simplify fault-tolerant failover.

- **Employ effective monitoring tools**—The use of effective monitoring tools helps you to identify problem areas quicker where fixes can be applied. Monitoring tools should complement your instrumentation techniques and event-throwing services and software modules.

Preparing Your Data Infrastructure

Mashups operate in a data-intensive atmosphere where the need for many views on the same data can be enormous. Therefore, an agile data infrastructure is needed to support current requirements as well as many unforeseen future requirements. This section discusses the issues and solutions to address when preparing your data infrastructure to handle the needs of a mashup environment.

Presentation Layer

In the presentation layer of a mashup infrastructure, data is typically handled by scripting code and usually takes the form of text; XML; an XML-based dialect such as RSS, RDF, or ATOM; or JSON. Proprietary formats are found but are not compatible with the open atmosphere in which mashups thrive.

The following sections address how you can prepare the presentation layer of your mashup infrastructure for efficient data handling.

POX *(Plain Old XML)*

XML is great for applying semantics to data and documents. It is great for describing data in a human-readable manner and also addresses internationalization in a powerful way. XML is a great format for serializing and transporting entire documents, and many specifications for business have mandated some dialect of XML as the payload format. Since XML was gaining such popularity as a universal document model, it seemed natural to design serialization techniques and technologies for it. However, XML is verbose and can be difficult to apply to programming language constructs. Mashups deal with data in smaller chunks, primarily from scripting languages running in a browser, and as such, XML was found to be a difficult fit at times.

Plain old XML (POX) is the name often given to XML when referring to it as a data-serialization format. POX was the original data format for which AJAX was developed. However, it was soon discovered that there was a need to reduce the size of payloads transported from browser to server and back. It was also apparent that more efficient techniques were needed to integrate payload data with scripting languages. JSON was developed to meet this need and is gaining widespread use and popularity.

JSON

JSON is a data format that is a subset of the JavaScript programming language and can embody simple data structures with a limited set of primitives that can be processed by most modern programming language. Objects can also be represented with JSON as associative arrays.

Listing 2.2 is an example of a corporate user object represented in JSON format.

Listing 2.2   *Example of a JSON User Object*

```
{
  "userName": "jdoe",
  "fullName": "John Doe",
  "employeeInfo": {
    "dept": "engineering",
    "title": "Senior Software Engineer",
    "employeeID": 12345
  },
  "emailAddresses": [
    "email1": "jdoe@example.org",
    "email2": "jdoe@example.com"
  ]
}
```

In Listing 2.2, the JSON user object is simply a human-readable JavaScript construct that can be processed using standard JavaScript language methods and techniques.

JSON has been gaining a tremendous amount of popularity in the AJAX and mashup community because it is an easy way to serialize small chunks of data in-and-out of a JavaScript environment such as a mashup or AJAX-enabled web page.

Techniques have been developed that exploit JSON and the dynamic ability to execute JavaScript on-the-fly to sidestep the browser security sandbox. Many widgets, gadgets, badges, and so on use these techniques and, therefore, many mashups depend on them.

RSS and Atom

RSS and Atom are XML dialects used to serialize web feeds such as blogs and news. An RSS or Atom document contains descriptive information about a feed such as a summary, description, author, published date, and other items.

RSS and Atom feed readers are used to enable a model in which users subscribe to feeds/blogs that will be periodically queried by the readers. The readers then display a brief summary of the feed/blog content to the user. This makes an effective means for receiving updates for content of interest to a user.

Mashups often use RSS feed data as content and as a means for obtaining summary information about a given topic or entity to add value to the content. This process requires the ability to parse the feed data using XML-parsing code, often in JavaScript when performed in a browser. Mashups also embed RSS and Atom readers in the page as a widget, gadget, or badge.

Microformats

Microformats is an approach to formatting snippets of HTML and XHTML data to create standards for representing artifacts such as calendar events, tags, and people semantically in browser pages.

For example, the hCard microformat shown in Listing 2.3 represents my information.

Listing 2.3   *Example of an hCard Microformat*

```
<div class="hCard">
  <div class="fn">J. Jeffrey Hanson</div>
  <div><span class="fn nickname">Jeff Hanson</span></div>
  <a class="url"
     href="http://www.jeffhanson.com/">
     http://www.jeffhanson.com/</a>
  <div class="country-name">USA</div>
</div>
```

Microformats use simple markup annotations meant to add semantic meaning to standard HTML and XHTML markup. The example in Listing 2.3 uses

HTML tag properties to annotate a block of markup representing my contact information.

Since microformats enable a more semantically rich web page, they are used in greater number to lend semantic meaning to mashup pages.

Data Layer

A mashup environment responds effectively to a resource-oriented data layer. In a resource-oriented data layer, anything that can be accessed over the HTTP protocol should be identified by and accessible with a URI. Therefore, it is essential to find a data model for your mashup infrastructure that lends itself well to resource-oriented, URI-referencing access methods.

The Resource Description Framework (RDF) standard is built on the notion that all resources are to be referenced using URIs. RDF also attempts to promote semantic meaning to data. This idea is central to the mashup environment, where data is a collection of loosely coupled resources. With respect to this knowledge, RDF makes a great fit as a universal data model for the data layer of your mashup infrastructure.

RDF as a Universal Data Model

RDF describes data as a graph of semantically related sets of resources. RDF describes data as subject-predicate-object triples, where a resource is the subject and the object shares some relation to the subject. The predicate uses properties in the form of links to describe the relationship between the subject and object. This interconnecting network of resources and links forms the graph of data that RDF seeks to define. More information about RDF can be found at http://www.w3.org/RDF/.

The following is an example of a simple RDF document:

```
<rdf:RDF
  xmlns:rdf="http://www.w3.org/1999/02/22-rdf-syntax-ns#"
  xmlns:em="http://www.example.org/email#">

<rdf:Description
  rdf:about="http://www.example.org/contacts/John Doe">
  <em:email>jdoe@example.org</em:email>
</rdf:Description>

<rdf:Description
  rdf:about="http://www.example.org/contacts/Bill Smith">
  <em:email>bsmith@example.org</em:email>
</rdf:Description>
</rdf:RDF>
```

Using URIs to expose access to your resources and using RDF to create the graph of relationships between resources makes RDF a natural choice for a universal data format.

Normalize Your Data

One of the first steps you should take when preparing the data layer of your mashup infrastructure is to normalize the views of your data. An effective method for normalizing views of your data is to model your data as URI-accessible resources defined by relationships in RDF. Once your data is normalized as RDF, you can transform to-and-from RDF according to useful semantics using standard, ubiquitous methods and tools.

A method referred to as "triple store" is used at times to store RDF statements in a relational database. With this method, an RDF subject-predicate-object triple is stored as one row with three distinct columns.

A useful example of normalizing data to RDF and using it in different scenarios is explained in the following steps. Note that in this example JSON is the ultimate data format consumed by presentation artifacts or other components:

1. Convert proprietary data and relational data to an XML dialect such as RSS, Atom, RDF, and microformat-annotated XHTML, depending on the type of consumer most likely to use the data.

2. Enable non-RDF, XML-dialect data with GRDDL transformations links, where applicable.

3. Transform GRDDL-enabled data to RDF. Transform non-GRDDL-enabled data to RDF with XSLT. A detailed discussion of GRDDL is presented later in this chapter.

4. Optionally, categorize RDF data using RDF-S and/or OWL

5. Convert RDF to JSON using utilities for the given programming language used by your process layer.

This process is illustrated in the diagram shown in Figure 2.9.

To understand this process, you must understand the relationships between RDF and RDF transformation technologies such as GRDDL. In this process, GRDDL and associated transformation documents are applied against an RDF document to produce the final transformed document.

RSS

Regarding the data layer, RSS is a good format for representing simple, categorized, dated, textual data. RSS data is easily consumable using standard XML

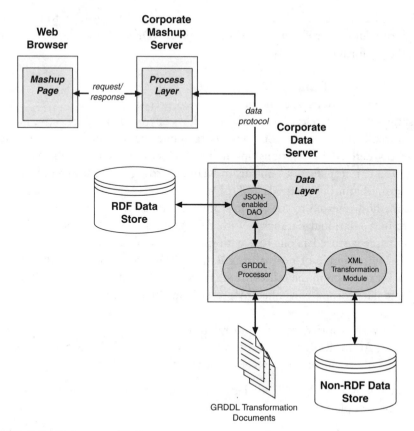

Figure 2.9   *Data normalization process*

tools. Also, many specific RSS libraries and tools are available in most programming languages.

RSS has a number of benefits including the ability to aggregate content easily
from multiple RSS data sources. The simplicity of the RSS structure is shown in
Listing 2.4.

Listing 2.4   *Example RSS 2.0 Document*

```
<?xml version="1.0"?>
<rss version="2.0">
  <channel>
    <title>Enterprise Mashup News</title>
    <link>http://www.jeffhanson.com/mashups/rss/index.rss</link>
    <description>
      Latest news about enterprise mashups.
    </description>
    <pubDate>Mon, 30 Jun 2008 05:02:00 GMT</pubDate>
    <lastBuildDate>Fri, 4 July 2008 10:22:01 GMT</lastBuildDate>
```

```
    <item>
      <title>Enterprise Mashups</title>
      <link>
        http://msdn.microsoft.com/en-us/library/bb906060.aspx
      </link>
      <description>
        This article describes the architecture of mashups,
        and explores how you can create mashups for use in your
        enterprise. We add wisdom gained from projects with
        systems integrators who have implemented mashups
        for the enterprise.
      </description>
      <pubDate>Wed, 2 July 2008 09:26:23 GMT</pubDate>
      <guid isPermaLink="true">
        http://msdn.microsoft.com/en-us/library/bb906060.aspx
      </guid>
    </item>

    <item>
      <title>
        Web and Enterprise Mashups for Web Services and Data
      </title>
      <link>
        http://www.developer.com/design/article.php/3755436
      </link>
      <description>
        This article discusses mashups and the differences
        between enterprise and web mashups, and
        data and application mashups. It also adds insight on
        tools that automate creation of enterprise mashups

      </description>
      <pubDate>Thu, 3 July 2008 11:14:54 GMT</pubDate>
      <guid isPermaLink="true">
        http://www.developer.com/design/article.php/3755436
      </guid>
    </item>
  </channel>
</rss>
```

Atom

Atom is another XML data format used for web feeds. The Atom format was developed primarily due to the many different incarnations of RSS and incompatibilities between RSS versions.

In contrast to RSS, Atom allows for a wide variety of content types including text, XML, and binary. Atom also allows references to external content and allows characters not contained in the ASCII character set.

Listing 2.5 is an example of an Atom document representing the same content shown in the RSS document in Listing 2.4.

Listing 2.5 *Example Atom Document*

```
<?xml version="1.0" encoding="utf-8"?>
<feed xmlns="http://www.w3.org/2005/Atom">
 <title>Enterprise Mashup News</title>
 <subtitle>Latest news about enterprise mashups.</subtitle>
 <link href="http://www.jeffhanson.com/mashups/atom/index.xml"/>
 <updated>2008-07-04T10:22:01Z</updated>

 <author>
   <name>J. Jeffrey Hanson</name>
   <uri>http://www.jeffhanson.com/contact</uri>
 </author>

 <entry>
   <title>Enterprise Mashups</title>
   <link
     href="http://msdn.microsoft.com/library/bb906060.aspx"/>
   <id>
     tag:jeffhanson.com,2008-07-02:/123456/enterprise-mashups
   </id>
   <updated>2008-07-02T09:26:23Z</updated>
   <summary>
     This article describes the architecture of mashups,
     and explores how you can create mashups for use in your
     enterprise. We also add wisdom gained from projects with
     systems integrators who have implemented mashups
     for the enterprise.
   </summary>
 </entry>

 <entry>
   <title>
     Web and Enterprise Mashups for Web Services and Data
   </title>
   <link
     href="http://www.developer.com/design/article.php/37554"/>
   <id>
     tag:jeffhanson.com,2008-07-03:/123457/enterprise-mashups
   </id>
   <updated>2008-07-03T11:14:54Z</updated>
   <summary>
     This article discusses what mashups are and the differences
     between enterprise and web mashups, and
     data and application mashups. It also adds insight on
     tools that automate creation of enterprise mashups
```

```
    </summary>
  </entry>
</feed>
```

GRDDL

Industries and enterprises are continually trying to find ways to standardize the representations of data that are transferred back and forth. XML dialects have been the most commonly used means for realizing this goal. With all of these standard XML dialects in place, a mechanism for extracting relevant data should be relatively easy. However, producing content that is relevant to a resource-oriented environment is not as simple. The GRDDL (Gleaning Resource Descriptions from Dialects of Languages) specification provides a means for producing resource-oriented content, specifically RDF content, from XML-based documents using transformation algorithms specifically formulated for a given XML dialect.

GRDDL attempts to associate specific transformation algorithms with a family of related XML documents by deriving semantics from the structure of the XML dialect. GRDDL allows URI-discoverable "namespace documents" or "profile documents" to declare that every document associated with a given namespace or profile contains semantically related data that can be extracted using the same algorithm. It also provides a means for linking to the algorithm to extract the data. Data extracted is most often used to create RDF documents.

In Listing 2.6, an XML document is declared as a source for potential GRDDL parsing and is linked to a GRDDL transformation.

Listing 2.6 *XML Document with GRDDL Transformation Link*

```
<contacts
   xmlns="http://example.org/contacts"
   xmlns:grddl='http://www.w3.org/2003/g/data-view#'
   grddl:transformation=
     "http://example.org/contacts/getEmail.xsl">
   <contact>
      <name>John Doe</name>
      <email>jdoe@example.org</email>
   </contact>
   <contact>
      <name>Bill Smith</name>
      <email>bsmith@example.org</email>
   </contact>
</contacts>
```

The XML in Listing 2.6 is linked to the transformation identified by http://www.example.org/contacts/getEmail.xsl. When the document is encountered by a GRDDL processor, getEmail.xsl transformation is applied against the document and the RDF document presented in Listing 2.7 is produced.

Listing 2.7   *RDF Document after GRDDL Transformation*

```
<rdf:RDF
  xmlns:rdf="http://www.w3.org/1999/02/22-rdf-syntax-ns#"
  xmlns:em="http://www.example.org/email#">

<rdf:Description
  rdf:about="http://www.example.org/contacts/John Doe">
  <em:email>jdoe@example.org</em:email>
</rdf:Description>

<rdf:Description
  rdf:about="http://www.example.org/contacts/Bill Smith">
  <em:email>bsmith@example.org</em:email>
</rdf:Description>
</rdf:RDF>
```

Process Layer

Preparing your process layer for mashup data is a process of accepting requests in a given format, returning responses in a given format, and providing mechanisms for supporting transformations from one format to another.

The following tasks prepare your process layer for mashup data handling:

- Support resource-oriented techniques such as mapping resource URIs to data sources.

- Enable a REST approach for handle service API requests.

- Return snapshots of data and cache when possible.

- Broadcast data changes to snapshot monitors to keep snapshots synchronized with data sources.

- Support a stateless communication model for service APIs.

- Combine results from multiple services using a normalized data model, such as RDF.

Preparing Your Implementation Strategy

Mashups can be easy to build from an unsecured, UI perspective. However, to address the constraints and requirements of a secure, scalable, and potent enterprise mashup, a comprehensive implementation strategy is needed. Preparing an infrastructure for the dynamic and agile nature of mashups requires tools and methodologies that are just as agile. This section discusses techniques and technologies to address when preparing your implementation strategy for a mashup environment.

Presentation Layer

The presentation layer of a mashup infrastructure must be enabled with that ability to change and evolve to meet the immediate influences of customers, industry trends, and market pressures.

The following sections address some of the tips and technologies that help to facilitate an agile and powerful presentation-oriented mashup layer.

A natural tendency when building a mashup is to stuff everything into the presentation layer since results can be seen so quickly. In fact, the popularity of mashups can be attributed to this phenomenon. However, when thinking in terms of an enterprise infrastructure that must evolve effectively and promote reuse across potentially many development groups, you must be careful to keep code where it may do the most good over a long period of time. Therefore, be careful to restrict code in the presentation layer to modules and scripts that fulfill the precise purpose of each particular mashup. Always monitor presentation layer development processes and make careful judgments about the interface abstractions and software modules involved to be sure to distribute logic to the most useful domain—that is, service platform, resource platform, data sources, presentation platform, and so on.

AJAX

AJAX is built on an HTTP communication mechanism from browser-to-server and back again that operates outside the normal user-instigated request/response process. This ability coupled with dynamic DOM manipulation techniques enables you to build richer web pages than traditional methods because it allows you to place a higher degree of application logic in the web page.

In a mashup environment AJAX can be exploited to process data and content from different sources and apply the data and content to a given web page dynamically. However, there are disadvantages to using AJAX in a mashup environment as well.

Following are some popular AJAX libraries:

- **The Yahoo! User Interface Library (YUI)**—http://developer.yahoo.com/yui/

- **dojo**—http://dojotoolkit.org/

- **jQuery**—http://jquery.com/

- **prototype**—http://www.prototypejs.org/

- **script.aculo.us**—http://script.aculo.us/

- **MooTools**—http://mootools.net/

IDEs and Editors

You need a development environment for your mashups. JavaScript editors and IDEs are typically the environments used; however, a number of mashup-specific tools are being introduced. The following are some of the more popular development environments for your presentation layer:

- **Eclipse**—http://www.eclipse.org/

- **MashupMaker**—http://www.webrpc.com/mm/edit.jsp

- **JackBe Presto**—http://www.jackbe.com/

- **Aptana Studio**—http://www.aptana.com/

- **Adobe Flex**—http://www.adobe.com/products/flex/

- **Yahoo! Pipes**—http://pipes.yahoo.com/pipes/

- **Google Mashup Editor**—http://code.google.com/gme/

- **Microsoft Popfly**—http://www.popfly.com/

Data Layer

Since data in a mashup infrastructure is most often accessed from many diverse consumers via resource URIs and/or service APIs, it is important to enable your data layer with frameworks that facilitate an agile data model. This implies a strict separation between your data and the data consumer, whether it is a UI client or a software component in your process layer.

Here are some of the more popular data access frameworks that enable agile development for your data layer:

- **iBATIS**—http://ibatis.apache.org/

- **Hibernate**—http://www.hibernate.org/328.html

- **ADO.NET Data Services**—http://msdn.microsoft.com/en-us/data/bb931106.aspx

- **Pear DB_DataObject**—http://pear.php.net/package/DB_DataObject

Resources in a mashup environment are considered to be current snapshots of a given piece of data. This assumption promotes the use of caching very easily.

Most web application environments can benefit to a certain degree from intelligent caching. Mashups and resource-oriented infrastructures can benefit to an even larger degree.

The following are some of the more popular caching frameworks that can be used for your data layer:

- **OSCache**—http://www.opensymphony.com/oscache/

- **Ehcache**—http://ehcache.sourceforge.net/

- **JBoss Cache**—http://www.jboss.org/jbosscache/

- **ASP.NET Caching**—http://msdn.microsoft.com/en-us/library/xsbfdd8c(VS.71).aspx

- **Zend_Cache**—http://framework.zend.com/manual/en/zend.cache.html

Process Layer

Preparing your process layer implementation strategy involves preparing for resource and service API support. This entails RESTful practices and loose-coupling techniques. Several specifications and frameworks are offered to help in this effort. There are some general principles that you can apply no matter which framework you choose.

The following is a list of some concepts you can apply to your process layer to implement an effective mashup implementation strategy:

- Create agile service APIs by enabling support for a number of different data formats.

- Make service APIs semantically rich by offering as much information as possible about what each API does in the API itself, for example, createNewUser, getUserAccount, deleteUsers, and so on.

- Standardize your service APIs and resource URIs. If you name a method to create a user "createNewUser," name other methods in a similar fashion, for example, createNewAccount, createNewProfile, and so on. In the same fashion, name resource URIs consistently. If one resource URI pointing to a bar chart is named http://resource.example.com/charts/v2/bar, name other URIs in the same manner, for example, http://resource.example.com/orders/v1/sales.

- Make each service API atomic so that it performs the function that it describes and nothing more.

- Respond to error conditions with very descriptive errors.

Several mature third-party frameworks exist that support a service-oriented environment. If you choose to use a third-party framework, be sure to choose one that supports loosely coupled relationships between software components and can be enabled to support a wide range of data formats.

Here are some of the more popular service-oriented frameworks that enable loosely coupled implementations for a mashup process layer:

- **Rogue Wave HydraSCA**—http://www.roguewave.com/products/hydra/hydrasca.php

- **Spring Dynamic Modules for OSGi Service Platforms**—http://www.springframework.org/osgi

- **Knoplerfish**—http://www.knopflerfish.org/

- **Apache Felix**—http://felix.apache.org/site/index.html

- **Eclipse Equinox**—http://www.eclipse.org/equinox/

- **WSO2 Web Services Framework for PHP**—http://wso2.com/products/wsfphp/

- **WSO2 Web Services Framework for Ruby**—http://wso2.com/products/wsfruby/

- **Microsoft Managed Services Engine**—http://www.codeplex.com/servicesengine

Preparing a Testing and Debugging Strategy

A testing and debugging strategy for a mashup infrastructure involves applying service-oriented and resource-oriented QA patterns along with patterns to test mashable UI artifacts and scripting code. Test patterns and tools should be agile enough to handle the dynamic nature of the mashup environment. This equates to patterns and tools configured with technologies that can change rapidly while still retaining the coverage needed to include tests for authentication, access control, governance, and so forth.

UI artifacts, service APIs, and data access, for example, must all be addressed in terms of code reviews, unit testing, and integration testing. However, because of the dynamic nature of the mashup environment, regression testing and performance testing must be very rigid and complete.

Presentation Layer

The presentation layer of a mashup infrastructure must be tested for its ability to change and evolve as the mashup domain evolves. It must also be able to meet typical UI constraints and requirements in an environment that processes content and input from a number of different sources.

The following tasks illustrate some of the issues that must be addressed when testing the presentation layer for your mashup infrastructure:

- Test input validation, including input that is simply being redirected through the presentation layer from one host to another.

- Test error handling from both internal and external hosts gracefully. Provide users with a consistent experience that gracefully handles errors no matter where they originate.

- Test internationalization and localization of content and UI artifacts that originate for internal hosts and external hosts.

- Test JavaScript performance and request/response interactions from AJAX calls.

- Apply automated test harnesses to JavaScript functions to apply strict regression tests.

- Apply rigorous integration and acceptance testing to be sure content and UI artifacts meet the standards for your organization no matter where they are hosted.

Following are some debugging tools:

- Venkman (http://www.mozilla.org/projects/venkman/)—A JavaScript debugging environment from Mozilla that supports Gecko-based browsers, such as Firefox and Flock. Venkman is distributed as a browser plug-in and runs as both a graphic debugger and a console debugger. Venkman supports evaluation of variables, object inspection, breakpoints, and call stack inspection. It also supports execution of JavaScript code snippets within the console.

- Firebug (http://www.joehewitt.com/software/firebug/)—A web development tool for Firefox that includes a JavaScript debugger. Firebug allows breakpoint setting, call stack inspection, evaluation of variables, evaluation of expressions, and performance profiling.

- **JsUnit (http://www.jsunit.net/introduction.html)**—A JUnit-styled unit testing framework for JavaScript.

- **JsUnit 1.3 (http://jsunit.berlios.de/)**—A unit testing framework for JavaScript that allows you to write automated tests and test suites. JsUnit is a part of JUnit 3.8.1, therefore, JsUnit 1.3 allows you to create unit test suites to effectively test each JavaScript function individually or as part of a suite of pages.

- **Fiddler (http://www.fiddler2.com)**—Fiddler is an HTTP debugging proxy that allows you to inspect and filter HTTP traffic on a Windows machine. Fiddler works automatically for applications based on the WinINET API such as Internet Explorer, Opera, and Safari. It can be manually configured to filter HTTP traffic received by Firefox.

Data Layer

Testing of the data layer in a mashup infrastructure must be concerned with loading data and querying data from many different consumers and in many different formats. Therefore, your testing strategy must be flexible and comprehensive.

Here are some of the tests that should be performed when testing your data layer:

- Test internationalization support. This usually takes the form of ensuring that UTF-8 is enabled for the data store and that all data is encoded consistently.

- Test database connections, deadlocks, and lock contention.

- Test queries to be sure they use the desired indexes.

- Test memory usage of cursors.

- Test data stores in a development "sandbox" to avoid destruction of vital data.

- Test data transformations to be sure they work according to configured business rules.

- Test performance of data writing and data queries to be sure they work within acceptable time periods.

Process Layer

The steps involved with preparing your process layer testing strategy must follow standard software-engineering testing practices but must also address service-oriented and resource-oriented issues. This means testing for REST-based inter-actions, loosely coupled services, and software modules.

The following are some of tests that should be performed in your process layer to address an effective mashup testing strategy:

- Test aggressively for system stability, including memory-leak detection, load handling, assertion failures, and other events.

- Encourage Test Driven Development (TDD).

- Apply rigorous regression and integration test suites.

- Be strict about expected test-case output.

- Test internationalization support throughout the codebase to ensure consistent encoding coverage.

- Throw and catch exceptions precisely to detect errors in the offending code.

- Trust source-code control tools rather than manual intervention to roll back changes.

Building a Simple Mashup

Preparing a mashup infrastructure involves a number of unique processes. Access to external data sources and service APIs must be established, application/API keys must be obtained, data sources must be prepared for agile access and transformation, services must be designed, and resource URIs must be mapped. Also, security must be analyzed across a broader spectrum of components, modules, and sub-systems than typical traditional systems. The following sections include pointers and examples of the ideas discussed in this chapter.

The deliverables for a mashup infrastructure are products of content and data from multiple sources. They are also dependent on good web development tools, including script editors and debuggers, service-oriented tools, and data access frameworks. The following are some of the items of interest for building your mashup infrastructure.

Registering with Service-API and UI Artifact Providers

Establish relationships with the service-API providers and UI artifact providers that you have chosen. Many well-known and trusted companies and enterprises provide powerful services and UI artifacts that are easily integrated. Some of these companies and enterprises are

- **USPS Web Tools for shipping labels, postal rates, address information, and so on**—http://www.usps.com/webtools/

- **National digital forecast database**—http://www.nws.noaa.gov/forecasts/xml/

- **Salesforce.com's developersource CRM services**—http://www.salesforce.com/developer/

- **Google Apps user provisioning**—http://code.google.com/apis/apps/gdata_provisioning_api_v2.0_reference.html

- **Doba eCommerce services**—http://www.doba.com/about/partners/about.html

- **ADP Employease HR management**—http://developer.employease.com/extend.html

- **Google AJAX Feed API**—http://code.google.com/apis/ajaxfeeds/

- **Dapper service for API creation**—http://www.dapper.net/developers/webservices/search.php

- **AOL Open Authentication API**—http://dev.aol.com/api/openauth

- **Yahoo! Browser-based authentication service**—http://developer.yahoo.com/auth/

- **buySAFE eCommerce Trust API**—http://developer.buysafe.com/

Normalizing Data to RDF

Jena is Java-based, semantic web development framework. It can be used to build applications and services that use RDF and OWL. It provides a number of different APIs including an RDF-creation API, an RDF-parser API, and rule-based inference APIs for RDFS and OWL.

Jena provides persistent storage of RDF data in relational databases including Oracle, Microsoft SQL Server, MySQL, HSQLDB, and PostgreSQL. A Jena database model is used to create a reference to a given database using an existing database connection, as shown in Listing 2.8.

Listing 2.8　*Creating a Database Reference for a Jena Database Model*
```
String dbURL = "jdbc:mysql://localhost/mashuprdf";
String dbUser = "jdoe";
String dbPasswd = "foobar";
String dbVendor = "MySQL";
String dbDriverClsName = "com.mysql.jdbc.Driver";

// load the driver class
Class.forName(dbDriverClsName);
```

```
// create a database connection
IDBConnection conn = new DBConnection(dbURL,
                                      dbUser,
                                      dbPasswd,
                                      dbVendor);

// create the DB model
ModelRDB model = ModelRDB.createModel(conn);
```

Once the model has been created, it can be used to store RDF resources and properties, as well as query for stored RDF resources.

Converting RDF and XML to JSON

The Java source code located at http://www.json.org/java/ provides simple yet sufficient functionality to convert XML text to JSON objects. To convert a string containing XML data to JSON object data involves one line of code similar to the following snippet:

```
org.json.JSONArray jsonArray =
  org.json.JSONML.toJSONArray(xmlText);
System.out.println(jsonArray.toString());
```

Consider applying the XML data presented in Listing 2.9 to the preceding code.

Listing 2.9 *Sample XML Data*
```
<contacts>
  <organization name="Example Inc."/>
  <contact>
    <name>John Doe</name>
    <email>jdoe@example.org</email>
  </contact>

  <contact>
    <name>Bill Smith</name>
    <email>bsmith@example.org</email>
  </contact>
</contacts>
```

The JSON object data shown in Listing 2.10 is produced.

Listing 2.10 *JSON Object Data Produced from XML*
```
["contacts",
 ["organization",{"name":"Example Inc."}],
 ["contact",
   ["name","John Doe"],
   ["email","jdoe@example.org"]
 ],
```

```
  ["contact",
    ["name","Bill Smith"],
    ["email","bsmith@example.org"]
  ]
]
```

Summary

A mashup infrastructure must address a very dynamic environment where the potential for change is vast. Therefore, it is essential that you prepare your infrastructure to handle this evolutionary process in areas such as potential load, error conditions, and data refactoring. An agile data infrastructure is needed to support current requirements as well as many unforeseen future requirements. Preparing an infrastructure for the dynamic and agile nature of mashups requires tools and methodologies that are just as agile.

This chapter discussed some of the preparations that should be made to create an infrastructure that is ready to handle the dynamic and agile environment of enterprise mashups.

Certain preparations must be made in a mashup infrastructure to address issues, including requirements and constraints, security, governance, stability, performance, data, implementation, testing, and performance, across all layers of functionality. Each area of concern has issues unique to enterprise mashups in respect to traditional enterprise software disciplines.

Chapter 3

Creating an Enterprise Mashup

An enterprise mashup infrastructure must present solutions for a very agile and evolutionary environment. Data sources can change rapidly, services are added and changed at any given time, presentation technologies are constantly being integrated with the system, marketing and sales departments are eager to apply the potential facilitated by the easy UI generation model, just to name a few of the things that can happen.

The dynamic nature of an enterprise mashup environment must be flexible and powerful enough to handle existing business operations as well as many new operations that arise out of the dynamic nature of the mashup development model.

This chapter discusses some of the common and uncommon problems that a mashup infrastructure can solve for a company. Also presented in this chapter is a foundation for an agile mashup development framework that can address the dynamic nature of an enterprise mashup environment.

Solving Enterprise Problems with a Mashup Infrastructure

An enterprise mashup infrastructure involves a lot of server-side processes and frameworks that can be used to update, access, and integrate unstructured and structured data from sources of all kinds. An enterprise mashup infrastructure can apply structure to extracted data that was previously unstructured. Such is the case when structure is applied to an ordinary HTML page using screen-scraping techniques.

An enterprise mashup infrastructure presents views of existing resources and data to other applications where they are restructured and aggregated to form new composite views that may even create new semantic meaning for the composite data and, therefore, for the enterprise itself.

An enterprise mashup infrastructure helps to solve non-UI integration problems as well as UI-related problems. Non-UI integration solutions enabled using the resource-oriented and semantic nature of an enterprise mashup infrastructure can be applied directly to specific business problems or indirectly through the orchestration and aggregation of the reusable components presented by the infrastructure.

Some of the features that can be provided with an enterprise mashup infrastructure are

- **Research projects**—Research efforts can be combined from multiple sources using information that is related semantically.

- **Financial analysis and reporting**—Financial decisions can pull from many different sources as well as from data obtained as a result of combining statistics and events from existing sources. Financial reports can enjoy a high-degree of accuracy and timeliness due to the ability to combine data from many different departments and organizations in real-time or near real-time.

- **Sales forecasting**—Sales estimates can be empowered using data pulled from a number of different sources, including accounting, customer support, and marketing surveys.

- **Purchasing accuracy**—Purchasing predictions can be more accurate due to the ability to combine production capabilities with current prices.

- **Inventory control**—On-hand inventory can be accurately matched with inventory, and predictions can be made based on up-to-date numbers pulled from many sources.

- **Defect tracking**—Defects can be tracked from a number of different sources including formal defect-tracking systems, customer support data, public forums, and private blogs.

- **Competitive pricing**—Prices can be compared to competitors' prices pulled from many sources including screen-scraped HTML of online stores.

- **Pinpoint marketing**—Products and services can be offered to customers based on interests posted to social sites, blogs, forums, and other web sites. Ads can be strategically placed in regions where demand matches supply points most accurately.

- **Personnel recruitment**—Open job requisitions can be matched to potential candidates using semantically rich data extracted from online resumes, blogs, and articles.

Potential Uses of Mashups for Your Enterprise

The dynamic and semantically rich nature of a mashup infrastructure can be applied in a number of different uses for an enterprise:

- **Identify potential customers**—Information pertaining to a given customer or company extracted from publicly available sources such as news feeds, stock reports, and search results can be combined with contact information and past sales efforts to more accurately identify potential customer needs.

- **Provide effective customer service**—Information about orders (for example, status, tracking, and delays) can be placed in the hands of your customer service personnel to enable them to provide accurate information and help to customers. Most shipping companies supply resource URIs and/or service APIs that provide up-to-the-minute information about a package in transit. This information can be combined with geomapping components and internal order-tracking systems in an aggregated web page to allow customer service personnel a precise view of packages as they are being shipped.

- **Enable your human resources departments**—Active job requisition requirements can be matched semantically with potential candidates' skill-sets, location, and experience level using data pulled from online profiles, blogs, job sites, or personal web sites. This leads to a deeper talent pool from which to draw as well as a more current pool.

- **Enable your IT departments**—Product defects and feature requests can be semantically aggregated with issue tracking software, online user-community data, customer support reports, and system monitoring data to discover bugs and feature requests earlier. Bugs can be more easily solved with a larger, more semantically accurate collection of data to use for analysis and bug re-creation.

- **Empower your R&D departments**—Research and development departments can exploit research data from a vast number of resources when using semantically enhanced resource mashup data. Data can be derived from

RSS feeds, screen-scraped sites, user forums, search results, government agency services, and semantically enhanced internal documents. Using data from different sources external and internal creates a virtual mindset that empowers your R&D departments with a far greater asset than just adding more head count.

- **Compete more effectively**—Provide your people with powerful tools with which to compete. Using data extracted from RSS feeds; search results; and competitor data such as financials, product prices, product news, acquisition announcements, and strategic partner agreements can be combined and delivered to your sales departments, marketing departments, and engineering departments, enabling them to keep a more watchful eye on the competition.

Uses of Mashups for Specific Enterprises

Mashups benefit enterprises in most every industry. Some benefits are evident. However, a number of industry applications are just now realizing the benefits of an agile mashup infrastructure.

The following items illustrate some of the unique industry benefits realized by a mashup environment:

- **Trucking and shipping**—Trucking and shipping companies can gather and analyze data from manufacturing companies, weather reporting sites, geomapping services, and road condition agencies to coordinate capacity, loading, and delivery for products.

- **Economic analysis**—Financial institutions and government agencies can combine and analyze data pulled from sources such as unemployment reports, interest rates, blue-chip company financials, foreign currency values, and mortgage-lending reports to make accurate assessments of the economy on macro and micro levels.

- **Intelligence gathering and analysis**—Government and defense agencies can gather and analyze data from external sources and internal sources to predict potential trouble situations and prepare more effectively.

Determining Relevant Application Patterns for Your Mashups

Applications built on a mashup infrastructure can take many forms. You should determine how your particular business needs will be best suited before beginning the design work for your mashup infrastructure.

A good way to start is by identifying the common business processes that are in place now and how they will be best served by UI artifacts, services, resources, and data formats.

Also, perform analysis of the target user audience for the mashups that will be created. Try to envision how each business process will be addressed from a user's perspective or from the perspective of another internal process.

Some of the common items to address when analyzing the potential uses of your mashup infrastructure are

- Serve specific business purposes with your mashup's perspective to meet market demands and solve business problems.

- Address user needs with your mashups to solve specific problems and to address necessary feature enhancements.

- Apply similar techniques and concepts used by other mashups in your industry that have solved the same problems.

- Realize ROI potential offered by a successful mashup infrastructure deployment.

- Solve integration issues using the semantic richness of an effective mashup infrastructure.

- Analyze existing internal systems and where they fall short of solving your business process challenges.

- Determine logical abstractions on your existing business logic that can be refactored as service APIs.

- Envision how future mashups will be used to form aggregate services and other applications or mashups by combining mashups.

- Examine your data sources to determine how they can best serve content in a semantically rich fashion.

A thorough analysis of the items described in the preceding list helps you to form rough designs of the primary components and artifacts to include in your mashup infrastructure, as well as helps you to understand the use cases that can be solved by the final product. Once this analysis is complete, you can start to identify sources of information from internal and external resources.

Identifying Sources of Information for Your Enterprise Mashups

Once you have identified the applicable uses for your mashups, you need to identify the sources of information from which your mashups will draw. Conversely, new uses will inevitably appear after sources are identified. The sources can include

- **Existing relational databases**—Data sources that are already in use by your organization.

- **Organizational documentation**—Documents, spreadsheets, sales reports, presentations, and forums that are available across servers and data stores throughout your organization.

- **Existing applications**—Information can be drawn from existing applications as event data, monitoring statistics, user trends, and so on.

- **Search results**—Search results can be filtered and structured to establish a semantic context that can be organized and stored as structured data.

- **External commentary**—Commentary from external sources about your organization. This can include analyst reports, news feeds, news sites, financial reports, competitor articles, online trade magazines, and user forums.

Identifying Services for Your Enterprise Mashups

Service APIs exposing functionality pertaining to the parts of your enterprise for which you want a public interface should be identified for your mashup infrastructure. These can be identified from a number of different mechanisms:

- **Legacy APIs**—Existing APIs that have no public interface can be refactored to expose a publicly available service API.

- **Composite services**—New functionality can be derived from the combination of multiple services or software modules. This functionality can then be exposed as service APIs.

- **Data access operations**—Data access operations often contain business semantics that may serve better as a service API. This can help to reduce couplings between data consumers and data sources, as well.

- **Search semantics**—Semantics of any search operations targeting content internal to your organization often indicate a need for business logic that is not yet available.

- **Events**—Events and notifications published by monitoring tools and software components can be combined to form complex events and service APIs.

Enterprise Mashup Design Tips

Designing your mashup infrastructure can entail some common principles as well as some unique techniques. Understanding the scope of these concepts can help you make the most effective use of resources and personnel. Some of these are as follows:

- **Optimize reuse**—Reuse is the primary benefit of a mashup environment. Promoting reuse promotes creativity. Seek to promote reuse by reducing couplings in code and by establishing effective internal documentation and policies in which software modules and services are clearly defined and promoted.

- **Always consider bandwidth**—Mashups tend to promote a high degree of network traffic due to the use of resources scattered across many diverse regions and sites. Be smart about making remote invocations and seek to keep payloads at a minimum. Use caching where applicable and try to transmit just changes in data rather than transmitting entire datasets over and over.

- **Promote the use of standards**—Doing this enables you to avoid proprietary and ad hoc data formats and protocols. This helps to present your mashups to more potential consumers, development tools, and client devices.

- **Establish a consistent look-and-feel**—Even though a mashup environment is dynamic and free-form, a consistent look-and-feel can be established for UI artifacts from which mashup builders can choose. Try to promote the look-and-feel even with external UI artifacts using CSS techniques, dynamic scripting techniques, and even refactoring data before it is presented.

- **Separate data models from presentation logic**—Keep data models and presentation logic separated. Markup languages provide a quick and easy way to present information in exciting views and forms. However, this can lead to the tendency to combine data and presentation logic in a tightly coupled page. Many presentation frameworks go to great lengths to keep logic and data separated, but they are only effective if this separation of data and logic is exploited in a strict manner.

Separation of data and presentation logic is essential for building agile teams of developers with different skill-sets. If data and presentation logic are separated, teams can work concurrently to produce deliverables much faster than a linear development approach.

One of the most effective technologies used by web page developers to realize separation of data and presentation logic is CSS. CSS allows look-and-feel for web pages to be completely separated from the actual data being presented. To modify the look-and-feel for single items, multiple items, or an entire web site, CSS classes and tags can be adjusted without any interaction with the presentation data.

Building the Foundation for an Enterprise Mashup Infrastructure

This section applies the concepts of this chapter to the construction of a foundation for an enterprise mashup infrastructure. The basis for the architecture used in this chapter is a multilayered platform as illustrated in Figure 3.1.

In the diagram shown in Figure 3.1, the layers for the mashup infrastructure will be embodied as interconnected service engines or kernels that will act as the primary segregation points of scalability and performance.

The service engines in this scenario will be implemented using OSGi objects, where each kernel can run independently from one another and manage service registrations, service invocations, and service lifecycles. Each kernel can be managed using JMX-based instrumentation, and each kernel can publish its registered services on which other kernels and software modules can make service invocations.

Implementing Infrastructure Layers Using OSGi

The foundation technology for each kernel will be the OSGi Service Platform (http://www.osgi.org). OSGi technology is ideally suited for any project that is

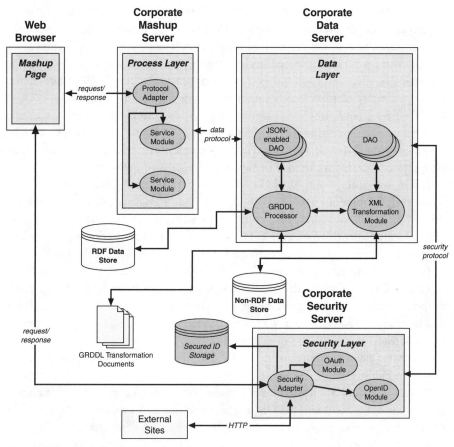

Figure 3.1 *High-level view of mashup infrastructure*

interested in principles of modularity, component-oriented, and/or service-orientated. OSGi technology combines aspects of these principles to define a dynamic service deployment framework that is amenable to remote management. OSGi also integrates nicely within management frameworks built on Java Management Extensions (JMX).

OSGi technology is the dynamic module system for Java. The OSGi Service Platform provides functionality to Java that makes Java the premier environment for software integration and thus for development. Java provides the portability required to support products on many different platforms. The OSGi technology provides the standardized primitives that allow applications to be constructed from small, reusable, and collaborative components. These components can be composed into an application and deployed.

The OSGi Service Platform provides the functions to change the composition dynamically on the device of a variety of networks, without requiring restarts. To minimize the coupling, as well as manage these couplings, the OSGi technology provides a service-oriented architecture that enables these components to dynamically discover each other for collaboration. The OSGi Alliance has developed many standard component interfaces for common functions such as HTTP servers, configuration, logging, security, user administration, XML, and many more. Plug-compatible implementations of these components can be obtained from different vendors with different optimizations and costs. However, service interfaces can also be developed on a proprietary basis.

OSGi technology adopters benefit from improved time-to-market and reduced development costs because OSGi technology provides for the integration of prebuilt and pretested component subsystems. The technology also reduces maintenance costs and enables unique new aftermarket opportunities because components can be dynamically delivered to devices in the field.

For the infrastructure discussed here, the OSGi implementation Apache Felix (http://felix.apache.org) will be used. Felix can be easily embedded into other projects and used as a plug-in or dynamic extension mechanism. This capability will be exploited to construct the service kernels for the OSGi kernel infrastructure discussed in the following example.

The basic class structure for each OSGi kernel will be similar to the diagram shown in Figure 3.2.

Notice in Figure 3.2 how the kernel relies on the Felix class. The Felix class is the primary entry point into the OSGi implementation provided by the Apache Felix project (http://felix.apache.org/site/index.html). With this infrastructure in place, services can be installed, updated, and uninstalled as OSGi bundles. Figure 3.2 illustrates the classes and interfaces making up the service layer (ServicePoller-Listener, ServicePoller, OSGiServicePoller, SimpleService, and ServicePollerEvent), the kernel foundation (Kernel, Daemon, OSGiKernel, KernelFactory, and KernelActivator), and OSGi classes from the Felix project (Felix, BundleContext, and Bundle).

Each kernel operates around the concept of polling for service bundles to be placed in a specified directory from which they will be deployed. When a service bundle is deployed, the services contained within will be registered with the specific kernel and available for use to other kernels and service consumers using local (in-VM) Java method calls.

The Kernel Daemon

Each kernel can be executed as a daemon thread in a stand-alone application or embedded within a running process. Once started, each kernel polls for new services, changed services, and removed services from a given directory.

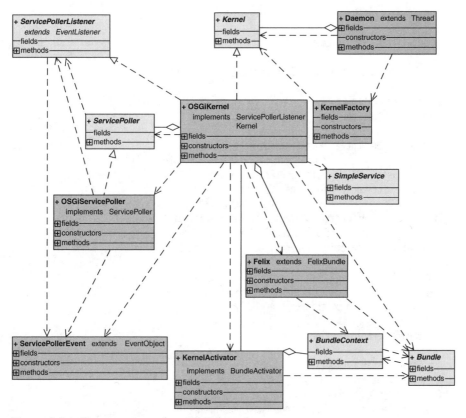

Figure 3.2 *Class structure of an OSGi kernel*

The code in Listing 3.1 illustrates the main entry point into an OSGi-based kernel.

Listing 3.1 *OSGI-Kernel Daemon Lifecycle Invocations*

```
Daemon daemon = new Daemon();
daemon.initialize();
daemon.startDaemon();
// wait until stopped
daemon.stopDaemon();
```

In Listing 3.2, a kernel daemon is instantiated, initialized, and started. From the point, work is done until the daemon is stopped as needed.

The methods invoked on the Daemon class operate on an instance of an abstract kernel interface made concrete through a kernel factory. In this case, the concrete kernel instance is an OSGi-based kernel instance.

Listing 3.2   *OSGI Kernel Daemon Details*

```java
/**
 * Initializes this daemon
 *
 * @throws KernelException - on error
 */
public void initialize()
  throws KernelException
{
  System.setProperty("com.jeffhanson.kernel",
                     "com.jeffhanson.kernel.osgi.OSGiKernel");
  String userDirPath = System.getProperty("user.dir");
  File servicesLocationDir = new File(userDirPath,
                                      "services");
System.out.println("Creating Kernel with service dir at [" +
                   servicesLocationDir + "]...");
  kernel = KernelFactory.newKernel(servicesLocationDir);
}

/**
 * Starts execution of this daemon
 *
 * @throws KernelException - on error
 */
public void startDaemon()
  throws KernelException
{
  Runtime.getRuntime().addShutdownHook(new Thread()
  {
    public void run()
    {
      System.out.println("Kernel daemon shutdown called");
      stopKernel();
    }
  });

  System.out.println("Starting Kernel...");
  kernel.start();

  Thread daemon = new Daemon();

  daemon.setDaemon(true);
  daemon.start();
}

/**
 * Stops execution of this daemon
 *
```

```
 * @throws KernelException - on error
 */
public void stopDaemon()
  throws KernelException
{
  System.out.println("Kernel daemon stopping...");
  running = false;
  stopKernel();
}
```

Notice how in Listing 3.2 the details of the kernel instance are hidden from the calling program via abstract interfaces and factories to allow different implementations of the kernel to be substituted as needed without forcing the caller to adapt.

The Mashup Infrastructure Kernel Using OSGi

The mashup infrastructure kernel is based on OSGi and uses the Apache Felix implementation to provide OSGi functionality for module, service, and bundle support.

The hidden details of the OSGi kernel are uncovered in Listing 3.3.

Listing 3.3   *OSGiKernel Details*
```
public class OSGiKernel
  implements ServicePollerListener,
             Kernel
{
  private static final int POLL_MILLIS = 30000;

  private KernelActivator m_activator = null;
  private Felix m_felix = null;
  private File m_cachedir = null;
  private ServicePoller m_servicePoller = null;
  private File m_servicesLocation = null;

  /**
   * Constructs an instance of this kernel
   */
  public OSGiKernel()
  {
  }

  public void initialize()
    throws KernelException
  {
    // Create a temporary bundle cache directory
    try
```

```
  {
    m_cachedir = File.createTempFile("osgikernel.cache",
                                     null);    }
  catch (IOException e)
  {
    throw new KernelException("Cache directory error: "
    + e);
  }
  m_cachedir.delete();

  // Create a case-insensitive configuration property map.
  //
  Map configMap = new StringMap(false);

  // Configure the Felix instance to be embedded.
  //
  configMap.put(FelixConstants.EMBEDDED_EXECUTION_PROP,
                "true");
  // Add core OSGi packages to be exported from the class path
  // via the system bundle.
  //
  configMap.put(Constants.FRAMEWORK_SYSTEMPACKAGES,
            "org.osgi.framework; version=1.3.0," +
            "org.osgi.service.packageadmin; version=1.2.0," +
            "org.osgi.service.startlevel; version=1.0.0," +
            "org.osgi.service.url; version=1.0.0," +
            "org.osgi.util.tracker; version=1.3.2," +
            "com.jeffhanson.service; version=1.0.0");
  // Explicitly specify directory to use for caching bundles.
  //
  String cacheDir = m_cachedir.getAbsolutePath();
  configMap.put(BundleCache.CACHE_PROFILE_DIR_PROP, cacheDir);
  configMap.put(BundleCache.CACHE_PROFILE_PROP",
                "OSGiMashupKernel");

  try
  {
    // Create kernel activator;
    //
    m_activator = new KernelActivator();
    List list = new ArrayList();
    list.add(m_activator);

    // Now create an instance of the framework with
    // our configuration properties and activator.
    //
    m_felix = new Felix(configMap, list);
```

```
        m_servicePoller =
            new OSGiServicePoller(m_servicesLocation,
                                  POLL_MILLIS);
        m_servicePoller.addServicePollerListener(this);
    }
    catch (Exception e)
    {
        throw new KernelException("Could not create OSGi kernel: "
                                  + e);
    }
}
```

In the construction and initialization phase of the OSGi kernel, a cache directory is established for temporary bundle storage. Also, various OSGi packages from the Felix project are specified and passed to the Felix class where an OSGi Service Platform will be created. A service-polling module is created and configured to poll for service changes at a given interval. The `OSGiKernel` instance is added to the service poller object as a `ServicePollerListener` object. This will enable the `OSGiKernel` instance to receive updates when a service is added, updated, and removed.

Service Methods

At this point, the kernel is initialized and started. Now, methods shown in Listing 3.4 can be invoked on the kernel to find services, add services, remove services, and make service invocations.

Listing 3.4 *Service-Related Methods of the OSGi Kernel*

```
/**
 * Retrieves a list of all installed services for this kernel
 *
 * @return a list of all installed services for this kernel
 */
public String[] getInstalledServiceNames()
{
    // Use the system bundle activator to gain external
    // access to the set of installed bundles.
    Bundle[] bundles = m_activator.getBundles();
    if (null != bundles && bundles.length > 0)
    {
        ArrayList<String> nameList = new ArrayList<String>();
        for (int i = 0; i < bundles.length; i++)
        {
            Bundle bundle = bundles[i];
            nameList.add(bundle.getSymbolicName());
        }
```

```java
    String[] names = new String[nameList.size()];
    nameList.toArray(names);
    return names;
  }

  return null;
}


/**
 * Retrieves a list of all installed services for this kernel
 *
 * @return a list of all installed services for this kernel
 */
public Object[] getInstalledServices()
{
  // Return the set of installed bundles.
  return m_activator.getBundles();
}


/**
 * Retrieves a service object by name
 *
 * @param serviceName - the name of the service to find
 * @return the service object or null
 */
public Object getServiceByName(String serviceName)
{
  Bundle[] bundles = m_activator.getBundles();
  if (null != bundles)
  {
    for (int i = 0; i < bundles.length; i++)
    {
      Bundle bundle = bundles[i];
      if (bundle.getSymbolicName().
          equalsIgnoreCase(serviceName))
      {
        return bundle;
      }
    }
  }

  return null;
}
```

The methods in Listing 3.4 return lists of services and individual services. Details about the objects returned are hidden to allow for implementation refactoring. Therefore, each object must be passed to the kernel when making invocations on a given service object.

Service Lifecycle Methods

The OSGi kernel has a simple lifecycle, consisting only of starting and stopping. Within these two lifecycle methods, the Felix framework is started and stopped. The service poller is also started and stopped.

Listing 3.5 illustrates the integration of Felix and the service poller with the OSGi kernel.

Listing 3.5 *Lifecycle Methods of the OSGi Kernel*

```
/**
 * Starts this kernel
 *
 * @throws KernelException
 */
public void start()
  throws KernelException
{
  // Start the felix framework when starting the kernel.
  try
  {
    m_felix.start();
    m_servicePoller.start();
  }
  catch (BundleException e)
  {
    throw new KernelException("Could not start OSGi kernel: +"
                              + e);
  }
}

/**
 * Stops this kernel
 *
 * @throws KernelException
 */
public void stop()
  throws KernelException
{
  // Stop the felix framework when stopping the kernel.
  try
  {
    m_servicePoller.stop();
    m_felix.stop();
    deleteFileOrDir(m_cachedir);
  }
  catch (BundleException e)
  {
    throw new KernelException("Could not stop OSGi kernel: +"
                              + e);
  }
}
```

The start and stop methods of the kernel do just what they imply—they stop and start the kernel. During this process the service poller is started and stopped, and the cache directory is emptied and deleted when stopped.

Service Deployment Methods

Services are registered with the kernel using the installService method and the uninstallService method. Services are deployed as OSGi bundles containing software components implemented as SimpleService instances. These components, when installed, provide the business logic and resource access logic for the mashup infrastructure.

Listing 3.6 illustrates the service deployment details of the OSGi kernel.

Listing 3.6 *Service Deployment Methods of the OSGi Kernel*

```
/**
 * Installs a service in this kernel
 *
 * @param serviceLocation
 * @return Object - the newly install service
 * @throws KernelException
 */
public Object installService(String serviceLocation)
  throws KernelException
{
  String tmpServiceLocation = serviceLocation;
  if (tmpServiceLocation.startsWith("file:/") == false)
  {
    tmpServiceLocation = "file:/" + tmpServiceLocation;
  }
  Object retVal =
    m_activator.installBundle(tmpServiceLocation);
  System.out.println(getClass().getName() +
                   " service installed: " +
                   serviceLocation);
  return retVal;
}

/**
 * Uninstalls a service from this kernel
 *
 * @param serviceLocation
 * @throws KernelException
 */
public void uninstallService(String serviceLocation)
  throws KernelException
{
  String tmpServiceLocation = serviceLocation;
  if (tmpServiceLocation.startsWith("file:/") == false)
```

```
    {
      tmpServiceLocation = "file:/" + tmpServiceLocation;
    }
    m_activator.uninstallBundle(tmpServiceLocation);
    System.out.println(getClass().getName() +
                    " service uninstalled: " +
                    serviceLocation);
  }
```

The installService method and the uninstallService method install OSGi bundles specified by a given file-system location. When the bundles are installed, the services within the bundle are registered as OSGi ServiceReference objects and made available for invocation requests.

Service Invocation Method

Services installed with a given kernel instance can be invoked via the kernel instance. The invokeService method provides the ability for a caller to make a generic call on any service installed with the kernel, provided the service is an instance of the SimpleService interface.

Listing 3.7 illustrates the service-invocation mechanism of the OSGi kernel.

Listing 3.7 *Service Invocation Method of the OSGi Kernel*

```
/**
 * Invokes a service installed in this kernel
 *
 * @param service - the service to invoke
 * @param props - any properties needed by the invocation
 * @return the return value from the invocation, or null
 * @throws KernelException
 */
public Object invokeService(Object service, Properties props)
  throws KernelException
{
  org.osgi.framework.Bundle bundle =
    (org.osgi.framework.Bundle)service;
  ServiceReference[] registeredServices =
    bundle.getRegisteredServices();
  if (null == registeredServices ||
      registeredServices.length <= 0)
  {
    throw new KernelException("Service not found ");
  }

  BundleContext bundleContext = bundle.getBundleContext();
  if (null == bundleContext)
  {
    throw new KernelException("Bundle context is null");
  }
```

```
Object serviceObj =
   bundleContext.getService(registeredServices[0]);
if (null != serviceObj)
{
  if (serviceObj instanceof SimpleService)
  {
    SimpleService simpleServiceObj =
       (SimpleService)serviceObj;
    return simpleServiceObj.execute(props);
  }
  else
  {
    throw new KernelException("Service object is invalid " +
                          bundle.getSymbolicName());
  }
}
else
{
  throw new KernelException("Service object is null for " +
                          bundle.getSymbolicName());
}
}
```

Service invocations are directed through the invokeService method (shown in Listing 3.7). A previously obtained service object is passed to the method along with any properties needed by the service. An Object instance or null is returned from the service invocation.

Each service is found by inquiring on a bundle object about its registered services. If a service is registered and is of type SimpleService, the invocation is made on the execute method of the SimpleService instance.

ServicePollerListener Method Implementations
The OSGi kernel registers itself with the service poller as an implementation of a ServicePollerListener to receive notifications when service bundles are added, updated, and removed from the services directory. That way, the kernel can register and unregister the bundles with the underlying OSGi framework.

Listing 3.8 illustrates the steps taken by the kernel to add bundles, update bundles, and remove bundles when notifications are received from the service poller.

Listing 3.8 *ServicePollerListener Implementation Methods of the OSGi Kernel*

```
/**
 * ServicePoller method
 *
 * @param evt
 */
```

```java
public void serviceAdded(ServicePollerEvent evt)
{
  try
  {
    installService(evt.getServiceLocation());
  }
  catch (KernelException e)
  {
    e.printStackTrace();
  }
}


/**
 * ServicePoller method
 *
 * @param evt
 */
public void serviceChanged(ServicePollerEvent evt)
{
  try
  {
    String serviceLocation = evt.getServiceLocation();
    uninstallService(serviceLocation);
    installService(serviceLocation);
  }
  catch (KernelException e)
  {
    e.printStackTrace();
  }
}


/**
 * ServicePoller method
 *
 * @param evt
 */
public void serviceRemoved(ServicePollerEvent evt)
{
  try
  {
    uninstallService(evt.getServiceLocation());
  }
  catch (KernelException e)
  {
    e.printStackTrace();
  }
}
}
```

The serviceAdded, serviceChanged, and serviceRemoved methods are implementations of the ServicePollerListener interface. These methods are called by the service poller when services are added to the service directory, removed from the service directory, or updated in the service directory.

The sequence of steps required to drive the OSGiKernel daemon through its complete lifecycle (initialize, start, and stop) is illustrated in Figure 3.3.

An instance of the OSGiKernel will dispatch service invocations through services that are registered with the kernel. The kernel relies on a service polling

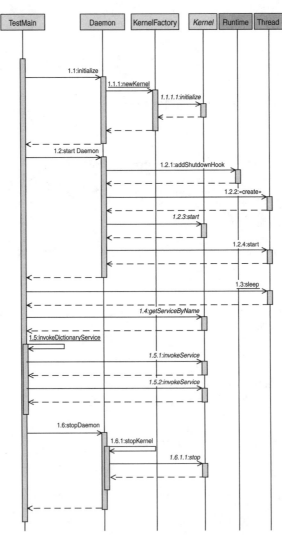

Figure 3.3 *Sequence diagram for lifecycle of an OSGi kernel*

mechanism that monitors a given service store, such as the file system or a database. The service poller registers new services as they are found, unregisters services as they are removed, and updates existing services as they are changed.

The Service Poller

The service polling mechanism allows hot-deployment of services at runtime without stopping and restarting the kernel.

Listing 3.9 illustrates the polling mechanism of the service poller.

Listing 3.9 *Service Polling Mechanism*

```
private void poll()
{
  File[] files = m_servicesLocation.listFiles();
  if (m_cachedFiles == null)
  {
    // add all new
    if (null != files && files.length > 0)
    {
      m_cachedFiles = new ArrayList<CachedFile>();
      m_cachedFiles.addAll(fileArrayToCachedList(files));
      fireServiceAddedForAll();
    }
  }
  else if (files.length <= 0)
  {
    // remove all
    fireServiceRemovedForAll();
  }
  else
  {
    // pick and choose
    List<File> newFileList = Arrays.asList(files);

    // find deleted files
    ArrayList<File> deletedFiles = new ArrayList<File>();
    Iterator<CachedFile> cachedFileIter =
        m_cachedFiles.iterator();
    while (cachedFileIter.hasNext())
    {
      CachedFile cachedFile = cachedFileIter.next();
      if (null == isFileInList(cachedFile.m_file,
                          newFileList))
      {
        deletedFiles.add(cachedFile.m_file);
      }
    }
```

```java
      // Remove deleted files from cache
      Iterator<File> deletedFileIter = deletedFiles.iterator();
      while (deletedFileIter.hasNext())
      {
        CachedFile cachedFile = cachedFileIter.next();
        System.out.println(getClass().getName() +
                          " service removed: " +
                          cachedFile.m_file.getAbsolutePath());
        removeFileFromCache(cachedFile.m_file);
      }

      // remove deleted files from new list
      newFileList.removeAll(deletedFiles);

      // find new and changed files
      Iterator<File> newFileIter = newFileList.iterator();
      while (newFileIter.hasNext())
      {
        File newFile = newFileIter.next();
        CachedFile cachedFile = isCachedFileInList(newFile,
                                            m_cachedFiles);
        if (null != cachedFile)
        {
          // test modified date
          if (newFile.lastModified() >
              cachedFile.m_lastModified)
          {
            System.out.println(getClass().getName() +
                              " service changed: " +
                              newFile.getAbsolutePath());
            fireServiceChanged(newFile);
          }
        }
        else
        {
          m_cachedFiles.add(new CachedFile(newFile));
          System.out.println(getClass().getName() +
                            " service added: " +
                            newFile.getAbsolutePath());
          fireServiceAdded(newFile);
        }
      }
    }
  }
}
```

As a service is discovered to be added, changed, or removed from the services location, the service poller adds it to its private cache and fires an event to all registered listeners conveying information about the service.

Event-Firing Mechanisms

The fireServiceRemoved, fireServiceAdded, and fireServiceChanged methods iterate through the list of listeners and invoke the appropriate method on each listener, passing a ServicePollerEvent object that contains information about the event and the service in question.

The methods in Listing 3.10 illustrate the implementation details for firing events from the service poller as services are added, removed, and modified.

Listing 3.10 *Event-Firing Methods*

```
private void fireServiceRemoved(File aFile)
{
  ServicePollerEvent evt =
    new ServicePollerEvent(this, aFile.getAbsolutePath());
  Iterator<ServicePollerListener> listenerIter =
    m_listeners.iterator();
  while (listenerIter.hasNext())
  {
    ServicePollerListener listener = listenerIter.next();
    listener.serviceRemoved(evt);
  }
}

private void fireServiceAdded(File aFile)
{
  ServicePollerEvent evt =
    new ServicePollerEvent(this, aFile.getAbsolutePath());
  Iterator<ServicePollerListener> listenerIter =
    m_listeners.iterator();
  while (listenerIter.hasNext())
  {
    ServicePollerListener listener = listenerIter.next();
    listener.serviceAdded(evt);
  }
}

private void fireServiceChanged(File aFile)
{
  ServicePollerEvent evt =
    new ServicePollerEvent(this, aFile.getAbsolutePath());
  Iterator<ServicePollerListener> listenerIter =
    m_listeners.iterator();
  while (listenerIter.hasNext())
  {
    ServicePollerListener listener = listenerIter.next();
    listener.serviceChanged(evt);
  }
}
```

The lifecycle methods, start and stop, on the ServicePoller object start and stop the necessary tasks and processes that a ServicePoller instance needs to effectively load and unload services as they are added and removed from the services directory.

Lifecycle Methods

The start method ensures that the services directory is created and then starts a timer that will run at intervals specified by the host component of the ServicePoller instance. The task associated with the timer is responsible for instigating the polling process that checks the services directory for service changes.

The methods in Listing 3.11 illustrate the implementation details of the lifecycle methods for the service poller.

Listing 3.11   *Service Poller Lifecycle Methods*

```
public void start()
    throws KernelException
  {
    if (m_servicesLocation.exists() == false)
    {
      m_servicesLocation.mkdir();
    }
    else if (!m_servicesLocation.isDirectory())
    {
      throw new KernelException(getClass().getName()
                    + ".start() invalid services location: "
                    + m_servicesLocation.getAbsolutePath());
    }

    TimerTask timerTask = new TimerTask()
    {
      public void run()
      {
        poll();
      }
    };
    m_timer = new Timer();
    m_timer.scheduleAtFixedRate(timerTask, 0, m_pollMillis);
  }

  public void stop()
    throws KernelException
  {
    m_timer.cancel();
    m_timer = null;
  }
```

Event Listener Support Methods

The `addServicePollerListener` method and the `removeServicePollerListener` method are responsible for respectively adding and removing listeners to the `ServicePoller` instance.

The methods in Listing 3.12 illustrate the implementation details of the event listener methods for the service poller.

Listing 3.12 *Service Poller Event Listener Methods*

```
public void
  addServicePollerListener(ServicePollerListener listener)
  {
    m_listeners.add(listener);
  }

  public void removeServicePollerListener(ServicePollerListener
                                          listener)
  {
    m_listeners.remove(listener);
  }
```

After a listener is added to the service poller it receives notifications as services are added, removed, and modified.

Summary

This chapter discussed some of the problems that a mashup infrastructure can solve for a company and also presented a framework that can serve as the foundation for an agile mashup infrastructure that responds to the dynamic and evolutionary nature of an enterprise.

An agile, semantically rich infrastructure promotes operations that update, access, and integrate diverse unstructured and structured data; presents access to existing resources and information in a manner that allows the data to be restructured and aggregated to form new views; and can solve non-UI and UI-related problems, including specific business problems, directly or indirectly via orchestration and aggregation of reusable components presented by the infrastructure.

The semantically rich nature of a mashup infrastructure can be exploited to identify potential customers, provide effective customer service, enable human resources and IT departments, empower R&D departments, and compete more effectively.

You must determine how your particular business needs will be best suited before beginning the design work for your mashup infrastructure, and then identify the sources of information from which your mashups will draw.

The mashup infrastructure described in this chapter is based on a service layer implemented using OSGi objects that can manage service registrations, service invocations, and service lifecycles. The service layer can publish registered services on which other software modules can make service invocations.

The framework described in this chapter lays the foundation for a flexible, modular service infrastructure. In subsequent chapters this foundation is expanded to enable a resource-oriented framework that works in unison with this service-oriented infrastructure. Chapter 4 introduces some of the fundamental concerns that should be addressed by all enterprise mashup infrastructures along with a detailed implementation that illustrates solutions to these concerns.

Chapter 4

Fundamental Concerns for Enterprise Mashups

As with any enterprise application environment, enterprise mashup infrastructures must address some fundamental concerns such as information management, security, governance, and system administration. In addition to the typical enterprise application concerns, mashup infrastructures must address an environment that seeks to fulfill dynamic requirements and flexible solutions to business issues.

In this chapter I discuss some of the most important concerns that all enterprise mashup infrastructures must address. I also discuss solutions for each concern and provide sample code at the end of the chapter.

Structuring and Managing Information

One of the biggest challenges facing an enterprise is the issue of managing and sharing data from disparate information sources. Legacy mechanisms for managing and sharing information typically kept data and metadata (data about the data) separated. Semantic techniques and technologies seek to bridge the gap between data and metadata to present a more effective means for applying meaning to information.

Choosing the fundamental format for data within your mashup infrastructure should be one of the first areas that you address. Mashup infrastructures derive much of their benefit from being able to apply and present semantic meaning to data and content. This enables consumers of the data and content to create aggregate components and content much more easily than traditional application environments.

Applying semantics to a repository of information involves extending typical data stores and content sources to provide structured meaning to the information stored within, thereby giving the information source features that better enable both machines and humans to understand the information. Once effective

125

semantic meaning has been applied to an information source, the data stored within can be discovered, aggregated, automated, augmented, and reused more effectively.

One of the best places to begin the quest for a semantic information foundation is the realm of formal specifications. These specifications currently include XML, the Resource Description Framework (RDF), the Web Ontology Language (OWL), RDF Schema (RDFS), and microformats.

Standards such as XML, microformats, RDF, RDF Schema and OWL are emerging as enabling technologies for semantic data interchange. The following is a brief overview of these technologies and how they seek to facilitate semantic interchange:

- **Semantics**—XML applies strict structure to document content. However, semantics are derived from separate schema documents and document type definition (DTD) documents.

- **Constraints and definitions**—XML Schema defines and constrains content stored within XML documents using an XML-derived syntax.

- **Relationships**—RDF is an XML-derived markup language that enables semantic meaning to resources using subject-predicate-object triples. Each triple can be used to form an understanding of the relationship between a subject and an object defining a resource.

- **Hierarchies**—RDF Schema describes RDF-defined resources using properties and classes. RDF Schema also provides features for defining semantically rich hierarchies of resource properties and classes.

- **Class relations**—OWL also describes resources using properties and classes and provides the ability to define relations between classes, cardinality, equality, enumeration, and so on.

- **Queries**—SPARQL (a recursive acronym that stands for SPARQL Protocol and RDF Query Language) is a language and remote protocol that is used to construct queries across assorted RDF-based data sources by using subject-predicate-object patterns.

- **Rules**—The Rule Interchange Format (RIF) is currently being defined and is seeking to be embraced as a means for creating an interchange format that can be used by disparate rule languages and inference engines.

The following sections discuss some of the data formats that are not necessarily semantically rich but are being used by semantic-based infrastructures to exchange data.

XML

XML is a general-purpose markup language for representing data. Data represented as XML is easy for humans to read and understand. Transforming XML data into other formats is easy using tools available in nearly every programming language. XML supports schema-based validation, and many formal enterprise data-format standards support XML. XML supports internationalization explicitly and is platform and language independent and extensible.

XML is verbose and is strictly a data markup specification. It does not seek to integrate with any one programming language intrinsically via support for primitives, arrays, and objects. Therefore, a distinctly separate process typically occurs between marshalling XML data to and from the programming language.

Data can be described easily in a human-readable manner with XML. XML is a great format for serializing and transporting entire documents, and many specifications for business such as ebXML, XBRL, FpML, OFX, and others have mandated some dialect of XML as the payload format. Since XML was gaining such popularity as a universal document model, it seemed natural to design serialization techniques and technologies for it. Semantic meaning within data and documents begins to be approached by XML using namespace context and metadata. For XML data to effectively embody semantic meaning, additional context must be applied in the form of such technologies as XSLT.

JSON

JavaScript Object Notation (JSON) is a JavaScript data format that offers the advantage of easy accessibility and parsing from within a JavaScript environment. JSON supports a limited number of simple primitive types allowing complex data structures to be represented and consumed easily from standard programming languages.

Namespaces and schema-based validation are not supported by JSON, and JSON is not currently accepted by nearly as many formal enterprise data-format standards as XML. JSON is a semantically challenged approach to data exchange, relying on tight couplings between data producer and data consumer to form an understanding of the data. However, where JSON lacks in semantic richness, it makes up for it in data terseness.

RSS and Atom

RSS and Atom are XML-based data formats for representing web feeds such as blogs and podcasts. Both formats are ideally suited for representing data that can be categorized and described using channels, titles, items, and resource links. An RSS or Atom document contains descriptive information about a feed such as a summary, description, author, published date, and so on.

Some of the same disadvantages that XML exposes are shared by RSS and Atom, and both are primarily focused on representing resources and feed data. However, both formats are being adopted for more general purpose needs. RSS and Atom address semantic meaning by describing resources and other entities using standard tags that explicitly define the purpose of each particular element, for example, title, creator, and published date.

Data Mediation

Mediation handles tasks such as protocol transposing, data-format conversions, and security validating to facilitate exchange between data producers and data consumers. Typically, mediation is an operation of a messaging framework used to simplify integration of systems, applications, services, or components. Processing data or messages as they are transported from one component to another is a typical function of mediation.

Mediator-driven data processing enables you to transform content from one format to another. This is especially helpful when a data producer and a data consumer embody some form of semantics defining the message or data, as the semantics can be applied during the mediation process. A mediator employs transformation and conversion using technologies such as XSLT transformations to perform the necessary data augmentation.

Mediation is a vital technology that enables separation of concerns between software components. Mediation frameworks operate on data as it travels from data producers to data consumers.

Mediation typically performs the following types of data augmentation:

- Transforming data from one format to another

- Embellishing data with additional data to fit the needs of the targeted data destination

- Routing data to one or more destinations based on routing rules, content, embedded attributes, and so forth

- Securing data in terms of authorization, authentication, signing, encryption/decryption, nonrepudiation, confidentiality, and enforcement of security constraints such as WS-Security and Kerberos

- Ensuring that data and/or the producer of the data is authorized to send to the targeted destination

Figure 4.1 illustrates a typical mediation framework and its relationship to a mashup server and service framework.

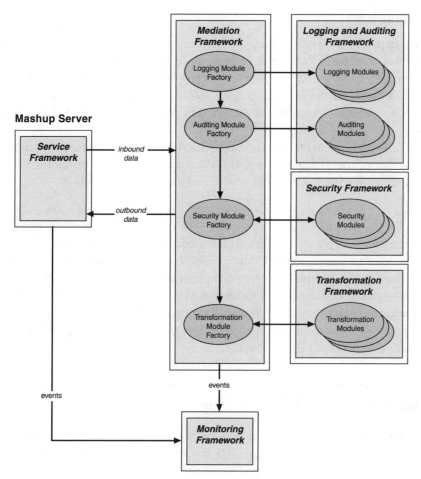

Figure 4.1   *High-level view of mediation framework*

As Figure 4.1 illustrates, data is directed from the service framework through the mediation framework and its components. The processed data is then routed to its final destination, also hosted in the service framework. As the data flows from the service framework, through the mediation framework, and back again to the service framework, events representing changes to the data such as exceptions, threshold attainments, and other events are registered with the monitoring framework. These events can then be viewed and used from management consoles and applications.

In the following sections, I discuss the components of the mediation framework and monitoring framework in greater detail.

Logging

Logging plays a vital role in a mediation framework and across a mashup infrastructure. As data is transferred from producer to consumer and across the different components that make up the mashup infrastructure, state changes, errors, time-sensitive events, and other information can be logged and used to optimize and stabilize the infrastructure. Logging is also a valuable tool used in distributed system debugging.

An effective logging framework can record system-level information to track the health of the system and individual components of the system as well as track the flow of data across the system and system components.

Auditing

Auditing features of a mediation framework enabled within a mashup infrastructure allow parties to track data at a level of interest to business and project managers. Audit information often complements a logging framework.

An auditing framework can validate data to ensure correctness according to business constraints and data-consumption requirements. Auditing frameworks can perform tasks to record the trail of data that can later be viewed and analyzed to ensure standards compliance.

Management and Monitoring

Management and monitoring are essential parts of the administration and optimization efforts within a mashup infrastructure. The decoupled and segregated nature of a mashup infrastructure makes the need for an effective management and monitoring framework even more important.

Management and monitoring also play an important part in maintaining a secure environment and enforcing policies (such as authorization, privacy, and auditing) and standards compliance. As components of a mashup infrastructure are executed and data is transported across the infrastructure, administration consoles and tools within an effective management and monitoring framework are used to record and direct information as transactions transpire.

Figure 4.2 illustrates the interactions and components of a typical monitoring framework as used in a mashup infrastructure.

In Figure 4.2, the mashup server and external event sources publish management event information such as JMX, SNMP, and/or proprietary notifications to the monitoring framework. The monitoring framework publishes management data to the mashup infrastructure where the data can be used by mashup components and admin consoles.

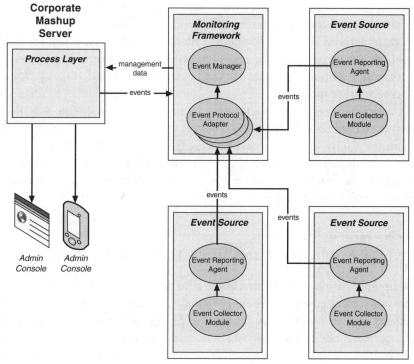

Figure 4.2 *High-level view of monitoring framework*

Performance or health monitoring is a specialized form of monitoring that entails collecting data reflecting conditions of a system or components that demand attention from administrative tools and personnel. Data collecting happens from your mashup infrastructure and its ancillary components and services during system runtime. This data should be comprised of a constant flow of information that reflects values that provide a fine-grained, detailed depiction of the health of services, components, and the infrastructure as a whole. A history of this information should be retained to establish baselines by which you can ensure the health of each component or system. This historical data can also be analyzed to determine the cause of problems.

Performance measurements are typically published from components that provide instrumented access to underlying software components, hardware components, and network interfaces. Performance measurement data can be published in a number of different formats including SQL query result sets, XML, and SNMP-related traps and notifications.

Each device or component from which performance data is published can publish the data directly or indirectly. Indirect publication occurs when events are measured by an external entity that extracts pertinent performance data and publishes it to management components and applications.

Each monitored device or component measures and collects data relating to its availability or performance and presents it to consumers. In this case the consumer is a monitoring framework. The data is presented via an API, event message, or other means.

As data is received by the monitoring agent from devices or components, the data is presented to administration consoles and mashup components to allow humans the ability to modify, view, and analyze using mashup UI artifacts.

Mashup infrastructure administration includes gathering and displaying monitored data, but other tasks are involved as well, such as facilitating configuration changes, registering services and components, and user account control.

Mashup Application and Infrastructure Administration

Mashup application and infrastructure administration must address the same tasks as a typical enterprise administration framework along with other tasks relating to the very dynamic and flexible environment in which mashups reside. Some of these additional tasks include categorizing and cataloging mashup components, managing API license keys, maintaining mashup component relationships, and others.

The following sections discuss some of the typical tasks that a mashup infrastructure administration framework must address.

Managing Mashup Configurations

Configuration management within a mashup environment must address the unique aspects of the mashup domain. This covers configuration management within the presentation layer, data layer, and process layer.

Some unique aspects related to managing configuration information within a mashup environment are as follows:

- **Categorizing and cataloging mashup components**—Mashup configurations typically maintain a catalog or repository of items that define the various components and services presented by the mashup infrastructure. In addition, external components and services are defined and categorized to enable effective reuse and reorchestration of each component.

- **Feeds**—Feeds are typically XML-based content, such as crime statistics for a given area, which is pulled from various sites to be consumed and viewed by a feed reader. Mashups often extract content from feeds and combine the extracted content with other types of components, such as geomapping components, to create new forms of content, such as a geomapping page with crime statistics for a given geographical region. Metadata for feeds is stored and maintained by a mashup administration framework to allow tools and developers a convenient mechanism for finding content to use in mashup pages and applications.

- **Widgets and other UI components**—Widgets are small UI components such as snippets of HTML, dynamic JavaScript, and embeddable widgets accessed from various sites. Metadata describing widgets and other UI components is stored within a repository or catalog of a mashup administration framework. The metadata can then be queried and accessed by mashup tools and developers to compose and orchestrate mashup pages and applications.

- **Mashup pages and applications**—A mashup page or application is a collection of data and widgets or other UI components. Mashup pages often apply filters to the data published by feeds and widgets to derive pertinent content for a given context. Filters are typically embodied by function and/ or operators that can be constrained and configured as needed to facilitate such tasks as sorting data, restricting data, and combining data. A mashup administration framework exposes tools that allow you to construct and modify filters in a graphical manner.

  Configuration data for each mashup page consists of the information about each component on the page and all the associated filters for each component. This information is stored and maintained within the catalog or repository of the mashup administration framework.

- **Mediation flows and configurations**—Mashup administration frameworks can present tools and applications to construct and configure messages and data transfers that flow through a mediation framework. The actual routes that messages and data transfers take as they travel from producer to consumer can be configured and maintained. Data mappings and transformation-constraints can be configured and maintained as well.

- **Security configurations**—an administration framework should provide facilities for managing security constraints and policies. User account information, transport-level security such as SSL, message-level security (WS-Security, encryption/decryption, and so on) for messages and data transfers, and certificates all need to be managed.

Mashup Administration Consoles

Mashup administration consoles must present interfaces for managing configuration data and for maintaining the items described previously. However, a mashup administration console should also present mechanisms for mashup page or application maintenance and deployment as well.

An effective mashup administration console is accessible from the web and provides the ability to install and uninstall new mashups and mashup pages on-the-fly. Interfaces for managing the lifecycle of mashup components, pages, and applications should also be presented by an administration console.

Visual orchestration tools where mashups can actually be constructed using drag-and-drop interfaces and property editors are often found in the same context as mashup administration consoles.

Administration consoles are often used to get a global view of the mashup infrastructure including views displaying alerts, errors, availability metrics, and performance metrics. Interfaces for taking actions necessary to correct errors and preempt critical situations can also be presented by mashup administration consoles.

Managing policies and standards compliance requires interfaces that can be presented by a mashup administration console. This encroaches on the area of governance within a mashup infrastructure, which is subject worthy of a separate discussion.

Governance in a Mashup Infrastructure

The creation, maintenance, and enforcement of lifecycles, policies, and standards compliance, often referred to as infrastructure governance, is essential for an enterprise mashup infrastructure. It is also a complex area of concern for a mashup infrastructure. Due to the dynamic nature of a mashup infrastructure, services, components, and mashup pages are constantly changing with new content and components frequently being introduced.

An important activity of mashup infrastructure governance takes place when the governance framework is powerful and comprehensive enough to provide sufficient policy and standards enforcement without being too restrictive, thereby inhibiting creativity and production.

Providing measures to ensure governance of security across the mashup infrastructure is a complex task in itself. You must be certain to not only secure your internal components and services, but you must also be certain to secure data that is often transmitted from your mashup pages or components to external sites and pages. A centralized framework where requests and data transfers are directed is often used to act as the enforcement agent of business policies and security.

Figure 4.3 illustrates a typical mediation framework that interacts with a governance framework to enforce security, privacy, and standards compliance.

As illustrated in Figure 4.3, a mediation framework can interact with a governance framework for enforcement of such things as data security, data privacy, and standards compliance.

Another aspect of mashup governance involves monitoring the creation and maintenance of mashups themselves. This aspect is responsible for overseeing

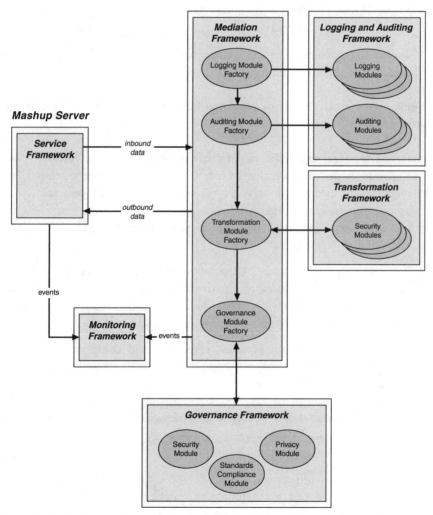

Figure 4.3 *Mediation framework interrelating with governance framework*

and enforcing which individuals have permission to create or enforce mashups. This is typically an exercise in role definitions and access management.

Some of the components of an effective governance framework include

- A registry or catalog to store and maintain services and mashup components to facilitate service or component discovery and reuse, and to allow related services or components to be discovered

- Mechanisms to facilitate policy enforcement across services, UI components, and data

- Mechanisms to facilitate validations and policy enforcement as data transfers and service requests transpire throughout the mashup infrastructure

- Tools and mechanisms to facilitate management of the lifecycle of services used within the mashup infrastructure

Some of the tasks central to your mashup component lifecycle governance process are as follows:

- **Define services, resources, and UI components**—Services, resources, and UI components must be discovered, designed, implemented, tested, and managed. Since mashup services, resources, and UI components will be accessed from a multitude of clients and in a vast number of scenarios, interface design is particularly important to ensure the greatest flexibility and stability.

- **Test services, resources, and UI components**—Services, resources, and UI components must be tested in a variety of ways to ensure asserted behavior performs in most any scenario. Be sure to test services, resources, and components in many composite applications and pages.

- **Manage the lifecycle for services, resources, and components**—Deployment of services, resources, and components can be a fragile process since the services, resources, and components may have direct and indirect dependencies from many diverse clients. It is important to maintain existing dependencies while applying new deployments with bug fixes and feature enhancements. A savvy versioning strategy is critical to ensure proper dependency management.

- **Manage security of services, resources, and UI components**—Maintaining a secure environment for deployment, maintenance, and invocations of your services, resources, and UI components is very important. You must ensure that only authorized individuals have rights to deploy and maintain each item. You must also ensure that only authorized clients invoke or access the services, resources, and UI components.

Since services, resources, and UI components can be shared among multiple applications and pages, a single bottleneck or point of failure can have a tragic ripple effect. It is therefore important to have a comprehensive monitoring framework in place along with easy-to-use administration consoles. The framework and consoles should allow administrators to monitor the global mashup infrastructure along with allowing a fine-grained view of each individual service, resource, and UI component providing details about performance, stability, and their current state. Service level agreements (SLAs) will depend greatly on your monitoring framework.

Interfaces and APIs for Services, Resources, and UI Components

Determining the proper interface for a service, resource, or UI component can have a tremendous impact on the usability of your mashup infrastructure. Since mashups depend on aggregating and orchestrating existing services, resources, and UI components, proper public interfaces are very important to a mashup infrastructure.

UI Component Interfaces

The interfaces for your mashup infrastructure's UI components are often the first point of access into the infrastructure. UI components are combined and orchestrated to form new functionality and new applications. It is therefore important that the interface for each UI component gives a clear depiction of what the component actually does. The interface of a component along with any documentation or descriptions should identify the functionality of the component along with some of the side effects from using the component. Side effects can be things such as whether the component changes the state of other software modules within the infrastructure or whether the component alters other components on the mashup page or within the mashup application.

Service Interfaces

Services can be invoked locally or remotely by service consumers. Interfaces can be applied to individual services to best suit the invocation model. For example, the interfaces published for local invocations are often more fine grained than interfaces published for remote invocations.

The transport protocol can have an effect on the interface by which a service is invoked. If the service is to be invoked across a TCP/IP network running the HTTP protocol, the interface must be compatible with a request/response interaction. To avoid continual network interplay, coarse-grained interfaces are often advocated for remote service invocations. Service invocations that send and return entire documents—typically XML-based documents—have become popular for many service invocations because of the inherent nature of this document-style interaction to be coarse grained.

Services available for remote invocation must be careful to serve clients in a timely manner to avoid adding to the response time delay inherent with networked communications. This requirement is often realized using some form of service instance pooling mechanism and stateless conversations between service consumer and service. In a stateless conversation, information from one request to another—that is, session information—is not maintained. This requires that each invocation carry with it the necessary information for the service to understand the entire semantics and goal of the invocation without regard to prior events.

Asynchronous service interfaces are beneficial in that invocations on the service can take place without noticeable blocking taking place in the consumer application or page. However, asynchronous interactions are not yet standard for an HTTP communication model. A number of mechanisms (AJAX polling, HTTP streaming, and HTML five server-sent events, for example) are seeking to solve and standardize this model.

Resource Interfaces

Mashup interactions are often interested in the exchange of data from one or more hosts. Data is often referred to as a resource. Therefore, it is important to provide coherent interfaces for resources exposed by your mashup infrastructure. A good model to follow is defined by the Representational State Transfer (REST), a resource-oriented architecture defined in a dissertation by Roy Thomas Fielding.

REST is a model for interaction with resources based on a common, finite set of methods. For the HTTP protocol, this is embodied by the methods GET, POST, PUT, DELETE, and sometimes HEAD. In a REST-based application or interaction, resources are identified are by a URI. The response for REST-based invocation is referred to as a representation of the resource.

REST is often realized using HTTP methods in the following manner: Create the resource (PUT), retrieve a representation of the resource (GET), delete the resource (DELETE), modify the resource (POST), and retrieve metadata about the resource (HEAD).

One of the primary issues with resource-oriented design is the problem of what should be considered a resource. A resource is often defined as any entity that can be directly referenced with a URI. Using this definition, anything that can be retrieved using a URI can be considered a resource. What an underlying infrastructure does to create the resource representation is of no concern to the resource consumer as long as the interface depicts a discrete and concrete chunk of data.

The interface for your mashup resources should be embodied represented as clearly defined URIs. Properly defined URIs for your mashup resources result in a more agile and usable infrastructure. An effective resource URI should include a unique name that identifies the resource clearly. Context information for the resource should be included in the URI if possible. For example, an individual user resource might be included in a context of users in the following manner: http://www.example.com/users/jdoe.

Building Mediation and Monitoring Frameworks for Mashups

As defined in the previous sections, mediation and monitoring are essential frameworks for an effective mashup infrastructure. This section applies the concepts of this chapter to the construction of a mashup.

The Mediation Framework

A mashup mediation framework provides components through which messages and/or data can flow to be augmented as needed to address business requirements. Figure 4.4 shows classes for a simple mediation framework along with their relationships to each other.

As illustrated in Figure 4.4, a message (or data item) is the central figure in a mediation framework. A mediator class is an aggregation of a number of components that are used to perform the necessary augmentation duties, such as transformation, logging, and auditing, on the message or data item.

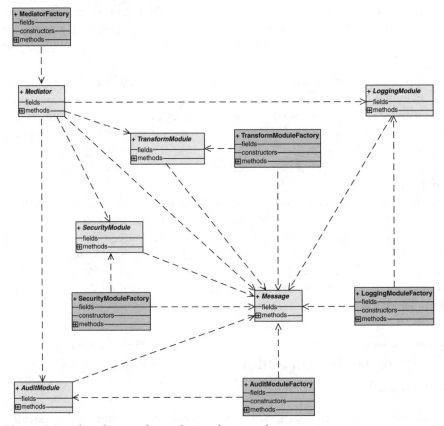

Figure 4.4   *Class diagram for mediation framework*

Figure 4.5 illustrates the sequence of interactions as a data item travels through this simple mediation framework.

In Figure 4.5, a message client creates a message that is then passed to a mediator instance to be augmented. A mediator factory is used to create the mediator instance. The specific mediator instance can be created based on configuration constraints, data producer attributes, message content or type, or a combination of all of the above.

Listing 4.1 shows a simple Java message client and the flow of control for creating a message and a mediator instance and for invoking the mediator to augment the message.

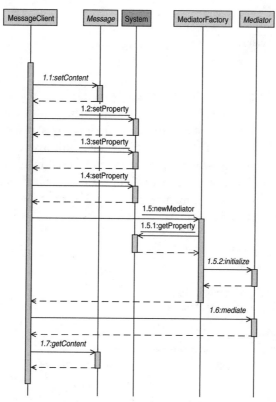

Figure 4.5   *Sequence diagram for mediation framework*

Listing 4.1   *The Message Mediator Client*
```
private void mediateMessage()
{
  Message message = new SimpleMessage("application/rdf+xml");
  message.setContent(RDF_CONTENT);

  try
  {
    System.setProperty("com.jeffhanson.audit.module",
                      SimpleAuditModule.class.getName());
    System.setProperty("com.jeffhanson.logging.module",
                      SimpleLoggingModule.class.getName());
    System.setProperty("com.jeffhanson.mediator",
                      SimpleMediator.class.getName());
    Mediator mediator = MediatorFactory.newMediator();
    mediator.mediate(message);
    System.out.println("\nMediated message:\n"
                      + message.getContent());
  }
```

```
  catch (Throwable t)
  {
    t.printStackTrace();
  }
}
```

As shown in Listing 4.1, the mediateMessage method of a message client creates a new RDF-based message. The message client then creates a mediator using a mediator factory, which uses a class name defined by a system property. The message client then passes the message to the mediator instance where it is augmented. The processed message is then ready to be used by its intended destination target. In this instance the target is simply the console display.

Listing 4.2 shows a simple mediator factory and the flow of control for creating a mediator instance.

Listing 4.2 *The Mediator Factory*

```
public class MediatorFactory
{
  public static Mediator newMediator()
    throws MediatorFactoryException
  {
    String mediatorClsName =
      System.getProperty("com.jeffhanson.mediator");
    if (null == mediatorClsName || mediatorClsName.length() <= 0)
    {
      throw new
        MediatorFactoryException("Mediator property not set");
    }

    try
    {
      Class cls = Class.forName(mediatorClsName);
      if (Mediator.class.isAssignableFrom(cls))
      {
        Object obj = cls.newInstance();
        Mediator mediator = (Mediator)obj;
        mediator.initialize();
        return mediator;
      }
      else
      {
        throw new
          MediatorFactoryException("Mediator system property "
                  + "is not derived from the Mediator class");
      }
    }
```

```
    catch (Exception e)
    {
      throw new MediatorFactoryException(e);
    }
  }
}
```

As shown in Listing 4.2, the mediator factory dynamically creates a new mediator instance using a class name set in a system property. The name could also be retrieved from configuration data found on the file system or a database. A default class name could be made available if desired to fulfill a situation where no alternative class name is provided.

Listing 4.3 shows a simple mediator interface and the methods by which individual mediation modules can be set using inversion of control (IoC) to populate each mediator instance.

Listing 4.3 *The Mediator Interface*
```
public interface Mediator
{
  void initialize();

  void mediate(Message message)
    throws MediationException;

  void setAuditModule(AuditModule auditModule);

  void setLoggingModule(LoggingModule loggingModule);

  void setSecurityModule(SecurityModule securityModule);

  void setTransformModule(TransformModule transformModule);
}
```

As shown in Listing 4.3, the mediator interface provides a method by which a mediator instance is initialized. The interface also provides setter methods that can be called by a mediator factory or other software component to set the individual mediation modules as needed.

Listing 4.4 shows a simple mediator and the steps it uses to process a given message using individual mediation modules.

Listing 4.4 *A Simple Mediator Implementation*
```
public class SimpleMediator
  implements Mediator
{
  private AuditModule auditModule = null;
  private LoggingModule loggingModule = null;
```

```java
private SecurityModule securityModule = null;
private TransformModule transformModule = null;

public SimpleMediator()
{
}

public SimpleMediator(AuditModule auditModule,
                      LoggingModule loggingModule,
                      SecurityModule securityModule,
                      TransformModule transformModule)
{
  this.auditModule = auditModule;
  this.loggingModule = loggingModule;
  this.securityModule = securityModule;
  this.transformModule = transformModule;
}

public void initialize()
{
}

public void setAuditModule(AuditModule auditModule)
{
  this.auditModule = auditModule;
}

public void setLoggingModule(LoggingModule loggingModule)
{
  this.loggingModule = loggingModule;
}

public void setSecurityModule(SecurityModule securityModule)
{
  this.securityModule = securityModule;
}

public void
setTransformModule(TransformModule transformModule)
{
  this.transformModule = transformModule;
}

public void mediate(Message message)
  throws MediationException
{
  try
  {
    if (null == auditModule)
```

```
  {
    auditModule =
      AuditModuleFactory.getAuditModule(message);
  }

  if (null == loggingModule)
  {
    loggingModule =
      LoggingModuleFactory.getLoggingModule(message);
  }

  if (null == securityModule)
  {
    securityModule =
      SecurityModuleFactory.getSecurityModule(message);
  }

  if (null == transformModule)
  {
    transformModule =
      TransformModuleFactory.getTransformModule(message);
  }

  auditModule.processInboundMessage(message);
  loggingModule.processInboundMessage(message);
  securityModule.processInboundMessage(message);
  transformModule.processInboundMessage(message);
  }
  catch (Exception e)
  {
    e.printStackTrace();
    throw new MediationException(e);
  }
 }
}
```

In Listing 4.4, the mediator uses aggregation to process a given message passed to mediation modules previously set in the mediator instance.

Listing 4.5 shows an implementation of an audit module factory. It illustrates the steps taken to create the audit module instance and to initialize the instance.

Listing 4.5 *The Message-Agnostic Audit Module Factory*
```
public class AuditModuleFactory
{
  public static AuditModule getAuditModule(Message message)
    throws AuditModuleFactoryException
  {
```

```
    String auditModuleClsName =
      System.getProperty("com.jeffhanson.audit.module");
    if (null == auditModuleClsName ||
        auditModuleClsName.length() <= 0)
    {
      throw new
        AuditModuleFactoryException("AuditModule property "
                                    + "is not set");
    }

    try
    {
      Class cls = Class.forName(auditModuleClsName);
      if (AuditModule.class.isAssignableFrom(cls))
      {
        Object obj = cls.newInstance();
        AuditModule auditModule = (AuditModule)obj;
        auditModule.initialize();
        return auditModule;
      }
      else
      {
        throw new
          AuditModuleFactoryException("Audit module property "
                  + " not derived from the AuditModule class");
      }
    }
    catch (Exception e)
    {
      throw new AuditModuleFactoryException(e);
    }
  }
}
```

As shown in Listing 4.5, the audit module factory dynamically creates a new audit module instance using a class name set in a system property. The name could also be retrieved from configuration data found on the file system or a database. A default class name could be made available if desired to fulfill a situation where no alternative class name is provided.

Listing 4.6 shows an implementation of a security module factory. It illustrates the steps taken to create the security module instance and to initialize the instance.

Listing 4.6 *The Message-Specific Security Module Factory*
```
public class SecurityModuleFactory
{
  public static
  SecurityModule getSecurityModule(Message message)
```

```
    throws SecurityModuleFactoryException
{
  try
  {
    Class cls = classForMessageType(message);
    if (SecurityModule.class.isAssignableFrom(cls))
    {
      Object obj = cls.newInstance();
      SecurityModule securityModule = (SecurityModule)obj;
      securityModule.initialize();
      return securityModule;
    }
    else
    {
      throw new
        SecurityModuleFactoryException("Security module class"
                   + " not derived from SecurityModule");
    }
  }
  catch (Exception e)
  {
    throw new SecurityModuleFactoryException(e);
  }
}

private static Class classForMessageType(Message message)
  throws SecurityModuleFactoryException
{
  String contentType = message.getContentType();

  if (contentType.equalsIgnoreCase("application/rdf+xml"))
  {
    return RDFSecurityModule.class;
  }

  throw new
    SecurityModuleFactoryException("Unknown message type "
               + "encountered in SecurityModuleFactory");
  }
}
```

As shown in Listing 4.6, the security module factory dynamically creates a new audit module instance using a class specifically intended for the type of message content. A default class could be made available if desired to fulfill a situation where no alternative class is found.

Listing 4.7 shows an implementation of a simple audit module and illustrates the steps it takes to process a given message.

Listing 4.7   *A Simple Audit Module Implementation*

```
public class SimpleAuditModule
  implements AuditModule
{
  public void initialize()
  {
  }

  public void processInboundMessage(Message message)
    throws AuditModuleException
  {
    if (null == message.getContentType() ||
        message.getContentType().length() <= 0)
    {
      throw new
        AuditModuleException("Message content type is not set");
    }

    if (null == message.getContent() ||
        message.getContent().length() <= 0)
    {
      throw new
        AuditModuleException("Message content is not set");
    }
  }
}
```

As shown in Listing 4.7, the audit module class uses the processInboundMessage to receive messages for which it will augment. The only processing performed in this case is to validate the message content type and the message content length.

Listing 4.8 shows an implementation of a transformation module that handles RDF data. It illustrates the steps it takes to process a given message and do a simple transformation by replacing the email address in a given message.

Listing 4.8   *A Transform Module Implementation for RDF Message Content*

```
public class RDFTransformModule
  implements TransformModule
{
  public void initialize()
  {
  }

  public void processInboundMessage(Message message)
    throws TransformModuleException
  {
    if (message.getContentType().
        equalsIgnoreCase("application/rdf+xml") == false)
    {
```

```java
    throw new
      TransformModuleException("Invalid content type: "
                              + message.getContentType());
}

String content = message.getContent();

InputStream inStream = null;

try
{
  URL url =
    new URL("http://example.org/enterprise/mashups");
  inStream = new ByteArrayInputStream(content.getBytes());
  final Graph rdfMemGraph =
    SortedMemoryJRDFFactory.getFactory().getNewGraph();
  Parser parser = new GraphRdfXmlParser(rdfMemGraph);
  parser.parse(inStream, EscapeURL.toEscapedString(url));

  ClosableIterator<Triple> iter = null;

  try
  {
    iter = rdfMemGraph.find(AnySubjectNode.ANY_SUBJECT_NODE,
                      AnyPredicateNode.ANY_PREDICATE_NODE,
                      AnyObjectNode.ANY_OBJECT_NODE);
    while (iter.hasNext())
    {
      Triple triple = iter.next();
      if (triple.getObject().
          toString().contains("@example.org"))
      {
        String objectStr = triple.getObject().toString();
        objectStr =
          objectStr.replace("@example.org",
                            "@jeffhanson.com");
        if (objectStr.startsWith("\""))
        {
          objectStr = objectStr.substring(1);
        }
        if (objectStr.endsWith("\""))
        {
          objectStr = objectStr.substring(0,
                            objectStr.length() - 1);
        }

        rdfMemGraph.add(triple.getSubject(),
                      triple.getPredicate(),
                      new LiteralImpl(objectStr));
```

```
                rdfMemGraph.remove(triple);
            }
        }

        iter.close();
        iter = null;

        ByteArrayOutputStream outStream =
            new ByteArrayOutputStream();
        MemRdfXmlWriter writer = new MemRdfXmlWriter();
        writer.write(rdfMemGraph, outStream);

        message.setContent(outStream.toString());
      }
      finally
      {
        if (null != iter)
        {
          iter.close();
        }
      }
    }
    catch (Exception e)
    {
      e.printStackTrace();
    }
    finally
    {
      if (null != inStream)
      {
        try
        {
          inStream.close();
        }
        catch (IOException e)
        {
          e.printStackTrace();
        }
      }
    }
  }
}
```

As shown in Listing 4.8, the RDFTransformModule class uses the processInboundMessage to receive messages for which it will augment. In this case the graph for an RDF message is traversed to find email addresses in which the hosts for the addresses are modified.

The Monitoring Framework

A mashup monitoring framework provides components that produce events containing data of interest to monitoring tools and consoles. This includes alerts, threshold-limit breaches, errors, warnings, and other events. Figure 4.6 shows classes for a simple monitory framework along with their relationships to each other.

As illustrated in Figure 4.6, management events are the central figures in a monitoring framework. Event sources are embodied by the ManagementEventSource interface. An event manager class uses protocol adapters to enable it to receive events remotely from management event sources across multiple protocols. The event manager then publishes events to administration console classes, in this case a command-line console class.

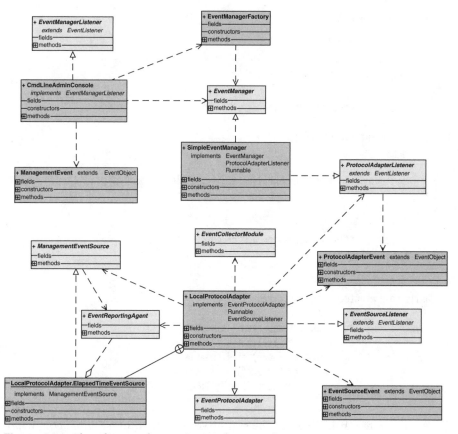

Figure 4.6 *Class diagram for monitoring framework*

Listing 4.9 shows part of a simple command-line console daemon class and the flow of control for creating an event manager and for receiving events from the event manager.

Listing 4.9   *An Implementation of a Command-Line admin Console*

```
private void monitorEvents()
  throws EventManagerFactoryException, EventManagerException
{
  System.setProperty("com.jeffhanson.event.manager",
                     SimpleEventManager.class.getName());
  final EventManager evtMgr =
    EventManagerFactory.newEventManager();
  evtMgr.addEventManagerListener(this);

  Runtime.getRuntime().addShutdownHook(new Thread()
  {
    public void run()
    {
      try
      {
        evtMgr.stop();
      }
      catch (EventManagerException e)
      {
        e.printStackTrace();
      }

      System.out.println("Command-line admin console stopped");
    }
  });

  System.out.println("Command-line admin console started");
  evtMgr.start();
}

public void eventOccurred(ManagementEvent evt)
{
  System.out.println("Encountered event: timestamp ["
                     + evt.getTimeStamp() + "], type ["
                     + evt.getType() + "], content ["
                     + evt.getContent() + "], source ["
                     + evt.getSource() + "]");
}
```

As illustrated in Listing 4.9 the monitorEvents method of a simple command-line console daemon class creates an event manager and then adds itself as a listener to the event manager. As events are received by the event manager, they are published to interested listeners. In this case, they will be published to the command-line console.

Listing 4.10 shows an example of output from the command-line console daemon class as events are received from the event manager.

Listing 4.10 *Output from Command-Line admin Console*
```
Encountered management event:
  timestamp [Sun Aug 03 23:29:20 MDT 2008],
  type [TIME_ELAPSED],
  content [Elapsed milliseconds: 5002],
  source [ElapsedTimeEventSource]
Encountered management event:
  timestamp [Sun Aug 03 23:29:25 MDT 2008],
  type [TIME_ELAPSED],
  content [Elapsed milliseconds: 5000],
  source [ElapsedTimeEventSource]
Encountered management event:
  timestamp [Sun Aug 03 23:29:30 MDT 2008],
  type [TIME_ELAPSED],
  content [Elapsed milliseconds: 5000],
  source [ElapsedTimeEventSource]
Encountered management event:
  timestamp [Sun Aug 03 23:29:35 MDT 2008],
  type [TIME_ELAPSED],
  content [Elapsed milliseconds: 5000],
  source [ElapsedTimeEventSource]
```

As illustrated in Listing 4.10, the events received by the event manager are published to the command-line console. In this case, the only management event source happens to just publish time-lapse events. Therefore, as time-lapse events occur, the console is notified and the events are displayed.

Listing 4.11 shows an implementation of an event manager factory. It illustrates the steps taken to create an event manager instance and to initialize the instance.

Listing 4.11 *The Event Manager Factory*
```
public class EventManagerFactory
{
  public static EventManager newEventManager()
    throws EventManagerFactoryException
  {
    String evtMgrClsName =
      System.getProperty("com.jeffhanson.event.manager");
    if (null == evtMgrClsName || evtMgrClsName.length() <= 0)
    {
      throw new
```

```
        EventManagerFactoryException("EventManager system "
                            + "property is not set");
    }

    try
    {
      Class cls = Class.forName(evtMgrClsName);
      if (EventManager.class.isAssignableFrom(cls))
      {
        Object obj = cls.newInstance();
        EventManager evtMgr = (EventManager)obj;
        evtMgr.initialize();
        return evtMgr;
      }
      else
      {
        throw new EventManagerFactoryException(
            "EventManager system "
            + " property is not derived from "
            + "the EventManager class");
      }
    }
    catch (Exception e)
    {
      throw new EventManagerFactoryException(e);
    }
  }
}
```

As shown in Listing 4.11, the event manager factory dynamically creates a new event manager instance using a class name set in a system property. The name could also be retrieved from configuration data found on the file system or a database. A default class name could be made available if desired to fulfill a situation where no alternative class name is provided.

Listing 4.12 snippet shows a simple event manager and the steps it uses to receive management events and to distribute the events to interested listeners.

Listing 4.12   *A Simple Event Manager Implementation*
```
public class SimpleEventManager
  implements EventManager,
             ProtocolAdapterListener,
             Runnable
{
  private ArrayList<EventProtocolAdapter>eventProtocolAdapters =
    new ArrayList<EventProtocolAdapter>();
  private ArrayList<EventManagerListener> listeners =
    new ArrayList<EventManagerListener>();
```

```java
private Thread workerThread = null;
private boolean running = false;

public SimpleEventManager()
{
  EventProtocolAdapter protocolAdapter =
    new LocalProtocolAdapter();
  eventProtocolAdapters.add(protocolAdapter);
  protocolAdapter.addEventReceivedListener(this);
}

public
SimpleEventManager(EventProtocolAdapter[] protocolAdapters)
{
  eventProtocolAdapters.addAll(Arrays.
                               asList(protocolAdapters));
}

public void run()
{
  running = true;

  System.out.println("SimpleEventManager started");

  while (running)
  {
    Thread.yield();
  }

  System.out.println("SimpleEventManager stopped");

  running = false;
}

public void
addProtocolAdapter(EventProtocolAdapter protocolAdapter)
{
  eventProtocolAdapters.add(protocolAdapter);
  if (running)
  {
    try
    {
      protocolAdapter.start();
    }
    catch (EventProtocolAdapterException e)
    {
      e.printStackTrace();
    }
  }
}
```

```java
public void
removeProtocolAdapter(EventProtocolAdapter protocolAdapter)
{
  int idx = eventProtocolAdapters.indexOf(protocolAdapter);
  if (idx >= 0)
  {
    try
    {
      protocolAdapter.stop();
    }
    catch (EventProtocolAdapterException e)
    {
      e.printStackTrace();
    }
    eventProtocolAdapters.remove(protocolAdapter);
  }
}

public void initialize()
  throws EventManagerException
{
}

public void
addEventManagerListener(EventManagerListener listener)
{
  listeners.add(listener);
}

public void start()
  throws EventManagerException
{
  Iterator<EventProtocolAdapter> iter =
    eventProtocolAdapters.iterator();
  while (iter.hasNext())
  {
    EventProtocolAdapter eventProtocolAdapter = iter.next();
    try
    {
      eventProtocolAdapter.start();
    }
    catch (EventProtocolAdapterException e)
    {
      e.printStackTrace();
      throw new EventManagerException(e);
    }
  }
}
```

```java
    workerThread = new Thread(this);
    workerThread.start();
  }

  public void stop()
    throws EventManagerException
  {
    Exception exception = null;

    Iterator<EventProtocolAdapter> iter =
      eventProtocolAdapters.iterator();
    while (iter.hasNext())
    {
      EventProtocolAdapter eventProtocolAdapter = iter.next();
      try
      {
        eventProtocolAdapter.stop();
      }
      catch (EventProtocolAdapterException e)
      {
        e.printStackTrace();
        exception = e;
      }
    }

    running = false;

    if (null != exception)
    {
      throw new EventManagerException(exception);
    }
  }

  public void eventOccurred(ProtocolAdapterEvent evt)
  {
    ManagementEvent mgmtEvt =
      new ManagementEvent(evt.getSource(),
                          evt.getTimeStamp(),
                          evt.getType(),
                          evt.getContent());

    Iterator<EventManagerListener> iter = listeners.iterator();
    while (iter.hasNext())
    {
      EventManagerListener listener = iter.next();
      listener.eventOccurred(mgmtEvt);
    }
  }
}
```

In Listing 4.12, the event manager uses one protocol adapter to receive events occurring in the same/local process. The event manager then runs in its own thread to listen for events passed to it from the protocol adapter.

Listing 4.13 shows the local protocol adapter and the steps it uses to receive management events from event sources and to distribute the events to interested listeners.

Listing 4.13   *An Event Protocol Adapter for In-Process (Local) Events*

```
public class LocalProtocolAdapter
  implements EventProtocolAdapter,
             Runnable,
             EventSourceListener
{
  // an event source class that reports time lapses
  //
  private static class ElapsedTimeEventSource
    implements ManagementEventSource
  {
    private static final String EVENT_TYPE = "TIME_ELAPSED";

    private ArrayList<EventCollectorModule> collectors =
      new ArrayList<EventCollectorModule>();
    private EventReportingAgent eventReportingAgent = null;
    private Date lastTimestamp = new Date();
    private Timer timer = null;

    public void
    setEventReportingAgent(EventReportingAgent evtAgent)
    {
      this.eventReportingAgent = evtAgent;
    }

    public void
    addEventCollectorModule(EventCollectorModule evtModule)
    {
      collectors.add(evtModule);
    }

    public void
    removeEventCollectorModule(EventCollectorModule
                                  eventCollectorModule)
    {
      collectors.remove(eventCollectorModule);
    }

    public void start()
    {
      TimerTask timerTask = new TimerTask()
```

```java
      {
        public void run()
        {
          Date currentTimestamp = new Date();
          long elapsedMillis =
           currentTimestamp.getTime() - lastTimestamp.getTime();
          EventSourceEvent evt =
            new EventSourceEvent("ElapsedTimeEventSource",
                                 new Date(),
                                 EVENT_TYPE,
                                 "Elapsed milliseconds: "
                                 + elapsedMillis)
          eventReportingAgent.reportEvent();
          lastTimestamp = currentTimestamp;
        }
      };

      timer = new Timer();
      timer.schedule(timerTask, 5000, 5000);

      System.out.println("ElapsedTimeEventSource started");
    }

    public void stop()
    {
      if (null != timer)
      {
        timer.cancel();
        timer = null;
      }

      System.out.println("ElapsedTimeEventSource stopped");
    }
  }


  // ====================================
  // member fields
  // ====================================

  private ArrayList<ManagementEventSource> eventSources =
    new ArrayList<ManagementEventSource>();
  private ArrayList<ProtocolAdapterListener> listeners =
    new ArrayList<ProtocolAdapterListener>();
  private boolean running = false;
  private Thread workerThread = null;

  public LocalProtocolAdapter()
  {
```

```java
    ManagementEventSource eventSource =
      new ElapsedTimeEventSource();

    this.eventSources.add(eventSource);

    // create a reporting agent that reports events
    // as local method calls
    //
    eventSource.setEventReportingAgent(new EventReportingAgent()
    {
      public void reportEvent(EventSourceEvent evt)
      {
        eventOccurred(evt);
      }
    });
  }

  public
  LocalProtocolAdapter(ManagementEventSource[] eventSources)
  {
    this.eventSources.addAll(Arrays.asList(eventSources));
  }

  public void run()
  {
    running = true;

    System.out.println("LocalProtocolAdapter started");

    while (running)
    {
      Thread.yield();
    }

    System.out.println("LocalProtocolAdapter stopped");

    running = false;
  }

  public void initialize()
    throws EventProtocolAdapterException
  {
  }

  public void
  addEventReceivedListener(ProtocolAdapterListener listener)
  {
    listeners.add(listener);
  }
```

```java
public void
  removeEventReceivedListener(ProtocolAdapterListener listener)
{
  listeners.remove(listener);
}

public void start()
  throws EventProtocolAdapterException
{
  Iterator<ManagementEventSource> iter =
    eventSources.iterator();
  while (iter.hasNext())
  {
    ManagementEventSource eventSource = iter.next();
    eventSource.start();
  }

  workerThread = new Thread(this);
  workerThread.start();
}

public void stop()
  throws EventProtocolAdapterException
{
  Iterator<ManagementEventSource> iter =
    eventSources.iterator();
  while (iter.hasNext())
  {
    ManagementEventSource eventSource = iter.next();
    eventSource.stop();
  }

  running = false;
}

public void eventOccurred(EventSourceEvent evt)
{
  ProtocolAdapterEvent protocolAdapterEvt =
    new ProtocolAdapterEvent(evt.getSource(),
                             evt.getTimeStamp(),
                             evt.getType(),
                             evt.getContent());

  Iterator<ProtocolAdapterListener> iter =
    listeners.iterator();
  while (iter.hasNext())
  {
    ProtocolAdapterListener listener = iter.next();
```

```
        listener.eventOccurred(protocolAdapterEvt);
      }
    }
  }
}
```

In Listing 4.13, the event manager receives events from one event source, a time-lapse event source. The protocol adapter runs in its own thread to listen for events passed to it from the event source. As events are received, the protocol adapter passes the events to interested listeners. In a remote protocol adapter, steps would be taken to distribute the events remotely.

Summary

This chapter discussed some of the most important concerns that all enterprise mashup infrastructures must address, including information management, governance, and system administration. In addition to the typical enterprise application concerns, mashup infrastructures must address an environment that seeks to fulfill dynamic requirements and flexible solutions to business issues.

Managing and sharing data from disparate information sources is a primary concern for mashup infrastructures. Rather than separating metadata from data, mashup infrastructures seek to provide a semantically rich environment where data and metadata are combined to present a more effective means for applying meaning to information. Therefore, choosing an effective fundamental format for data within your mashup infrastructure is a primary concern. This enables consumers of the data and content to create aggregate components and content much more easily than traditional application environments. Standards such as XML, microformats, RDF, RDF Schema, and OWL are emerging as enabling technologies for semantic data interchange.

Mediation is a primary component of mashup infrastructures for enabling separation of concerns between software components. Mediation frameworks operate on data as it travels from data producers to data consumers.

Management and monitoring are also essential for administrating and optimizing a mashup infrastructure. The decoupled and segregated nature of a mashup infrastructure makes the need for an effective management and monitoring framework vital.

Mashup governance including the creation, maintenance, and enforcement of lifecycles, policies, and standards compliance is vital for an effective enterprise mashup infrastructure. It is also a complex area of concern for a mashup infrastructure. Due to the dynamic nature of a mashup infrastructure, services, components, and mashup pages are constantly changing with new content and components constantly being introduced.

Determining the proper interface for a service, resource, or UI component has great impact on the usability of your mashup infrastructure. Since mashups depend on aggregating and orchestrating existing services, resources, and UI components, proper public interfaces are very important to a mashup infrastructure.

The next chapter discusses some patterns that can be applied to a mashup development environment, and example implementations for some of the patterns are presented.

Chapter 5

Enterprise Mashup Patterns

Mashup design and implementation share many of the same development issues as traditional software engineering. Therefore, many of the same techniques and methodologies that provide successful results to traditional software paradigms work equally as well with mashup development. Software patterns are one of the most widely used methodologies in traditional software engineering and are also strongly suggested as a mechanism for addressing mashup design and development scenarios.

This chapter discusses some patterns that can be applied to a mashup development environment to aid in finding common solutions to typical mashup problems. All the patterns discussed were created by Michael Ogrinz in his book *Mashup Patterns: Designs and Examples for the Modern Enterprise* (Addison-Wesley, March 2009), and a more detailed discussion of these patterns can be found there. Also presented in this chapter are example implementations for some of the patterns presented.

An Introduction to Patterns

Software design patterns present tested and proven blueprints for addressing recurring problems or situations that arise in many different design and development scenarios. By defining a design/development solution in terms of a pattern, problems can be solved without the need to rehash the same problem over and over in an attempt to provide a custom solution each time.

Using design patterns for software development is a concept that was borrowed from architecture as it applied to building homes, workplaces, and cities. The idea revolved around the concept that looking at problems abstractly presented common solutions to different architectural problems. The same concept was applied to software engineering and proved to work equally as well.

Applying patterns to software design and development scenarios really gained momentum when Erich Gamma, Richard Helm, Ralph Johnson, and

165

John Vlissides (The Gang of Four as they are collectively called) introduced their book *Design Patterns: Elements of Reusable Object-Oriented Software*.

A software design pattern is typically presented using a standard format containing most of the following items:

- **Name and classification**—A unique description used to identify the pattern

- **Intent**—The reason or goal for the pattern

- **Motivation and/or applicability**—A description of the scenarios or contexts in which the pattern applies

- **Structure**—A graphical depiction of the pattern, such as a class diagram

- **Consequences**—Side effects and/or results from use of the pattern

- **Participants**—Classes and/or objects used in the pattern along with their role in a design

- **Related patterns**—Other patterns that share a relationship with the pattern along with a discussion of each

- **Collaboration**—A discussion of the interactions between classes and objects used in the pattern

- **Implementation and/or sample code**—An example of a concrete implementation of the pattern

The Importance of Patterns within a Mashup Infrastructure

Since mashups address many different, dynamic scenarios and technologies, finding any sort of common ground on which to base design and implementation decisions can be a great help to software practitioners.

Mashups can be very data-intensive. Therefore patterns that define common solutions to the conversion or adaptation of different data formats offer a substantial benefit to developers. A pattern defining a common solution for enriching data as the data is transferred from one module to another offers significant benefits, as well.

Mashups seek to provide rich experiences for client-side users. Therefore, patterns defining common solutions applied to AJAX, JavaScript, XML, and CSS can provide benefits to UI developers.

With many of the processes in a mashup running externally in the Internet cloud, it is extremely desirable to find common patterns that address issues such as scalability, security, and manageability within this nebulous environment.

Core Activities of a Mashup

Many of the patterns in a mashup infrastructure can be divided into activities that describe the core functionality of the infrastructure. These core activities can be defined in a manner as to describe generic functionality on which most enterprise mashup infrastructures are based. The patterns in this chapter are discussed in the context of these core activities.

When analyzing the types of solutions that a mashup infrastructure seeks to address, developers can gain an understanding of the common scenarios that are likely to emerge. These scenarios can be dissected to uncover the core activities that should be presented by the mashup infrastructure.

The directions taken by a development staff may be significantly altered as the core activities of the mashup infrastructure are discovered. This makes it important to uncover the core activities of the infrastructure as early as possible in the analysis stage.

Some of the common core activities that are likely to be discovered in many mashup design efforts are discussed in the following sections.

Publishing and Promoting Content and Artifacts

With the open communication avenues that the web offers today, it is easy enough to find an outlet for publishing your opinions and experiences, and/or for sharing your knowledge. However, finding and enticing an audience is increasingly difficult as the web becomes more and more flooded with blogs, sites, and video and audio streams.

The mashup space has introduced a new avenue for publishing that allows creative-minded individuals to produce exciting new experiences for users and readers in the consumer realm. Businesses are exploring the enterprise mashup space and are seeking to capitalize on the wave of excitement of the consumer mashup space and to implement similar technologies and techniques to promote and publish business content, as well as products and services. Several challenges stand in the way of enterprise mashups by which consumer mashups are not burdened. Not the least of which is the challenge of allowing the openness of the mashup environment to promote creativity for the business model while managing this openness to ensure compliance and security of business content and data.

Semantic Formats and Patterns for Data Access and Extraction

As businesses move to the enterprise mashup space they find that much of their content and many of their data sources are confined by nonpublic and tightly coupled data access APIs. It becomes immediately apparent that a standard and more open data model is needed to expose content and data to mashup tools and developers. This need for an open, standard data model has led enterprises to adopt data formats and technologies that present a semantically rich data interface such as RSS, RDF, microformats, and others.

Semantic data formats and related patterns enable mashup tools and developers to find and use relevant data and content much easier than traditional data formats. RSS, RDF, microformats, and others expose data in standard ways with a great deal of semantic meaning presented with the actual content. This allows data to be extracted and used in a dynamic fashion to build mashups to serve an ever-changing business environment.

Semantic Formats and Patterns for Data Transfer and Reuse

As applications and pages evolve in the mashup space, data is transferred between sites, applications, and pages and is used to populate pages and/or UI artifacts along the way. Data must be transformed to meet the constraints of each individual page or UI artifact. Transformation of data is needed to adapt to different security constraints, different form field constraints, and entirely different data formats.

As with data access and extraction, data transfer and reuse are being facilitated by adoption of semantic data formats and related patterns. When data is presented in a semantically rich model, it is much easier for content to be found and transformed for reuse. Presenting text content as RSS data allows a software component to find the author, subject, and/or content of the text in a standard way that is not possible with proprietary or nonsemantic data formats. Presenting user-centric data as an FOAF (friend of a friend) microformat allows the user's name, gender, email address, and so on to be reused easily by each page or UI artifact as the data is transferred from one site to another.

Patterns and Methods for Data Presentation

Once data is extracted, transferred, and transformed it is ready to be presented. Although not all mashups are graphical (pure data or process mashups, for example), it is important to understand the patterns and methods used for constructing a graphical presentation when needed.

The presentation of data in a mashup can be facilitated with internal or external APIs, services, and UI artifacts. Both internal and external presentation methods have advantages and disadvantages.

Using external APIs (such as Amazon web service APIs and eBay web service APIs), services, and UI artifacts allows you to take advantage of a much greater pool of talent than is possible with most internal IT departments. However, using external APIs, services, and UI artifacts can reduce the workload of your internal IT staff but requires the transfer of control and sometimes sensitive data into the hands of third parties. This requires establishing and maintaining a high degree of trust between your organization and third parties.

Using internal APIs, services, and UI artifacts allows you to control the security and compliance of data very closely. It also enables fine-grained control of the look-and-feel of content as it is presented in a mashup.

Sequences of interval values as found in a time-series related pattern can be presented easily using external charting services. However, customizing charts to fit corporate branding may not be possible to the degree needed by a given company or application. In this case, internal APIs, services, and UI artifacts must be used to fill the requirement.

Presenting data in map-based UIs using internal resources is just not a possibility for most organizations. Also, enabling a single sign-on solution that spans multiple sites is by definition only possible using a third-party facility.

Patterns and Methods for Scheduling and Observation

Most enterprises coordinate activities based on data collected from a number of different places such as branch offices. This data must be collected using notifications as thresholds are exceeded or on a regular basis using automated batch tasks.

Collecting data using automated tasks promotes a consistent and accurate view of an organization's operations without relying on manual intervention. Periodic execution of a task to collect time-series data can enable accurate charting capabilities for a mashup that presents views into an organization's online computing resources or bandwidth.

Periodic task-execution schedules can be determined by many different factors such as business hours of operation, geographical constraints, and available resources. An organization that has geographically dispersed offices typically needs to collect data from each office at regular intervals. As data is received, a centralized framework might report changes using an application consisting of the data and maps generated by a third party. The requirements of the application may be such that changes must be reported as they happen. This requirement falls in line with an event-driven framework and can use many of the same patterns applied in a typical event-driven or asynchronous enterprise application. These patterns include publish-subscribe, command-observer, background-worker, and others.

Content Reuse with Clipping

Another core activity is a technique referred to as "clipping," "screen scraping," or "web clipping." Clipping refers to the process of capturing a portion of a web site and reusing it in another web page. A clipping or clip can be a single UI artifact found on a web page, multiple UI artifacts, textual content from the page, or the entire web page itself. Clipping is typically used to combine subsets of HTML data/content from external web sites without requiring changes to the mashup server infrastructure.

Rather than extracting discrete values from a web page, clipping captures UI artifacts and snippets in a manner that allows the clippings to be reused in another page. For example, the process of extracting company performance statistics might return textual content representing values signifying the performance data. A clipping would simply return the actual HTML or other markup to redisplay it on another page.

To unify the process of capturing clippings from multiple, disparate sites, industry standards (XML, JSON, RDF, and so on) and common transformation technologies (XSLT, for example) should be supported by your clipping services. This helps to facilitate common data formats, HTML tags, and CSS classes. One such common capability is overriding CSS classes and styles in the clippings with company-approved classes and styles.

Normalizing Content Using Data/Content Augmentation Patterns

It is rare when you find multiple legacy sites exposing content in a common format. The inconsistencies can vary from variations in UI artifacts, to CSS styles, to differences in currencies and languages. A normalized and uniform data standard should be deployed to ensure proper transformation of data and clippings retrieved from other sites and/or pages.

Data/content augmentation is the process of transforming and/or enriching data or content prior to transferring the data or content to a final destination. Web page data rarely has any data type information associated with it. Most data or content is simply text. A mashup infrastructure should work to solve the problem of data mismatches using patterns that define services and processes that facilitate data augmentation. Some of the patterns to use include the message translator pattern, the content-enricher pattern, the content filter pattern, the canonical data model pattern, and others.

Assembling a Canvas of Mashup Components

Artifacts gathered from data augmentation and clipping core activities must be assembled and orchestrated to give them directed purpose. This can be regarded in the same manner as the activity of an artist assembling colors, shapes, and layers on a canvas to produce a painting.

Data entities need to be assembled to be used in an intelligent manner in the same way that visual artifacts need to be assembled. In this respect, a virtual canvas is used as the arena in which data is assembled and orchestrated. Metadata is important for a virtual data canvas in that it allows tools and processes to discover similarities between data entities and, hopefully, semantic relevance through which aggregate entities might be derived.

UI artifacts are assembled on a literal canvas where visual arrangement is required. Metadata for visual components is also important for interlinking components that share similarities in context and functionality.

With an effective layer of metadata instrumentation applied to data and UI artifacts, the act of assembling components together is greatly simplified. If the metadata is semantically rich and sufficiently contextual, much of the assembly work can be automated using programmatic techniques. This can produce a mashup infrastructure that enables a robust environment for building new components, services, and applications using a small amount of manual intervention.

Patterns and Purposes for Notifications and Alerts

Enterprise applications are often required to respond to changes reported by other systems, devices, and subsystems. Techniques for enabling a mashup infrastructure to react to these changes include periodic polling of each device or subsystem to query for changes or transmitting the changes dynamically from the device or subsystem to the mashup infrastructure as the changes take place.

Periodic polling has been the typical technique used in many HTTP-based systems since the HTTP protocol does not support a mechanism for dynamically transmitting or "pushing" data. Therefore, ascertaining changes that have taken place in a device or subsystem typically requires a manual query of the device or subsystem on a periodic basis. This leads to a number of problems including bandwidth congestion from unnecessary HTTP traffic and latency of information discovery. If it is crucial to discover changes as soon as possible, HTTP requests must be made frequently, which can cause large amounts of unnecessary bandwidth usage. It is far more efficient to transmit data from devices or subsystems to a mashup infrastructure as changes take place.

Some applications or protocols are designed around a notification or push model, such as SNMP (Simple Network Management Protocol), MOM (Message-Oriented Middleware), SMTP (Simple Mail Transfer Protocol), RSS, and others.

SNMP is designed around a model for issuing events called "traps" or notifications containing information about the status of networked devices. Status information is sent from SNMP agents to SNMP management entities at pre-defined intervals. Interested listeners, such as monitoring or management applications, can use this data to inform network managers of faults, performance statistics, and so on. Patterns used for SNMP notification handling include adapter, proxy, bridge, mediator, and others.

MOM frameworks provide support for asynchronous message processing using a publish/subscribe model. In this model, interested listeners can subscribe with message stores known as "topics" to which message publishers send notification messages. When a topic receives a message, the message is relayed to all subscribers. This model allows a decoupled message-passing interaction between message publishers and message subscribers. Patterns used for MOM message handling include broker, composite application, message bus, pipes and filters, and others.

SMTP is a protocol that facilitates another form of push-based message communication. Although not typically used for mission-critical event notifications, SMTP can be an efficient means for distributing message data asynchronously. Patterns used for SMTP message handling include observer, chain of responsibility, decorator, pipes and filters, and others.

Types of Mashup Patterns

Patterns can be applied to a mashup infrastructure with the same amount of success that is enjoyed by other types of software development infrastructures. In fact, with a mashup infrastructure being responsible for hosting many new applications and services not foreseen at first, it makes even more sense to apply common patterns to the framework to provide as much structure to the development environment as possible.

The following sections describe some types of patterns that can be used within a mashup infrastructure.

UI Artifact Mashup Pattern

The UI artifact pattern defines the activity of assembling UI artifacts (related and unrelated) on a page. The artifacts may have no commonalities; they may just individually fulfill a given purpose that adds to the value or usability of the page. The UI artifacts are usually just embedded within the page as distinct objects. Pages resembling portals that are composed of widgetlike components are typical examples of this.

Figure 5.1 illustrates the relationships of components and modules that embody a typical UI artifact design pattern in a mashup environment.

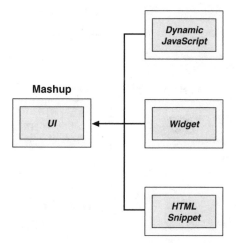

Figure 5.1 *UI artifact mashup pattern*

As shown in Figure 5.1, UI artifacts can be produced from a number of different technologies and markup languages. The artifacts are typically arranged on a page side-by-side with no common features shared between neighboring components. The UI object in the diagram can refer to such things as a web page, a desktop application, or a mobile device display.

Presentation Layer Mashup Pattern

The presentation layer mashup pattern defines a model for producing a visual mashup page using data and content from remote sources such as web service APIs, RSS feeds, and so on. Many of the visual components produced in this model are generated using data that is fed to the page using dynamic techniques involving JavaScript, DOM manipulation, CSS, and user-agent detection. This dynamic environment allows multiple components to share data and functionality, therefore exposing a more integrated look-and-feel than the UI artifact pattern.

Figure 5.2 illustrates the relationships of data and content present in a typical presentation layer design pattern environment.

Figure 5.2 shows multiple sources feeding data and content to the presentation layer of a mashup. The data and content can be used to dynamically generate UI artifacts that have many common features and share some of the same attributes. This model is used in many AJAX-based applications, since AJAX allows data to be retrieved in the background and used to update individual components on a page.

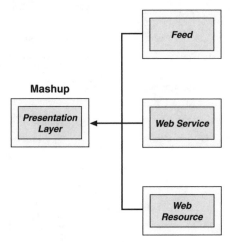

Figure 5.2   *Presentation layer mashup pattern*

Process Layer Mashup Pattern

The process layer pattern defines a model that combines data or content together before it reaches the visual page. This typically occurs on the server side of a mashup environment. The advantage of this model is that tools and programming languages on the server side are typically more mature when it comes to integrating data. Other issues such as data security can be managed and controlled easier when handled on the server side.

Figure 5.3 illustrates a typical process layer design pattern and the relationships of modules and services in a framework using the pattern.

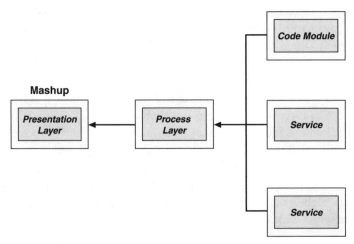

Figure 5.3   *Process layer mashup pattern*

As Figure 5.3 illustrates, data and content are fed to the process layer from multiple sources such as services and code modules. The data and content are integrated in the process layer before being distributed to the presentation layer. This model is found in many systems exposing service APIs and UI artifacts that have been produced from the process layer as data and content are combined.

Data Layer Mashup Pattern

The data layer pattern defines a model in which data is integrated using standard toolsets and technologies such as relational databases, XML-based data feeds, and service API results. Significant advances have been introduced by database vendors, service providers, and others in regards to their abilities to provide tools and features that allow disparate data to be easily integrated.

Figure 5.4 illustrates a typical data layer design pattern showing how components and modules feed data to the data layer to be augmented and integrated.

In Figure 5.4 databases, external feeds, and service APIs provide data to the data layer to be processed. The data layer can then enrich and transform the data prior to feeding it to the process layer. This enables a model where semantically sparse data can be augmented with semantics that can be easily used by the process layer to further aggregate data and content.

Alerter Pattern

The alerter pattern describes a model where notifications and alerts are passed to interested listeners. A framework designed around the alerter pattern can provide

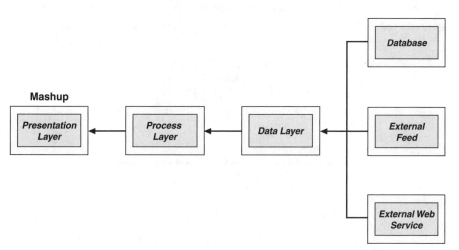

Figure 5.4 *Data layer pattern*

responsive interactions to components and frameworks with which it interacts due to the ability to provide real-time or near real-time updates and events. Mashup infrastructures can exploit this responsiveness by providing dynamically updateable datasets and UI artifacts that are used in mashup applications.

In addition to pushing notifications to listeners, an instance of the alerter that represents a watched resource can be queried or polled at regularly scheduled intervals to retrieve status updates.

Instances of the alerter pattern can interact effectively with nonhuman agents. This allows gathering of data to take place in background processes where the data can be evaluated and used in an aggregate form to feed statistical modeling software and other management tools.

Mashups do not need to regularly interact with an end user to add value. Intelligent agents can be used to alert applications and services of significant events.

Figure 5.5 illustrates a typical alerter design pattern as applied to event sources and event sinks.

In Figure 5.5, multiple event sinks are interested listeners to a single event source. In practice, event sinks might be registered as interested listeners to multiple event sources. Event sinks may take the form of data components, processes, and UI artifacts.

Time Series Pattern

The time series pattern defines a model for tracking time series data. A "time series" is a chain of related data accumulated across scheduled intervals. Applying statistical models against the accumulated time series data, future events can be predicted and acted on. This data can also be used for historical trend analy-

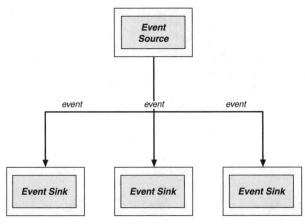

Figure 5.5 *Alerter pattern*

sis and applied to the decision-making process for setting future directions. For example, in his book *Mashup Patterns: Designs and Examples for the Modern Enterprise* Michael Ogrinz points out that "studying past conditions can provide answers to the following questions:

- Which drug will most effectively combat the spread of a particular disease?

- How much gas should be refined for the upcoming holiday weekend?

- When will a particular assembly-line robot need to be replaced?

- What food items sell best under particular weather conditions?"

Ogrinz goes on to state that time series data can be harvested in four distinct steps: identification, collection, transformation, and scheduling and storage.

Time series data can be retrieved from internal sources such as IT operations systems and external sources such as publicly available sites including utility companies, government agencies, and others.

Figure 5.6 illustrates the interactions between components and modules that embody a typical time series design pattern in a mashup environment.

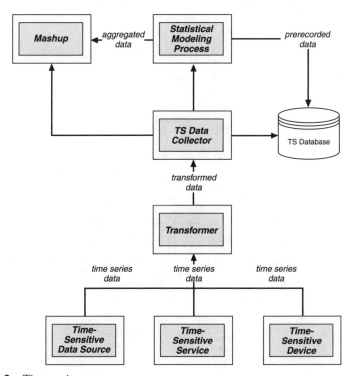

Figure 5.6 *Time series pattern*

As Figure 5.6 illustrates, data is fed to a data collector from multiple time-sensitive data sources via a transformer module. The transformer module normalizes the data before it reaches the data collector. The data collector then feeds the data to interested listeners such as a mashup or a statistical modeling process. The data collector can also store the data for future use.

Super Search Pattern

The super search pattern defines a model for enabling generic search capabilities across a wide range of disparate search technologies and other traversable resources. An instance of the super search pattern aggregates results retrieved from search engines, external service providers, databases, and so on and presents the aggregated results to search consumers. As long as a resource or service provides the means to crawl, navigate, or traverse result sets relating to the resource, a super search instance can apply search queries against the resource.

Figure 5.7 illustrates the relationships of components and modules that embody a typical super search design pattern in a mashup environment.

As Figure 5.7 illustrates, search data is retrieved from disparate sources to a super search instance using multiple retrieval mechanisms. The super search instance normalizes and aggregates the results before it is fed to a search consumer, such as a mashup.

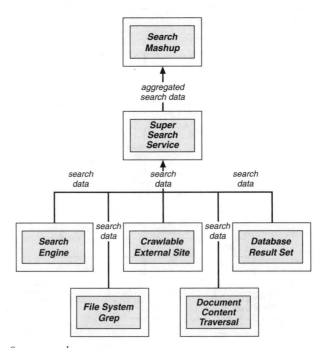

Figure 5.7 *Super search pattern*

Feed Factory Pattern

The feed factory pattern defines a model for traversing sites and pages of interest to collect information that can be used within a local module, service, or page.

RSS and Atom feeds are provided by many sites and authors. The content from these feeds is typically retrieved by feed readers or aggregators and presented as a collection of snippets describing the content of each feed item. The feed factory used within a mashup environment expands on traditional feed-aggregation methods by enabling a model where data can be fed from virtually any data source using any data format. In *Mashup Patterns: Designs and Examples for the Modern Enterprise*, Michael Ogrinz points out that "it is theoretically possible to RSS enable web sites, binary files (e.g., spreadsheets), databases, and more."

Sources of information participating with a feed factory instance can be dynamic in nature, such as in the case where notifications are pushed to the feed factory instance by alerter pattern instances or search results returned from super search pattern instances.

Figure 5.8 illustrates a typical feed factory design pattern in a mashup environment and how the components interact with each other in the use of the pattern.

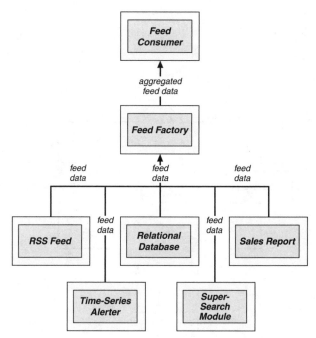

Figure 5.8 *Feed factory pattern*

As Figure 5.8 illustrates, data is fed from disparate sources to a feed factory. The feed factory module normalizes and aggregates the data before it is fed to a consumer module.

Workflow Pattern

The workflow pattern defines a model for organizing interactions between humans and business processes and for tracking the status of business processes and resources. Workflows define organized tasks that are repeated on a regular basis. Since so many business processes rely on software to perform associated tasks, software is a vital part of workflows.

Software-based workflow frameworks are typically concerned with business processes and the systems that participate in these processes. The systems participating in a given workflow direct the flow of information as it moves through each business process. Workflow definitions can be modified by altering (editing, adding, and deleting) the individual activities contained within each workflow definition.

Figure 5.9 illustrates a typical workflow design pattern and its participating processes as used in a mashup environment.

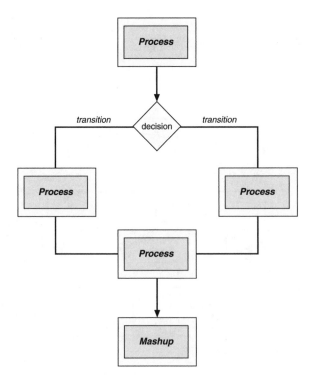

Figure 5.9 *Workflow pattern*

As Figure 5.9 illustrates, information and control transition from process to process based on the result of decisions made along the way. A formal software-based workflow typically embodies this flow in a document defining business rules and transitions.

Pipes and Filters Pattern

The pipes and filters pattern defines a chain of interconnected modules through which data flows. The data is enriched and augmented as it travels from one module to the next towards its final destination. The result of one module's enrichment and augmentation becomes the input for the next module in the chain.

Figure 5.10 illustrates a chain of modules that might be found in a typical pipes-and-filters design pattern in a mashup environment.

As Figure 5.10 illustrates, data transitions along a chain of modules where enrichment and augmentation of the data take place. The result from the final module in the chain is passed to the intended destination where it is used. In this case, a mashup is the final destination. The mashup could also act as a module in a larger chain performing even more enrichment and augmentation in a dynamic way.

Data Federation Pattern

The data federation pattern defines a mechanism for integrating and abstracting structured and unstructured data from multiple, disparate data sources. Instances of the data federation pattern seek to apply semantic metadata views

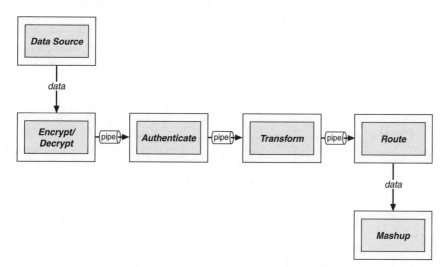

Figure 5.10 *Pipes and filters pattern*

to data sources and data relationships to transform and normalize data from various sources.

Data federation instances are traditionally embodied by federation servers that apply relational concepts to structured and unstructured data sources. In this scenario data consumers apply standard relational queries to the federation server, which performs the necessary conversions to apply the semantics of the queries to nonrelational data sources.

Figure 5.11 illustrates the relationships of components and modules that embody a typical data federation design pattern in a mashup environment.

As Figure 5.11 illustrates, disparate data sources are abstracted from the data layer by the data federation server. Processes and other data consumers can send queries to the data layer, which in turn, passes the queries on to the data federation server. The data federation server does the necessary conversions to apply the queries to each individual data source that is abstracted by the server.

Software as a Service (SaaS) Pattern

The software as a service (SaaS) pattern defines a model for delivering functionality to consumers across a network connection using a subscription model. An instance of the SaaS pattern delivers functionality to multiple consumers using standard web-based technologies such as HTML, CSS, and JavaScript.

SaaS reduces costs in a number of ways since SaaS typically operates in a browser or purely programmatic environment, little or no software is actually installed on an end user's system. Specifically, costs for testing across multiple

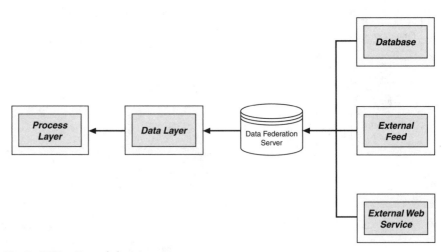

Figure 5.11 *Data federation pattern*

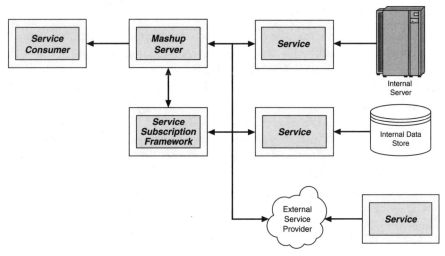

Figure 5.12 *Software as a service pattern*

hardware configurations and operating systems are all but eliminated since typically the only operating environment concerned is either a web browser or an external tool that consumes the functionality as a web service API result.

Figure 5.12 illustrates the components and modules that embody a typical SaaS design pattern in a mashup environment and the relationships between each component and module.

As Figure 5.12 illustrates, services exposing functionality for various services and service providers are registered with a service subscription framework. The service subscription framework then acts as the main point of contact between service consumers and service providers. The service subscription framework manages subscriptions for the service consumer.

Applying Patterns to an Enterprise Mashup Infrastructure

As defined in the previous sections, the time series pattern and the workflow pattern are used extensively in enterprise systems and frameworks. Implementations for each pattern can provide for an effective mashup infrastructure.

This section applies the concepts of the time series pattern and the workflow pattern to the construction of a mashup.

Time Series Framework

The software components of a simple time series framework can be minimal. To provide functionality for the basic concepts of a time series pattern the framework should supply components to support time periods, intervals of values and time periods, listeners, and a time series itself.

Figure 5.13 illustrates the primary classes participating in a simple time series framework and the relationships of each.

As Figure 5.13 illustrates, the main point of contact in a simple time series framework is the TimeSeries class. The TimeSeries class interacts with listener classes, time period classes, interval classes, and so on to provide a standard interface through which time series data providers can operate.

The sequence of invocations from a time series consumer and the time series framework is illustrated in Figure 5.14.

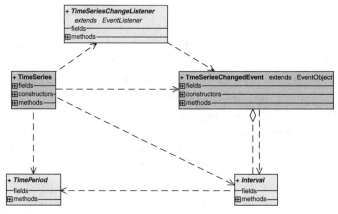

Figure 5.13   *Class diagram for the time series framework*

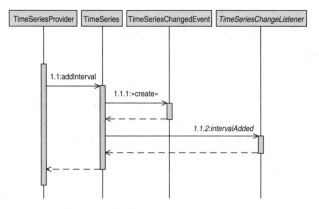

Figure 5.14   *Sequences for a simple time series interaction*

As shown in Figure 5.14, a time series provider interacts directly with the TimeSeries class. The time series provider adds interval values and time periods to the TimeSeries class. The TimeSeries class dispatches notifications to interested listeners as new intervals are added.

Listing 5.1 provides the details for a simple TimeSeries class in which listeners can register and time series providers can interact.

Listing 5.1 *TimeSeries Class*

```
public class TimeSeries
{
  private LinkedHashMap<TimePeriod, Double> intervals =
    new LinkedHashMap<TimePeriod, Double>();
  private String name = "";
  private ArrayList<TimeSeriesChangeListener>
    timeSeriesChangeListeners =
      new ArrayList<TimeSeriesChangeListener>();

  public TimeSeries(String name)
  {
    this.name = name;
  }

  public void addInterval(final TimePeriod period,
                          final double value)
  {
    intervals.put(period, value);

    Interval interval = new Interval()
    {
      public TimePeriod getPeriod()
      {
        return period;
      }

      public double getValue()
      {
        return value;
      }
    };

    TimeSeriesChangedEvent event =
      new TimeSeriesChangedEvent(this, interval);

    Iterator<TimeSeriesChangeListener> iter =
      timeSeriesChangeListeners.iterator();
    while (iter.hasNext())
    {
```

```
        TimeSeriesChangeListener timeSeriesChangeListener =
          iter.next();
        timeSeriesChangeListener.intervalAdded(event);
    }
  }

  public int getIntervalCount()
  {
    return intervals.size();
  }

  public String getName()
  {
    return name;
  }

  public TimePeriod getKey(int i)
  {
    return (TimePeriod)intervals.keySet().toArray()[i];
  }

  public Double getValue(int i)
  {
    return intervals.get(i);
  }

  public void
  addTimeSeriesChangeListener(TimeSeriesChangeListener
                              timeSeriesChangeListener)
  {
    timeSeriesChangeListeners.add(timeSeriesChangeListener);
  }

  public void
  removeTimeSeriesChangeListener(TimeSeriesChangeListener
                                 timeSeriesChangeListener)
  {
    timeSeriesChangeListeners.remove(timeSeriesChangeListener);
  }
}
```

As Listing 5.1 points out, interested listeners register and unregister with the TimeSeries class using the respective methods, addTimeSeriesChangeListener and removeTimeSeriesChangeListener. Time series data providers use the addInterval method to add time series data values and time periods. Intervals are stored in a data structure ensuring predictable iterations on retrieval. Ancillary methods allowing retrieval of specific intervals and the total number of intervals stored are provided.

A specific time period stored as part of an interval is defined by the `TimePeriod` interface. A simple incarnation of the interface, as shown in Listing 5.2, provides a `Timestamp` property. The interface should be enhanced to provide a more robust definition of time periods, specifically, with ranges of time periods in mind.

Listing 5.2 *TimePeriod Interface*
```
public interface TimePeriod
{
  public Date getTimestamp();
}
```

Implementations of the `TimePeriod` interface must provide support for the `getTimestamp` method. The timestamp returned is a simple Java Date type. Enhancements to the interface might provide a more robust definition of a timestamp to provide information about the time period such as timestamp authorities, digital signing information, and other information.

A given interval defining a time period and a value is defined by the `Interval` interface. The interface shown in Listing 5.3 provides a period property and a value property.

Listing 5.3 *Interval Interface*
```
public interface Interval
{
  public TimePeriod getPeriod();

  public double getValue();
}
```

Implementations of the `Interval` interface must provide support for the `getPeriod` method and the `getValue` method. Note the value returned from `getValue` is a primitive Java double type.

Interested listeners to the `TimeSeries` class must register themselves as implementations of the `TimeSeriesChangeListener` interface. This interface provides support for passing notifications of intervals being added to an instance of the `TimeSeries` class.

Listing 5.4 provides a detailed illustration of the `TimeSeriesChangeListener` interface.

Listing 5.4 *TimeSeriesChangeListener Interface*
```
public interface Interval
public interface TimeSeriesChangeListener
  extends EventListener
{
  void intervalAdded(TimeSeriesChangedEvent event);
}
```

Implementations of the `TimeSeriesChangeListener` interface must provide support for the `intervalAdded` method. As a new interval is added to the `TimeSeries` class, listeners are notified via the `intervalAdded` method. A `TimeSeriesChangedEvent` object containing details about the interval is passed to the `intervalAdded` method. Listeners can then access the information in the `TimeSeriesChangedEvent` to find out about the specific interval.

The `TimeSeriesChangedEvent` class defines an object that contains information about a given time series event; specifically, information about intervals. Instances of the interface are passed to interested listeners of the `TimeSeries` class as new intervals are added.

Listing 5.5 shows details of the `TimeSeriesChangedEvent` class.

Listing 5.5 *TimeSeriesChangedEvent Interface*
```
public class TimeSeriesChangedEvent
  extends EventObject
{
  private Interval interval = null;

  public TimeSeriesChangedEvent(Object source,
                                Interval interval)
  {
    super(source);

    this.interval = interval;
  }

  public Interval getInterval()
  {
    return interval;
  }
}
```

As shown in Listing 5.5, instances of the `TimeSeriesChangedEvent` class provide details about a time series event. This information consists of the source of the event and a specific interval containing a time period and a value.

Testing the time series framework is a process of instantiating the `TimeSeries` class, registering a listener with the `TimeSeries` instance, and then passing intervals to the `TimeSeries` instance on a periodic basis.

Listing 5.6 demonstrates a simple class that tests the basic functionality of the `TimeSeries` framework.

Listing 5.6 *Interaction with a Simple Time Series*
```
  private void testTimeSeries()
  {
    final TimeSeries timeSeries =
      new TimeSeries("Test Series");
```

```java
timeSeries.addTimeSeriesChangeListener(new
  TimeSeriesChangeListener()
{
  public void intervalAdded(TimeSeriesChangedEvent event)
  {
    System.out.println("Interval added to "
        + ((TimeSeries)event.getSource()).getName() + ": "
        + event.getInterval().getPeriod().getTimestamp()
        + " = " + event.getInterval().getValue());
  }
});

new Thread(new Runnable()
{
  public void run()
  {
    long startTime = System.currentTimeMillis();
    long currTime = startTime;
    while ((currTime - startTime) < 20000)
    {
      final double factor = 0.90 + 0.2 * Math.random();
      lastValue = lastValue * factor;
      final Date timestamp = new Date();
      final TimePeriod timePeriod = new TimePeriod()
      {
        public Date getTimestamp()
        {
          return timestamp;
        }
      };

      timeSeries.addInterval(timePeriod, lastValue);

      try
      {
        Thread.sleep(500);
      }
      catch (InterruptedException e)
      {
        e.printStackTrace();
      }

      currTime = System.currentTimeMillis();
    }
  }
}).start();
}
```

Listing 5.6 demonstrates a simple example of interplay with the time series framework. In the example, an instance of the TimeSeries class is instantiated, with which an instance of the TimeSeriesChangeListener interface is registered. A new thread is then started that adds random value intervals to the TimeSeries class instance roughly every one-half second. Each time an interval is added, the registered TimeSeriesChangeListener instance is notified via its addInterval method.

TimeSeries notifications can be transmitted to interested listeners in a web environment using technologies such as asynchronous AJAX, Comet, HTTP streaming, and so on.

A basic implementation of a workflow framework is discussed and illustrated in the following section.

Workflow Framework

A basic workflow framework should provide support for defining a set of rules by which the flow of work should follow. As part of the rule set, transitions should be defined to direct the flow of control as specific conditions are met. As the workflow traverses through a set of rules, tasks are executed and the results evaluated to determine subsequent steps. The workflow framework supports the definition and execution of workflows.

Figure 5.15 illustrates the relationships and definitions of the primary classes participating in a rudimentary workflow framework.

As Figure 5.15 illustrates, relationships between classes and interfaces in a simple workflow framework revolve around tasks, a workflow, and a workflow

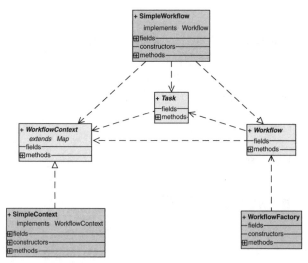

Figure 5.15 *Class diagram for the workflow framework*

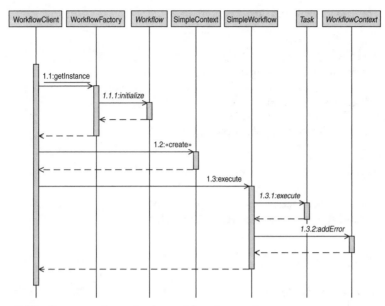

Figure 5.16   *Sequences for a simple workflow interaction*

context. The SimpleWorkflow class implements the Workflow interface and directs the
flow of control through a given set of tasks operating within a workflow context.

The sequence of invocations as flow-of-control traverses through the workflow framework is illustrated in Figure 5.16.

As shown in Figure 5.16, a workflow client retrieves an instance of the Workflow interface from the WorkflowFactory class. An instance of the WorkflowContext is
then created and passed to the Workflow instance, where the WorkflowContext
instance is passed along the chain of tasks executed by the workflow.

Listing 5.7 provides the details for a WorkflowFactory class in which instances
of Workflow implementations are created and returned.

Listing 5.7   *WorkflowFactory Class*

```
public class WorkflowFactory
{
  public static Workflow getInstance(String workflowConfigName)
    throws WorkflowFactoryException
  {
    try
    {
      String clsName =
        System.getProperty("com.jeffhanson.workflow");
      if (null == clsName || clsName.length() <= 0)
      {
```

```
      clsName = SimpleWorkflow.class.getName();
    }

    Class cls = Class.forName(clsName);
    if (Workflow.class.isAssignableFrom(cls))
    {
      Object obj = cls.newInstance();
      Workflow instance = (Workflow)obj;
      instance.initialize(workflowConfigName);
      return instance;
    }
    else
    {
      throw new WorkflowFactoryException(
        "Workflow object not derived from Workflow class");
    }
  }
  catch (Exception e)
  {
    throw new WorkflowFactoryException(e);
  }
 }
}
```

As detailed in Listing 5.7, the WorkflowFactory class looks at a system property to determine the name of the class implementing the Workflow interface that is to be instantiated and returned. If the system property is not found, the SimpleWorkflow class is instantiated and returned. Before the Workflow implementation instance is returned, its initialize method is called with the name of a configuration file containing the set of rules for the workflow.

A specific workflow is defined by an implementation of the Workflow interface. As shown in Listing 5.8, the Workflow interface is comprised of methods allowing management of tasks, initializing with a workflow configuration, and an execute method that instigates the workflow process.

Listing 5.8 *Workflow Interface*
```
public interface Workflow
{
  void addTask(String name,
               Task task,
               String onSuccessTransition,
               String onErrorTransition);

  Task getTask(String name);

  Iterator getTaskNames();
```

```
  void initialize(String workflowConfigName)
    throws WorkflowInitializationException;

  void execute(WorkflowContext workflowContext)
    throws WorkflowExecutionException;
}
```

Implementations of the Workflow interface are required to provide bodies for the addTask, getTask, getTaskNames, initialize, and execute methods. Tasks that are added to a Workflow instance are added to the workflow defined by the configuration file passed to the initialize method. In the initialize method, the workflow configuration is loaded and the set of rules defined within are parsed and added to the workflow. Tasks and transitions are evaluated and a flow of control is created according to the set of rules. The execute method embodies the functionality for actually executing the flow of control, including tasks and transitions defined by the set of rules in the workflow configuration.

Listing 5.9 shows a simple implementation of the Workflow interface. This class stores tasks and transitions in a data structure with predictable iteration. The tasks and transitions are evaluated when the execute method is called. Transitions consist of simple on-error or on-success decisions.

Listing 5.9 *Simple Workflow Class*

```
public class SimpleWorkflow
  implements Workflow
{
  private static class TaskData
  {
    Task task = null;
    String onSuccessTransition = null;
    String onErrorTransition = null;

    private TaskData(Task task,
                     String onSuccessTransition,
                     String onErrorTransition)
    {
      this.task = task;
      this.onSuccessTransition = onSuccessTransition;
      this.onErrorTransition = onErrorTransition;
    }
  }

  private LinkedHashMap<String, TaskData> tasks =
    new LinkedHashMap<String, TaskData>();

  public void initialize(String workflowConfigName)
    throws WorkflowInitializationException
```

```
{
  ClassLoader cl =
    Thread.currentThread().getContextClassLoader();
  if (cl == null)
  {
    cl = SimpleWorkflow.class.getClassLoader();
  }

  InputStream inStream =
    cl.getResourceAsStream(workflowConfigName);
  if (null == inStream)
  {
    throw new WorkflowInitializationException(
      "Workflow config [" + workflowConfigName
      + "] not found");
  }

  try
  {
    Document doc =
      DocumentBuilderFactory.newInstance().
        newDocumentBuilder().parse(inStream);
    NodeList taskNodes =
      doc.getElementsByTagName("task");
    if (taskNodes.getLength() <= 0)
    {
      throw new WorkflowInitializationException(
        "No task nodes found in workflow file.");
    }

    for (int i = 0; i < taskNodes.getLength(); i++)
    {
      Node taskNode = taskNodes.item(i);
      NamedNodeMap attributes = taskNode.getAttributes();
      String taskName = XMLUtils.loadAttrValue(attributes,
                                               "name");
      if (null != taskName && taskName.length() > 0)
      {
        String taskClsName =
          XMLUtils.loadAttrValue(attributes,
                                 "class");
        if (null != taskClsName && taskClsName.length() > 0)
        {
          Class cls = Class.forName(taskClsName);
          if (Task.class.isAssignableFrom(cls) == false)
          {
            throw new WorkflowInitializationException(
              "Class defined in workflow config "
```

```
                + "file for task [" + taskName
                + "] is an invalid type.");
          }

          String onSuccessTransition = null;
          String onErrorTransition = null;

          Node onSuccessNode =
            XMLUtils.findFirstNamedChild(taskNode,
                                  "onsuccess");
          if (null != onSuccessNode)
          {
            NamedNodeMap onSuccessNodeAttrs =
              onSuccessNode.getAttributes();
            onSuccessTransition =
              XMLUtils.loadAttrValue(onSuccessNodeAttrs,
                                  "transition");
          }

          Node onErrorNode =
            XMLUtils.findFirstNamedChild(taskNode,
                                  "onerror");
          if (null != onErrorNode)
          {
            NamedNodeMap onErrorNodeAttrs =
              onErrorNode.getAttributes();
            onErrorTransition =
              XMLUtils.loadAttrValue(onErrorNodeAttrs,
                                  "transition");
          }

          Task taskObj = (Task)cls.newInstance();
          taskObj.setName(taskName);
          taskObj.initialize();
          addTask(taskName,
                  taskObj,
                  onSuccessTransition,
                  onErrorTransition);
        }
      }
    }
  }
  catch (Exception e)
  {
    throw new WorkflowInitializationException(e);
  }
}
```

```java
public void execute(WorkflowContext workflowContext)
  throws WorkflowExecutionException
{
  Iterator<TaskData> iter = tasks.values().iterator();
  if (iter.hasNext())
  {
    TaskData taskData = iter.next();
    while (null != taskData)
    {
      Task task = taskData.task;
      try
      {
        task.execute(workflowContext);
        taskData = tasks.get(taskData.onSuccessTransition);
      }
      catch (Exception e)
      {
        workflowContext.addError(task.getName()
                                 + "-ERROR", e);
        taskData = tasks.get(taskData.onErrorTransition);
      }
    }
  }
}

public void addTask(String name, Task task,
                    String onSuccessTransition,
                    String onErrorTransition)
{
  TaskData taskData = new TaskData(task,
                                   onSuccessTransition,
                                   onErrorTransition);
  tasks.put(name, taskData);
}

public Task getTask(String name)
{
  TaskData taskData = tasks.get(name);
  if (null == taskData)
  {
    return null;
  }
  return taskData.task;
}

public Iterator getTaskNames()
{
  return tasks.keySet().iterator();
}
}
```

As shown in Listing 5.9, an XML-based workflow configuration is used to define the set of rules for the workflow. The XML configuration document contains nodes defining task classes along with the names of transitions in which to target for successful completion of each task or on unsuccessful completion of each task.

Each task executed in a given workflow is embodied within an implementation of the Task interface, as illustrated in Listing 5.10.

Listing 5.10   *Task Interface*

```
public interface Task
{
  void execute(WorkflowContext workflowContext)
    throws Exception;

  void setName(String name);

  String getName();

  void initialize();
}
```

As shown in Listing 5.10, the Task interface defines a name property, an initialize method, and an execute method. The execute method is called by a workflow instance during execution of the workflow. Work for each task occurs in the execute method of the Task interface implementation.

A simple implementation of the Task interface is shown in Listing 5.11. The execute method simply prints a message to System.out and adds a key/value pair to the workflow context passed to the method.

Listing 5.11   *SimpleTask Class*

```
public class SimpleTask
  implements Task
{
  private String name = "";

  public void execute(WorkflowContext workflowContext)
    throws Exception
  {
    System.out.println("SimpleTask");
    workflowContext.put("SimpleTask results", "success");
  }

  public void setName(String name)
  {
    this.name = name;
  }
```

```
public String getName()
{
  return name;
}

public void initialize()
{
}
}
```

Note in Listing 5.11, how name/value pairs can be added to the workflow context. This allows each task to leave tracks, so to speak, inside the workflow context. This trail of tracks can then be evaluated on termination of the workflow for auditing and management tasks.

A workflow context is defined by the WorkflowContext interface. The purpose of this interface is to define an object that can be passed throughout the execution of a workflow to each task in the workflow and provide a point of reference to the tasks. The context can also be used to store information about the execution of the chain of tasks. As shown in Listing 5.12, a workflow context provides methods to facilitate storage and retrieval of errors that occur as a workflow is executed.

Listing 5.12 *WorkflowContext Interface*
```
public interface WorkflowContext
  extends Map
{
  String getID();

  void addError(String errorName, Object errorObj);

  Iterator getErrorNames();

  Object getError(String errorName);
}
```

Listing 5.13 shows a simple implementation of the WorkflowContext interface. The java.util.Properties class is used as the data structure to store name/value pairs and errors as a hosting workflow passed an instance of the class throughout a workflow.

Listing 5.13 *SimpleContext Class*
```
public class SimpleContext
  implements WorkflowContext
{
  private String id = "";
  private Properties properties = new Properties();
  private Properties errors = new Properties();
```

```java
public SimpleContext(String id)
{
  this.id = id;
}

public String getID()
{
  return id;
}

public void addError(String errorName, Object errorObj)
{
  errors.put(errorName, errorObj);
}

public Iterator getErrorNames()
{
  return errors.keySet().iterator();
}

public Object getError(String errorName)
{
  return errors.get(errorName);
}

public int size()
{
  return properties.size();
}

public boolean isEmpty()
{
  return properties.isEmpty();
}

public boolean containsKey(Object key)
{
  return properties.containsKey(key);
}

public boolean containsValue(Object value)
{
  return properties.containsValue(value);
}

public Object get(Object key)
{
  return properties.get(key);
}
```

```
public Object put(Object key, Object value)
{
  return properties.put(key, value);
}

public Object remove(Object key)
{
  return properties.remove(key);
}

public void putAll(Map t)
{
  properties.putAll(t);
}

public void clear()
{
  properties.clear();
}

public Set keySet()
{
  return properties.keySet();
}

public Collection values()
{
  return properties.values();
}

public Set entrySet()
{
  return properties.entrySet();
}
}
```

In Listing 5.13, the methods defined by the java.util.Map interface must be embodied. The body for these methods is implemented by simply delegating each call to an associated java.util.Properties instance, which implements the java.util.Map.

Listing 5.14 defines an XML-based workflow configuration file that defines tasks as child elements of a parent workflow element. Each task element has a name and class attribute and child elements defining the transitions to make in the event of a successful execution or in the event of an error.

Listing 5.14 *A Sample Workflow*

```
<workflow name="SampleFlow">
  <task name="Step1"
```

```
        class="com.jeffhanson.workflow.Step1">
    <onsuccess transition="Step2" />
    <onerror transition="Abort" />
  </task>

  <task name="Step2"
        class="com.jeffhanson.workflow.Step2">
    <onsuccess transition="Step3" />
    <onerror transition="Abort" />
  </task>

  <task name="Step3"
        class="com.jeffhanson.workflow.Step3">
    <onsuccess transition="End" />
    <onerror transition="Abort" />
  </task>

  <task name="End"
        class="com.jeffhanson.workflow.End"/>

  <task name="Abort"
        class="com.jeffhanson.workflow.Abort"/>
</workflow>
```

Note in Listing 5.14 that terminating tasks, such as End and Abort do not require transition elements.

As demonstrated in Listing 5.15, testing the workflow framework is simply a matter of retrieving a workflow instance from the workflow factory, creating a context to pass to the workflow instance, and calling the execute method on the workflow instance.

Listing 5.15 *Testing the Workflow*
```
public class TestWorkflow
{
  public static void main(String[] args)
    throws Exception
  {
    Workflow workflow =
      WorkflowFactory.getInstance("test-flow.xml");
    SimpleContext workflowContext =
      new SimpleContext("TEST_CONTEXT");
    workflow.execute(workflowContext);
  }
}
```

Note in the call to WorkflowFactory.getInstance in Listing 5.15 how the name of the workflow configuration file is passed. In a production environment the location of the configuration file should be defined by a more flexible means such as a URL.

The time series pattern and the workflow pattern provide useful functionality to enterprise systems. In a mashup environment, these and other patterns discussed in this chapter can be exploited further to provide dynamic components and UI artifacts that can be used by mashup creators to build powerful applications, management consoles, dashboards, and other useful utilities.

Summary

Software design patterns are tested and proven blueprints that provide solutions for common design and implementation issues that occur in many enterprise application scenarios. Using patterns to address design and development issues allows issues to be addressed with common solutions that have been tested and proven over time.

Traditional enterprise software design and implementation have many of the same issues as mashup design and implementation. As such, many of the same design patterns that prove useful to traditional software engineering and design work just as well with mashup engineering and design.

This chapter discussed some of the patterns that can be applied to a mashup development environment to provide common solutions to typical mashup problems. Also discussed were example implementations for some of the patterns presented.

The next chapter discusses fundamental security issues that must be addressed when designing and implementing mashup components, processes, and artifacts.

Chapter 6

Applying Proper Techniques to Secure a Mashup

A mashup development model is very open by definition. This openness introduces many new security risks; therefore, security must be a primary concern when developing a mashup infrastructure.

Traditional mechanisms such as firewalls and DMZs are not sufficient for the granularity of access that mashups require for UI artifacts and data. The mashup infrastructure itself must be prepared to deal with issues such as cross-site request forgery (CSRF), AJAX security weaknesses, cross-site scripting, and secure sign-on across multiple domains.

This chapter discusses fundamental security issues that must be addressed when designing and implementing mashup components, processes, and artifacts. Solutions for these issues are discussed, and sample code is presented at the end of the chapter.

An Overview of Web Application Security

Early development efforts for the web were directed towards presenting static HTML pages to a browser client. This simplified model limited the types of interactions afforded to a user. However, this model also presented a number of possible security vulnerabilities. It wasn't long before developers and businesses realized that a more dynamic model of interaction was possible and desired by users of web sites.

A dynamic interaction with web site users started with the introduction of server-side scripting languages that could create custom pages based on input from a given user and/or input resulting from changes in business data. Now, users could interface with a web site in an interactive manner. This interactive means of interchange between client and server garnered an exponentially significant amount of momentum in a very short time. This momentum overwhelmed the technologies available at the time and led ingenious developers to create dynamic sites using programmatic side-steps, hacks, and proprietary trickery with languages such as Perl, C, C++, and others. This chaotic development environment created a breeding ground for security vulnerabilities and holes. Some of the most notorious vulnerabilities included buffer overflows, denial of service, and SQL injections.

Standards committees and programming language vendors scrambled to reign in the chaotic development activity surrounding dynamic site development that had surfaced in an attempt to create an environment conducive for executing secured electronic commerce (e-commerce). Out of this activity, sandboxing, managed programming spaces, digital signing, encryption, and other solutions emerged. This has produced a space where, today, e-commerce takes place with great regularity with a high-degree of confidence in the security of transactions. However, the era of mashups has emerged and is creating another round of side-steps and hacks that are leading to more security problems.

The Need for Security in a Mashup

The fact that a mashup is a page or application built typically using data combined from more than one site, illustrates the manner in which security vulnerabilities can multiply quickly. As new invocations are added to access resources or to call service APIs, new security vulnerabilities become possible. In addition, external mashups can embed your components and UI artifacts, thereby combining your functionality and data with components and UI artifacts of unknown origin. These wide open integration possibilities make it imperative to ensure that your data and functionality are not open to hacker attempts and other forms of intrusion.

The intrinsic openness of a mashup environment and the inability to predict exactly how components of a mashup infrastructure will be used in the future imply the need to address security at every aspect of the development lifecycle. Therefore, security must be a primary part of a development team's code review and testing processes.

A mashup environment most likely uses components and UI artifacts developed externally. This means that testing external components must be included in a development team's testing process right alongside an organization's own components. External components should be tested individually and in aggregate with other components of a given mashup.

Enterprise Mashup Security Guidelines

One of the most important steps for any organization is to institute best practices and mashup security policies based on standards established by industry, government, and compliance groups. The following are some guidelines for instituting a security policy:

- **Be determined to create a thorough security policy**—Once you have committed your organization to establishing a thorough security policy, meeting fundamental security needs will fall into place. Security must be a first-class citizen if you hope to be successful in securing your entire mashup infrastructure. Your security policy should outline which risks are acceptable and which risks are absolutely unacceptable.

- **Establish a proper authentication and authorization plan**—Manage user credentials effectively using industry standards and trusted identity management systems. Secure processes and services with role-based authorizations. Secure resources using access control lists (ACLs) based on security contexts.

- **Allow for flexibility**—Create modular authentication and authorization frameworks to support multiple security providers and specifications. Allow mashup component consumers to choose the desired privileges for a given component or resource. Guard components and resources using pre-established trust relationships.

- **Employ message-level and transport-level security**—To protect data and messages during transfer, digital signatures should be employed to ensure message integrity. Data and messages should also be encrypted to ensure data privacy. Transport-level security protects data and messages from one point to another, but does not secure the message payload or data itself. Message-level security protects the contents of a message by signing and encrypting all or part of the payload, thereby ensuring privacy of sensitive information until the message or data reaches its intended destination.

- **Support industry security standards**—Commit your organization to support industry security standards set by organizations such as W3C (http://www .w3.org), OASIS (http://www.oasis-open.org), Web Service Interoperability group (http://www.ws-i.org), Liberty Alliance project (http://projectliberty.org), OpenAjax Alliance (http://www.openajax.org), Trusted Computing Group (http://www.trustedcomputinggroup.org), and the Open Web Application Security Project (http://www.owasp.org).

Many standards and specifications are currently being promoted as solutions for securing web services transmitting SOAP and XML-based payloads. SOAP is an XML-based data format and protocol that was designed as a mechanism for exchanging messages across a network within a payload known as an "envelope." Like XML, SOAP is platform and language independent and extensible. SOAP is a specific incarnation of XML that is supported and sometimes mandated for many formal enterprise data-format standards.

One of the more prominent of these solutions is the WS-Security specification. WS-Security discusses, among other things, a standard set of extensions to SOAP that should be used to secure message content and confidentiality. This specification lies at the foundation for many other standards and specifications aimed at building secure web services.

Figure 6.1 illustrates the correlations between WS-Security and some of the most widely mentioned specifications and standards participating in the current stack of security standards for web services, XML, and SOAP.

Figure 6.1 illustrates an extensive stack of standards and specifications that are currently being promoted as solutions for securing web services transmitting SOAP and XML-based payloads. This stack is not complete by any means but does show most of the prominent players in this arena. These standards and specifications are briefly defined as follows:

- **WS-Security (http://en.wikipedia.org/wiki/WS-Security)**—Specifies extensions to SOAP messaging to ensure message content integrity and message

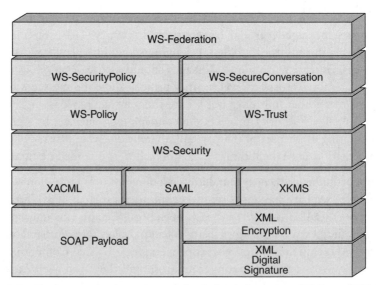

Figure 6.1 *Current stack of security standards for web services, XML, and SOAP*

confidentiality using a variety of security models such as PKI, SSL, and Kerberos

- **XML Digital Signature (http://www.w3.org/TR/xmldsig-core/)**—Specifies syntax for applying digital signatures to XML data

- **XML Encryption (http://www.w3.org/TR/xmlenc-core/)**—Specifies mechanisms for encrypting XML data

- **XML Key Management (XKMS) (http://www.w3.org/2001/XKMS/)**—Specifies mechanisms and protocols for registering and distributing public keys to be used with XML signatures and XML encryption

- **WS-SecureConversation   (http://www.ibm.com/developerworks/library/specification/ws-secon/)**—Specifies rules and mechanisms for sharing of security contexts between web service providers and consumers using token-based sessions

- **WS-SecurityPolicy (http://www.ibm.com/developerworks/library/specification/ws-secpol/)**—Specifies how web services set constraints and requirements as policy assertions to be applied to SOAP message security within the context of the WS-Security, WS-Trust, and WS-SecureConversation specifications

- **WS-Trust (http://www.ibm.com/developerworks/library/specification/ws-trust/)**—Specifies extensions and mechanisms for establishing trust relationships between messaging partners. Trust relationships are established via the process of issuing, validating, and renewing security tokens

- **WS-Federation (http://www.ibm.com/developerworks/library/specification/ws-fed/)**—Specifies mechanisms for allowing parties involved with security identities to transfer identities, attributes, and authentication information

- **Security Assertion Markup Language (SAML) (http://en.wikipedia.org/wiki/SAML)**—Specifies the means for exchanging XML-based authentication and authorization data between identity providers and identity consumers

- **XACML (http://en.wikipedia.org/wiki/XACML)**—Specifies an XML-based, access-control policy language and interpretation model for processing policies

- **WS-Federation—(http://www.ibm.com/developerworks/library/specification/ws-fed/)**—Specifies mechanisms for passing identity information, retrieving identity information, and establishing authentication and authorization claims between federation partners

Once you have established firm and effective policies and promoted use of industry specifications and standards throughout your organization, implementation details for securing mashup components and processes must be addressed.

The following sections discuss implementation specifics for securing vital parts of your mashup infrastructure.

Securing Input Data with Validation Techniques

Input validation is the foundation for securing a mashup application. Many intruder attempts including SQL injection, cross-site request forgery, and cross-site scripting can be prevented with a sound input validation model.

Your server-side validation framework should complement and support your client-side validation framework. Client-side frameworks can be side-stepped quite easily by clever individuals, so server-side validation is the final line of defense for protecting data and processes.

An effective input-validation framework should be mindful of the following items:

- Constraining input to a well-defined list of values.

- Validating the type of input data, as well as the input data length, range, and format.

- Reusing regular expressions on the client (via JavaScript, for example) and on the server with Java or other programming language that supports regular expressions. This enables a consistent validation framework on client and server.

- Scrubbing input data for invalid characters.

Once input is validated, data transferred between client and server should be sure to constrain content transferred between each other. This includes escaping of special characters, as discussed next.

Escaping Special Characters to Avoid Dynamic Exploits

All mainstream web browsers can interpret scripts dynamically downloaded from a server and embedded within a web page. Dynamic scripts such as these may include malicious HTML tags or scripting code that can exploit security vulnerabilities such as cross-site scripting. This problem can be averted by ensuring that scripts are checked and content is encoded to prevent execution of malicious code. An example of this is shown as follows:

```
<div>
This is some text
</div>
```

An escaped version of the preceding example would appear as follows:

```
&lt;div&gt;
This is some text
&lt;/div&gt;
```

Mashup pages often contain HTML snippets and scripts that are generated dynamically. Dynamically generated data should be validated and scrubbed to be sure that the data does not contain any unexpected special characters, such as HTML tags. If the dynamic data contains unexpected HTML markup, a web browser can interpret the data as HTML markup and/or scripting code and inadvertently execute the code as it is encountered by the browser. For this reason, dynamic content must be validated to identify unexpected special characters, such as HTML tags or scripting code. Unexpected special characters should be escaped to prevent inadvertent execution. Note that escaping in this context should not be confused with "output encoding," which typically refers to setting the character set for a given page or document, as in the following example:

```
<xsl:output method="html" encoding="ISO-8859-1" indent="no"/>
```

Data that is not validated and scrubbed for special characters runs the risk of encountering the following security vulnerabilities:

- Data integrity compromised

- Cookies created and/or accessed by unwanted parties

- User input, such as passwords and credit card data, intercepted and accessed by unwanted parties

- Execution of unwanted scripts within a trusted context or domain

The HTML specification is a good resource for identifying special characters. However, some characters are only special within the context used, such as block-level elements, attribute values, and URLs. Therefore a comprehensive analysis of each context is warranted to be sure to escape only characters that could cause problems within each context. Many frameworks such as Apache

Commons Lang, Django, and web2py are freely available for addressing each context and applying filtering to each context.

Defending against Session Fixation

Session fixation occurs when server-side code authenticates a user without first invalidating existing sessions. This exposes the opportunity for intruders to intercept authenticated sessions. An intruder can also create a new, legitimate session with a server and record the session ID. This ID can then be used maliciously in the event that another legitimate user creates a session that is identified by the same session ID. Hacking techniques are often employed to force this situation.

Listing 6.1 shows sample Java code where a user is authenticated without first invalidating the existing session using `HttpSession.invalidate()`.

Listing 6.1 *Example of Session Fixation Vulnerability*
```
private boolean authenticateUser(HttpServletRequest req)
{
  // session.invalidate() should have been called prior to this
  // to invalidate an existing session

  HttpSession session = req.getSession(false);
  if (null != session)
  {
    // session is assumed to existing and valid
    // an intruder can exploit this situation
    return true;
  }

  if (validateCredentials(req) == true)
  {
    // create a new session
    req.getSession();
    return true;
  }

  return false;
}
```

The code in Listing 6.1 can be exploited in a situation where a session exists and the browser is redirected back to the login page. If a new user provides login information to the server, the server simply assumes that it is the same session and returns a response to the user in the same manner as when a new session is created. This allows the owner of the existing session to potentially record and exploit data that is transferred between the browser and the server as long as the session exists. Cross-site scripting is often employed by attackers in this situation to bypass browser restrictions and to redirect data to an alternate site for recording.

Techniques to stop this type of attack include session timeouts, explicit session invalidation via logout buttons and links, forcing the user to reenter authentication data whenever sensitive data is accessed, storing session IDs in HTTP cookies rather than in GET or POST variables, regenerating the session ID on each request, and validating ancillary data during session activity.

The Spring Framework (http://www.springsource.org/) offerings provide features that attempt to address session fixation.

Preventing Cross-Site Request Forgery Attacks

Cross-site request forgery (CSRF) attacks occur when malicious code, originating from a third-party site, fools a browser into sending unwanted requests to a trusted site, such as a corporate mashup server.

The same-origin policy does not prevent requests being sent *from* a third-party site; it only prevents requests being sent *to* a third-party site. Therefore, the same-origin policy does not protect against CSRF attacks.

CSRF attacks depend on the assumption made by most servers that as long as a request comes from the same browser that originally authenticated a session with the server, any request or response transmitted over that authenticated session is valid. Most standard authentication mechanisms—including cookies, username/password, and SSL certificates—are at risk for CSRF attacks since each mechanism authenticates sessions between a browser and the server and not between a user and a server.

A CSRF attack occurs when a third-party site fools the browser into sending a request to the mashup server over the authenticated session. The mashup server assumes the request is a normal authenticated request from the mashup page and performs the necessary actions as usual. The response is then transmitted unknowingly to the third-party site. During a CSRF attack, a mashup page establishes an authenticated session with the mashup server. Requests are then passed from the mashup page to the mashup server across the authenticated session. The mashup server confirms that the mashup page is authenticated and allows each request to be performed. A CSRF attack sequence is illustrated in Figure 6.2.

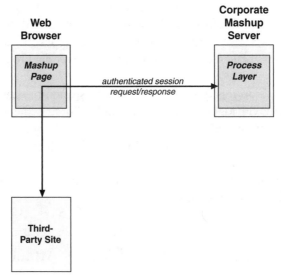

Figure 6.2   *Sequence of events during a CSRF attack*

Figure 6.2 illustrates a third-party site making authenticated requests to the mashup server via the mashup page. This can only happen if the third-party site can get the mashup page to make the requests in-proxy to the corporate mashup server for the third-party site. HTML exposes ways to make this happen.

The HTML <img> tag causes a web browser to access any URI specified as the src attribute. A CSRF-attacker can expose a page with the following <img> tag embedded:

```
<img src="http://somebank/transfer?amount=15000&
        sourceaccount=12345& destinationacct=67890">
```

If a user visits the page containing that <img> tag, while the user is authenticated to somebank, the <img> tag would instigate the browser into loading the URL specified as the src attribute, and the server at somebank would assume the request is valid and perform the requested action.

The preceding example instigates an HTTP GET request. This specific CSRF attack could be averted by making sure the server at somebank does not use GET requests to initiate changes on the server. Rather, require that only POST requests can be used to initiate changes.

A simple mechanism for preventing CSRF attacks involves requiring each HTTP request to include a user-specific request token, in addition to a standard cookie. The user-specific request token is embedded in the body of each POST request and in the URL of each GET request.

Securing On-Demand JavaScript

On-demand JavaScript is a technique in which a <script> tag and its accompanying JavaScript source are embedded in an HTML page. When the <script> tag is encountered, it is evaluated, and the JavaScript source is executed. One reason for using on-demand JavaScript is to bypass the same-origin policy and retrieve content from multiple sites. This mechanism is typically exploited by mashups by retrieving <script> snippets from a server after the page has been loaded, thereby only updating the portion of the page affected by the JavaScript source.

Listing 6.2 illustrates an example of three instances of on-demand JavaScript embedded in an HTML page.

Listing 6.2 *JavaScript Include Examples*

```
<html>
  <head>
    ...
  </head>
  <body>
    <script type="text/javascript" src="snippet1.js"></script>
    <script type="text/javascript" src="snippet2.js"></script>
    <script type="text/javascript" src="snippet3.js"></script>
  </body>
</html>
```

In this example, all three instances will be evaluated and executed when the HTML page is loaded.

On-demand JavaScript is often employed using AJAX and calls to a server via the XMLHttpRequest object. In this scenario, a response from the server is formatted as JavaScript. When the browser receives the response, it evaluates it and the JavaScript is executed. Any actions specified in the JavaScript affecting UI components are seen as the JavaScript is executed and the DOM is manipulated.

On-demand JavaScript has some obvious security vulnerabilities. Mainly, since the same-origin policy is bypassed and embedded scripts are executed as they are encountered, malicious code from external domains have a dangerous degree of access to data and processes available to the page in which the scripts are embedded. Specifically

- Scripts from external sites can access cookies associated with the hosting page.

- Scripts are executed immediately as they are evaluated, leaving no course of action to validate the scripts for potential security threats.

The typical solution currently employed to defend against on-demand security vulnerabilities involves constraining on-demand JavaScript to a hidden iframe. The hidden iframe then communicates with the main page to alter UI components on the page. In this manner, scripts can be parsed and evaluated prior to execution, thereby allowing a mashup to validate the script before execution. The script can be passed to the mashup server for further validation if needed, and results can be communicated from the server back to the iframe or to the parent page itself if desired.

Securing JSON

JSON is an acronym for JavaScript Object Notation, which aptly indicates that JSON data is actually an integral part of the JavaScript programming language. This means that JSON data can be used, as is, in a JavaScript function or statement. Specifically, the eval() function can be used to evaluate/interpret JSON data.

Observe the sample JSON data in Listing 6.3.

Listing 6.3   *A Typical JSON Object*

```
[
  {
    name: "object 1",
    message: "Hello from object 1",
    evil: alert("You should not see this!")
  },
  {
    name: "object 2",
    message: "Hello from object 2"
  },
  {
    name: "object 3",
    message: "Hello from object 3"
  },
  {
    name: "object 4",
    message: "Hello from object 4"
  },
  {
    name: "object 5",
    message: "Hello from object 5"
  },
  {
    name: "object 6",
    message: "Hello from object 6"
  }
]
```

When the JSON data shown in Listing 6.3 is interpreted, any valid JavaScript instructions embedded in the JSON data are executed. This mechanism is useful for receiving data responses from a server using the XMLHttpRequest object and used in a mashup page. However, this mechanism also presents some significant security vulnerabilities.

When JSON data is dynamically loaded, as with an XMLHttpRequest response, it can be easily interpreted on-the-fly and converted into standard JavaScript. Any executable JavaScript embedded within the JSON data is executed immediately as it is interpreted. JavaScript's eval() function, shown in the following example, is a common mechanism used to interpret JSON data dynamically.

```
var jsonObj = eval('(' + responseText + ')');
```

JSON data interpreted by the preceding eval() function executes immediately. If the data is retrieved from an attacker site (as is possible in a proxy-server scenario) and contains a malicious script, sensitive data can be stolen and used—and the attacker can now execute any code within the mashup page.

The example in Listing 6.4 illustrates JSON data that is preceded by a while(1); statement. This technique assumes that the client will remove the while(1); statement before using the JSON data. If the while(1); statement is not removed and the JavaScript eval() function is called, the browser will go into an endless loop as the while(1); executes.

Listing 6.4 *A JSON Object Preceded by a while Loop*
```
while(1);
  [
    {
      name: "object 1",
      message: "Hello from object 1",
      evil: alert("You should not see this!")
    },
    {
      name: "object 2",
      message: "Hello from object 2"
    },
    {
      name: "object 3",
      message: "Hello from object 3"
    },
    {
      name: "object 4",
      message: "Hello from object 4"
    },
    {
      name: "object 5",
      message: "Hello from object 5"
    },
```

```
      {
        name: "object 6",
        message: "Hello from object 6"
      }
    ]
```

Another technique for processing JSON data safely is to use the JSON.parse function from the libraries provided at http://www.json.org/ instead of eval() to eliminate risk of executing embedded functions, as in Listing 6.5.

Listing 6.5   *Removing while Loop from a JSON Object*
```
// include the json2 libraries
<script type="text/javascript" src="js/json2.js"></script>

// use JSON.parse instead of eval
var jsonObj = JSON.parse(jsonTxt);
```

The example in Listing 6.6 illustrates JSON data that is wrapped between comments. The comments prevent functions embedded within the JSON data from executing. The comments must be removed on the client before using.

Listing 6.6   *A JSON Object Wrapped in Comments*
```
/*
  [
    {
      name: "object 1",
      message: "Hello from object 1",
      evil: alert("You should not see this!")
    },
    {
      name: "object 2",
      message: "Hello from object 2"
    },
    {
      name: "object 3",
      message: "Hello from object 3"
    },
    {
      name: "object 4",
      message: "Hello from object 4"
    },
    {
      name: "object 5",
      message: "Hello from object 5"
    },
    {
      name: "object 6",
```

```
      message: "Hello from object 6"
    }
  ]
*/
```

The JavaScript function in Listing 6.7 removes comments from a JSON string and can, therefore, be used to remove comments from the JSON data in Listing 6.6.

Listing 6.7 *Removing Comments from a JSON Object*
```
function removeComments(jsonStr)
{
  return jsonStr.replace(/\/\/\*|\*\//g, "");
}
```

JSON data provides a useful and optimized means for retrieving JavaScript-compatible data from a server dynamically and used in mashup pages. However, this usefulness comes at the price of some significant security issues. With proper parsing of JSON data on the client, these security issues can be resolved and disaster averted.

Sanitizing HTML

Mashup pages are constructed from artifacts of code and data in many forms. Some of these artifacts take the form of HTML fragments dynamically inserted into a web page by manipulating the DOM for the page. Many of the HTML fragments used in mashups are snippets of JavaScript code embedded within <script> tags. As the embedded scripts are encountered, they are executed immediately by the browser. This technique can be dangerous if the JavaScript contains malicious code. Therefore, HTML fragments should be validated or "sanitized" before using.

Data returned from dynamic requests, such as those executed via the XMLHttp-Request object should be validated. Regular expressions can be used to verify that the data is properly formed. Listing 6.8 shows an example of a JavaScript function that validates a string and only allows brackets, digits, dashes, and spaces between 1 and 20 characters long.

Listing 6.8 *Validating Input Data*
```
function validateString(aStr)
{
  var regex = /^[\d\-\(\)\s]{1,20}$/gi;
  return regex.exec(aStr);
}
```

Once data has been validated, it should be sanitized prior to applying to the HTML page to prevent malicious content from being embedded in the page. The JavaScript function in Listing 6.9 illustrates a mechanism that inserts data into the DOM of a page as plain text, therefore preventing the data from executing if it contains malicious HTML.

Listing 6.9   *Sanitizing Data Prior to Rendering*

```
function sanitize(textData)
{
  var text = document.createTextNode(textData);
  // script won't be executed;
  document.getElementById('foo').appendChild(text);
}
```

Setting the content type explicitly can help to prevent security flaws due to data not being validated in its intended encoding. The following line sets the Content-Type for a page to UTF-8 encoding:

```
<meta http-equiv="Content-Type"
      content="text/html;charset=UTF-8">
```

Dynamic insertion of HTML fragments is a prevalent mechanism for building mashup pages today. However, potential security vulnerabilities can be exploited if the fragments are not validated and sanitized.

Securing iframes

Inline frames (iframes) are embedded HTML components that allow UI rendering and HTTP communication as separate entities. iframes are effective mechanisms for building secure UI artifacts and content snippets used in mashups. One reason for this is that iframes present a technique for isolating potentially untrusted content within a browser page, since content placed inside an iframe cannot manipulate the DOM or other browser components residing outside the iframe.

iframes are constructed using HTML code similar to Listing 6.10.

Listing 6.10   *Example of an iframe*

```
<iframe src="http://example.com/iframe1.html" />
<iframe src="http://example.com/iframe2.html" />
```

An iframe containing visual UI components is typically rendered in a browser using an embedded window with a border/frame, scrollbars, and other elements. However, iframes can be hidden and often are hidden to use as communication vehicles within a browser document. Figure 6.3 illustrates this concept.

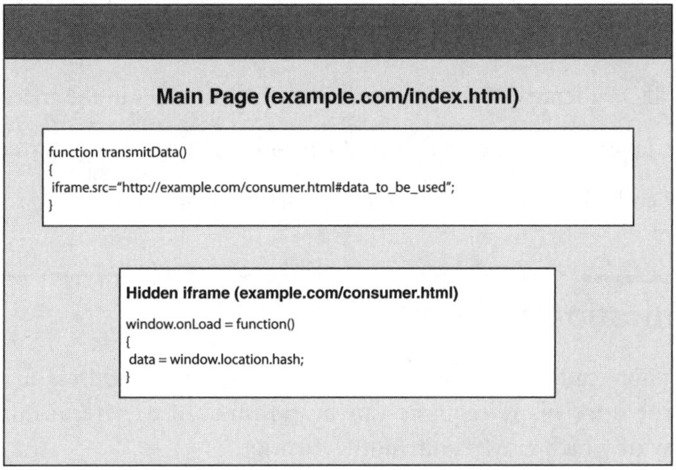

Main Page (example.com/index.html)

```
function transmitData()
{
  iframe.src="http://example.com/consumer.html#data_to_be_used";
}
```

Hidden iframe (example.com/consumer.html)

```
window.onLoad = function()
{
  data = window.location.hash;
}
```

Figure 6.3 *Data passing between an iframe and main browser page*

Figure 6.3 illustrates a main page that is embodied by index.html found at example.com. A hidden iframe is embedded within the main page document. The hidden iframe is constructed with content found at example.com/consumer.html. The JavaScript function, transmitData sets the src URL for the hidden iframe to consumer.html#data_to_be_used. The portion of the src URL following the hash mark (fragment identifier) can be extracted using the window.location.hash element. This is exactly what the function defined for the onLoad event does. Therefore, when the main document loads, the hidden iframe can retrieve the data following the fragment identifier of its own src URL and use it as it wants. This interplay is often used to communicate data between iframes or between containing documents and child iframes.

There is a security vulnerability using the "src URL" data-passing mechanism. Specifically, the src URL can be set by any component on the main page. If a UI artifact or content snippet is embedded in the page from an external site and the snippet or UI artifact contains malicious code, the iframe can be compromised. If the iframe is interacting with server-side code, data can be tainted or stolen.

The following tasks prevent attacks exploiting iframe fragment-identifier data passing:

* Validate the domain modifying fragment-identifiers to ensure that data is accepted from white-listed domains. JavaScript can be employed to monitor data passing and apply white-listing validation.

- Encrypt fragment-identifier data using the public key of the domain for the main web page.

- Include the identity of the fragment-identifier modifier in the encrypted data.

- Filter JavaScript embedded in fragment-identifier data.

- Filter embedded iframes in fragment-identifier data.

Authentication and Authorization

Authentication and authorization are complex issues to address in a mashup environment since many requests can be transmitted to several different services, many of which may require authentication.

A scenario where multiple authentication requests are needed to construct a mashup page using disparate services on several different sites is a fundamental concern for mashup developers. A few different single sign-on standards are emerging to address this concern, such as OpenID, OAuth, and others.

OpenID is a decentralized standard and framework gaining momentum as a single sign-on solution. OpenID allows the use of an existing URL owned by a user as the account ID that can be used to authenticate a user on any site supporting OpenID. The OpenID framework and standard requires the user to maintain only one set of credentials to be used for multiple sites.

OpenID enables single sign-on by using a URL as a user's identity. A site needing authentication credentials from a user utilizes the user's URL (blog site address, personal web site, social site URL, and so on) as the primary identifier of the user. This URL along with one username/password pair allows OpenID providers to authenticate a user with many different services and sites.

Many mainstream services are already supporting OpenID, therefore making it possible for users of their services to use the URL associated with their services as OpenID URLs. Some of the services supporting OpenID are

- Blogger

- AOL

- Flickr

- MySpace

- Technorati

- Yahoo!

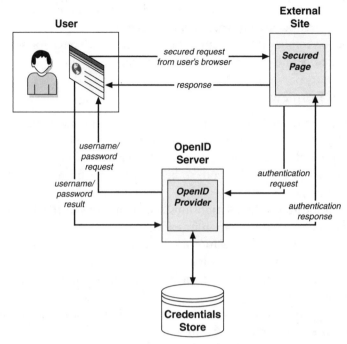

Figure 6.4 *Basic OpenID interaction between involved parties*

MyOpenID.com is a service that allows you to create an OpenID account to be used with any OpenID provider.

Figure 6.4 illustrates the typical relationships and interactions between OpenID services and parties.

In Figure 6.4, a user makes a request from her browser to a site requiring authentication. The user offers her OpenID URL to the site, and the site passes this OpenID to an OpenID provider. The OpenID provider requests a username and password from the user. If the username and password are valid, the OpenID provider returns a response to the site requiring authentication and the user's request is completed. The username and password remain the same regardless of which OpenID-supported site the user sends requests.

Applying Security to a Mashup Infrastructure

As defined in the previous sections, dynamic data and code are used extensively to pass requests to mashup servers and to construct mashup pages from data received from mashup servers and external sites. This dynamic data must be validated and sanitized before using to avoid the many potential security risks that abound with the use of dynamic data processing.

This section applies the concepts discussed in this chapter for securing and validating data before it is applied to the construction of a mashup.

Validation Framework

The software components of an input validation framework are used to process data received from a browser client. To provide functionality supporting proper input validation, the framework can use components based on regular expression parsing. This allows validation code to be shared on the client as JavaScript and on the server as Java.

Figure 6.5 illustrates the relationships and definitions of the primary classes participating in an input validation framework.

As Figure 6.5 illustrates, relationships between classes and interfaces in a simple validation framework revolve around a Validator interface. The Contacts-Validator class implements the Validator interface and contains logic for validating contact information.

The sequence of invocations as flow-of-control traverses through the validation framework is illustrated in Figure 6.6.

As shown in Figure 6.6, a Validator client retrieves an instance of the Validator interface from the ValidatorFactory class. Values are then passed to the Validator instance to be validated against given field names. A boolean result is returned indicating the result of each validation attempt.

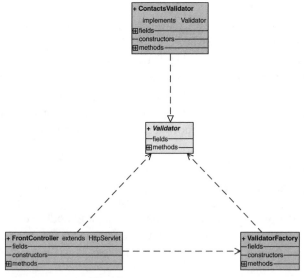

Figure 6.5   *Class diagram for the validation framework*

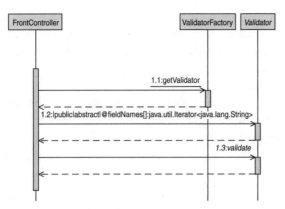

Figure 6.6 *Sequences for a simple validation interaction*

Listing 6.11 provides the details for a ValidatorFactory class in which instances of Validator implementations are created and returned.

Listing 6.11 *ValidatorFactory Class*

```
public class ValidatorFactory
{
  public static final String CONTACTS_VALIDATOR = "Contacts";

  public static Validator getValidator(String validatorName)
  {
    try
    {
      if (validatorName.equalsIgnoreCase(CONTACTS_VALIDATOR))
      {
        return
          new com.jeffhanson.mashups.web.ContactsValidator();
      }
      else
      {
        throw new Exception("Validator: "
                  + validatorName + " is not supported in "
                  + "ValidatorFactory.getValidator()");
      }
    }
    catch (Exception e)
    {
      e.printStackTrace();
    }

    return null;
  }
}
```

As detailed in Listing 6.11, the `ValidatorFactory` class does a simple string lookup to find the name of the class implementing the `Validator` interface that is to be instantiated and returned. If the name is invalid an exception is thrown and null is returned.

An input validator is defined by the `Validator` interface. As shown in Listing 6.12, the `Validator` interface is comprised of a method allowing retrieval of all field names supported by a given validator implementation and a method that validates a given value for a field name. A simple boolean value is returned from the `validate` method indicating whether the value passes the validation test.

Listing 6.12   *Validator Interface*

```
public interface Validator
{
  Iterator<String> fieldNames();
  boolean validate(String fieldName, String fieldValue);
}
```

Listing 6.12 illustrates the methods required for classes implementing the `Validator` interface. The `fieldNames` method must return a list of all fields that are to be validated for the class. The `validate` method must validate values for a given field supported by the class.

Listing 6.13 shows the details for a class that validates fields typically found in a form that gathers contact information. The class implements the `Validator` interface with bodies for the `fieldNames` method and the `validate` method. The validate method employs the same regular expression used by client-side JavaScript input validation.

Listing 6.13   *ContactsValidator Class*

```
public class ContactsValidator
  implements Validator
{
  public static final String CONTACT_NAME = "contact_name";
  public static final String CONTACT_ADDRESS =
    "contact_address";
  public static final String CONTACT_CITY = "contact_city";
  public static final String CONTACT_STATE = "contact_state";
  public static final String CONTACT_ZIP = "contact_zip";
  public static final String CONTACT_PHONE = "contact_phone";
  public static final String CONTACT_EMAIL = "contact_email";

  public static final String[] STATES = {
    "AL", "AK", "AZ", "AR", "CA", "CO", "CT", "DE", "DC", "FL",
    "GA", "HI", "ID", "IL", "IN", "IA", "KS", "KY", "LA", "ME",
    "MD", "MA", "MI", "MN", "MS", "MO", "MT", "NE", "NV", "NH",
    "NJ", "NM", "NY", "NC", "ND", "OH", "OK", "OR", "PA", "RI",
```

```
  "SC", "SD", "TN", "TX", "UT", "VT", "VA", "WA", "WV", "WI",
  "WY"
};

private static final ArrayList<String> fieldNames =
  new ArrayList<String>()
{{
  add(CONTACT_NAME);
  add(CONTACT_ADDRESS);
  add(CONTACT_CITY);
  add(CONTACT_STATE);
  add(CONTACT_ZIP);
  add(CONTACT_PHONE);
  add(CONTACT_EMAIL);
}};

public Iterator<String> fieldNames()
{
  return fieldNames.iterator();
}

public boolean validate(String fieldName,
                        String fieldValue)
{
  if (fieldName.equalsIgnoreCase(CONTACT_NAME))
  {
    return fieldValue.matches("^([a-z A-Z]+)$");
  }
  else if (fieldName.equalsIgnoreCase(CONTACT_ADDRESS))
  {
    return fieldValue.matches("^([a-z A-Z1-9]+)$");
  }
  else if (fieldName.equalsIgnoreCase(CONTACT_CITY))
  {
    return fieldValue.matches("^([a-z A-Z]+)$");
  }
  else if (fieldName.equalsIgnoreCase(CONTACT_STATE))
  {
    for (int i = 0; i < STATES.length; i++)
    {
      if (fieldValue.equalsIgnoreCase(STATES[i]))
      {
        return true;
      }
    }
  }
  else if (fieldName.equalsIgnoreCase(CONTACT_ZIP))
  {
```

```
      return fieldValue.matches("(^\\d{5}$)|(^\\d{5}-"
                          + "\\d{4}$)");
   }
   else if (fieldName.equalsIgnoreCase(CONTACT_PHONE))
   {
      return fieldValue.matches("^\\(([1-9]\\d{2}\\))\\s?"
                          + "\\d{3}\\-\\d{4}$");
   }
   else if (fieldName.equalsIgnoreCase(CONTACT_EMAIL))
   {
      return fieldValue.matches("(^[a-z]([a-z_\\.]*)"
                          + "@([a-z_\\.]*)([.]"
                          + "[a-z]{3})$)|(^[a-z]"
                          + "([a-z_\\.]*)@([a-z_"
                          + "\\.]*)(\\.[a-z]{3})"
                          + "(\\.[a-z]{2})*$)");
   }

   return false;
  }
}
```

Implementations of the `Validator` interface are required to provide bodies for the `fieldNames`, and `validate` methods. Values are validated for specific field names by applying regular expressions against values. The regular expressions are shared with JavaScript embedded in a browser page, thereby providing a consistent validation model across client and server.

Listing 6.14 shows a front controller servlet that handles HTTP requests. The request parameters are retrieved and passed to the `validator` class to determine whether they pass validation. If an invalid value is encountered, an error is returned and the user is allowed to go back and correct the error.

Listing 6.14   *FrontController Class*

```
public class FrontController extends HttpServlet
{
  protected void doGet(HttpServletRequest req,
                       HttpServletResponse res)
    throws ServletException, IOException
  {
    res.setContentType("text/html");
    PrintWriter out = res.getWriter();
    out.println("<h3>GET processed successfully</h3>");
  }

  protected void doPost(HttpServletRequest req,
                        HttpServletResponse res)
    throws ServletException, IOException
  {
```

```
    Validator validator =
      ValidatorFactory.
        getValidator(ValidatorFactory.CONTACTS_VALIDATOR);

    res.setContentType("text/html");
    PrintWriter out = res.getWriter();

    Iterator<String> iter = validator.fieldNames();
    while (iter.hasNext())
    {
      String fieldName = iter.next();
      String fieldValue = req.getParameter(fieldName);
      if ((null == fieldValue) || fieldValue.length() <= 0)
      {
        out.println("<h3>" + fieldname
                    + " not found. Press back button.</h3>");
      }
      else if (!validator.validate(fieldName, fieldValue))
      {
        out.println("<h3>" + fieldname
                    + " is invalid. Press back button.</h3>");
      }
    }

    out.println("<h3>POST data validated successfully</h3>");
  }

  protected void doPut(HttpServletRequest req,
                       HttpServletResponse res)
    throws ServletException, IOException
  {
    res.setContentType("text/html");
    PrintWriter out = res.getWriter();
    out.println("<h3>PUT processed successfully</h3>");
  }

  protected void doDelete(HttpServletRequest req,
                          HttpServletResponse res)
    throws ServletException, IOException
  {
    res.setContentType("text/html");
    PrintWriter out = res.getWriter();
    out.println("<h3>DELETE processed successfully</h3>");
  }
}
```

As Listing 6.14 illustrates, request parameters are checked for valid input by the specific validator returned from the validator factory. The validator is assumed to be the "contacts" validator in this scenario. Production implementations of the front controller would determine the name of the validator based on the request content and context.

Listing 6.15 shows an HTML page that provides a JavaScript validation framework that validates every field for a contacts form on the page. Regular expressions that are shared with the server-side validation are applied against the form values to determine whether they are valid. If a value is found to be invalid, an error alert is presented to the user and the input focus is returned to the field containing the invalid value.

Listing 6.15 *HTML Form Validation with JavaScript Regular Expressions*

```
<!DOCTYPE HTML PUBLIC "-//W3C//DTD HTML 4.01 Transitional//EN"
       "http://www.w3.org/TR/html4/loose.dtd">
<html>
<head>
  <title>Validation test</title>
  <script type="text/javascript">
  //<![CDATA[

  function validateName(val)
  {
    var valRegExp  = /^([a-z A-Z]+)$/;
    return valRegExp.test(val);
  }


  function validateAddress(val)
  {
    var valRegExp  = /^([a-z A-Z1-9]+)$/;
    return valRegExp.test(val);
  }


  function validateCity(val)
  {
    var valRegExp  = /^([a-z A-Z]+)$/;
    return valRegExp.test(val);
  }


  function validateZip(val)
  {
    var valRegExp  = /(^\d{5}$)|(^\d{5}-\d{4}$)/;
    return valRegExp.test(val);
  }


  function validatePhone(val)
  {
    var valRegExp  = /^\(([1-9]\d{2}\)\s?\d{3}\-\d{4}$/;
    return valRegExp.test(val);
  }
```

```
function validateEmail(val)
{
  var valRegExp =
    /(^[a-z]([a-z_\.]*)@([a-z_\.]*)([.][a-z]{3})$)|
    (^[a-z]([a-z_\.]*)@([a-z_\.]*)(\.[a-z]{3})
    (\.[a-z]{2})*$)/;
  return valRegExp.test(val);
}

function validateFormInput(form)
{
  if (form.contact_name.value == "")
  {
    alert("Please enter your name.");
    form.contact_name.focus();
    return false ;
  }
  if (!validateName(form.contact_name.value))
  {
    alert("Name contains invalid characters.");
    form.contact_name.focus();
    return false ;
  }

  if (form.contact_address.value == "")
  {
    alert("Please enter your address.");
    form.contact_address.focus();
    return false ;
  }
  if (!validateAddress(form.contact_address.value))
  {
    alert("Address contains invalid characters.");
    form.contact_address.focus();
    return false ;
  }

  if (form.contact_city.value == "")
  {
    alert("Please enter your city.");
    form.contact_city.focus();
    return false ;
  }
  if (!validateCity(form.contact_city.value))
  {
    alert("City contains invalid characters.");
    form.contact_city.focus();
    return false ;
  }
```

```
  if (form.contact_zip.value == "")
  {
    alert("Please enter your zip.");
    form.contact_zip.focus();
    return false ;
  }
  if (!validateZip(form.contact_zip.value))
  {
    alert("Zip code must be in the form of "
          + "nnnnn or nnnnn-nnnn.");
    form.contact_phone.focus();
    return false ;
  }

  if (form.contact_phone.value == "")
  {
    alert("Please enter your phone.");
    form.contact_phone.focus();
    return false ;
  }
  if (!validatePhone(form.contact_phone.value))
  {
    alert("Phone number must be in the form of "
          + "(nnn) nnn-nnnn or (nnn)nnn-nnnn.");
    form.contact_phone.focus();
    return false ;
  }

  if (form.contact_email.value == "")
  {
    alert("Please enter your email address.");
    form.contact_email.focus();
    return false ;
  }
  if (!validateEmail(form.contact_email.value))
  {
    alert("Email address must be in the form of "
          + "cccccccc@ccc.com, cccccccc@ccc.org, etc.");
    form.contact_email.focus();
    return false ;
  }

  // form.action.value = "process.cgi";

  return true ;
}

//]]>
</script>
```

```html
</head>
<body>

<table border="1">
  <form method="POST"
      action="http://localhost:8080/validate/v/test"
      onsubmit="return validateFormInput(this);"
      name="ValidateInputTestForm">
    <tr><td>Name:</td><td colspan="5"><input type="text" name="contact_name" size="100"
maxlength="40"/></td></tr>
    <tr><td>Address:</td><td colspan="5"><input type="text" name="contact_address"
size="100" maxlength="40"/></td>
</tr>
    <tr><td>City:</td><td><input type="text"
                                name="contact_city"
                                size="44"
                                maxlength="20"/>
    </td>
    <td>State:</td>
      <td>
        <select name="contact_state">
          <option value="AL">AL</option>
          <option value="AK">AK</option>
          ...
          <option value="WI">WI</option>
          <option value="WY">WY</option>
        </select>
      </td>
    <td>Zip:</td><td><input type="text"
                                name="contact_zip"
                                size="24"
                                maxlength="10"/></td>
    </tr>
    <tr><td>Phone:</td><td colspan="5"><input type="text"
    name="contact_phone" size="20" maxlength="14"/></td>
    </tr>
    <tr><td>Email:</td><td colspan="5"><input type="text"
    name="contact_email" size="100" maxlength="50"/></td>
    </tr>
    <tr><td colspan="6" align="center"><input type="submit" value="Submit"
name="submit"/></td></tr>
  </form>
</table>

</body>

</html>
```

As illustrated in Listing 6.15 the validateFormInput JavaScript function is called when the submit button is clicked. If the function returns true, the form directs an HTTP POST request at a URL pointing to the server containing the front controller servlet. The input values, passed as HTTP request parameters, are then validated by the server validation framework before allowing the actions of the HTTP request to execute.

As shown in the preceding section, a proper input validation framework should provide a consistent validation model on the client and server.

Secure JSON Framework

The framework described in this section provides functionality for protecting JSON data transmissions between server and client. The framework provides software components that reside in a client-side browser page as JavaScript and on server-side processing logic as Java. To provide functionality supporting proper input validation, the framework can use components based on regular expression parsing. This allows validation code to be shared on the client as JavaScript and on the server as Java.

The component interactions as flow-of-control traverses through the secure JSON framework are illustrated in Figure 6.7.

As shown in Figure 6.7 the secure JSON framework is concerned with retrieving JSON data from the data layer, preparing the data for delivery to a client browser, and then passing the data to the client as responses to HTTP requests invoked by the client.

Listing 6.16 illustrates the JavaScript components used by client code embedded in a browser page to invoke AJAX requests to server-side processes where the server performs business logic and returns results as JSON data.

The AJAX requests sent from the code in Listing 6.16 are all invoked synchronously. AJAX requests are performed synchronously to receive responses from the server before returning control to the caller.

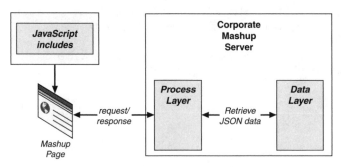

Figure 6.7 *Component interactions for secure JSON framework*

Listing 6.16 *ajax.js*

```
//====================================================
// initializes the XMLHTTP object
//====================================================
function getHTTPObject()
{
  var xmlhttp = null;
  var success = false;

  // List of MS XMLHTTP versions - newest first
  var MSXML_XMLHTTP_PROGIDS = new Array(
      'MSXML2.XMLHTTP.5.0',
      'MSXML2.XMLHTTP.4.0',
      'MSXML2.XMLHTTP.3.0',
      'MSXML2.XMLHTTP',
      'Microsoft.XMLHTTP'
  );

  for (var i = 0;
       i < MSXML_XMLHTTP_PROGIDS.length && !success;
       i++)
  {
    try
    {
      xmlhttp = new ActiveXObject(MSXML_XMLHTTP_PROGIDS[i]);
      success = true;
      return xmlhttp;
    }
    catch (e)
    {
      xmlhttp = false;
    }
  }

  if (!xmlhttp && typeof XMLHttpRequest != 'undefined')
  {
    try
    {
      xmlhttp = new XMLHttpRequest();
    }
    catch (e)
    {
      xmlhttp = false;
    }
  }

  return xmlhttp;
}
```

```
//===================================================
// performs a synchronous Ajax request
//===================================================
function ajaxSyncRequest(apiURL,
                         getOrPost,
                         requestData,
                         callbackFunc)
{
  var xmlRequest = getHTTPObject();

  xmlRequest.open(getOrPost, apiURL, false);
  xmlRequest.send(requestData);

  if (xmlRequest.status == 200)
  {
    if (callbackFunc)
    {
      if (xmlRequest.responseText)
      {
        callbackFunc(xmlRequest.responseText);
      }
    }
  }
  else
  {
    alert("ajaxSyncRequest failed with status: "
          + xmlRequest.status);
  }
}
```

The caller of the ajaxSyncRequest function passes a callback function that is invoked when the AJAX invocation completes. The AJAX response is passed as text to the callback function for processing.

Listing 6.17 illustrates how the ajaxSyncRequest function can be called and provided with a callback function. The callback function in this example is testResultHandler. This function receives the AJAX invocation result as JSON data formatted as plain text. The JSON data then must be interpreted or parsed to use it as actual JavaScript code.

Listing 6.17 *index.jsp*

```
<html>
<head>
<title>Test for secure JSON</title>

  <script type="text/javascript" src="js/json2.js"></script>
  <script type="text/javascript" src="js/ajax.js"></script>
```

```javascript
<script type="text/javascript">

//<![CDATA[

//==================================================
// removes comments wrapped around a JSON object
//==================================================
function removeComments(jsonStr)
{
  return jsonStr.replace(/\/\*|\*\//g, "");
}


//==================================================
// test callback
//==================================================
function testResultHandler(responseText)
{
  if (responseText)
  {
    alert("Raw results = " + responseText);

    var jsonTxt = removeComments(responseText);

    alert("Sanitized results = " + jsonTxt);

    try
    {
      // Use JSON.parse instead of eval(jsonTxt) to,
      // among other things,
      // eliminate risk of executing embedded functions
      var jsonObj = JSON.parse(jsonTxt);
      for (var i in jsonObj)
      {
        alert("JSON obj " + i + " = "
              + JSON.stringify(jsonObj[i]));
      }
    }
    catch (e)
    {
      alert("Embedded functions caused exception in JSON.parse");
    }
  }
  else
  {
    alert("testResultHandler responseText is null");
  }
}
```

```
//]]>

</script>
</head>

<body>
<form method="GET"
      action="javascript:ajaxSyncRequest(
                'http://host/json/commented',
                'GET',
                'rigma',
                testResultHandler)"
      name="getCommentedDataForm">
  <input type="submit"
         value="Get Commented JSON Data"
         name="submit"/>
</form>

<p/>

<form method="GET"
      action="javascript:ajaxSyncRequest(
                'http://host/json/evilfuncs',
                'GET',
                'rigma',
                testResultHandler)"
      name="getEmbeddedFuncsDataForm">
  <input type="submit"
         value="Get JSON Data with Embedded Functions"
         name="submit"/>
</form>

</body>
</html>
```

Listing 6.17 illustrates how the JSON.parse is used to create a JSON object from text returned from an AJAX invocation. The JSON.parse method is found in the json2.js library. The JSON.parse method prevents embedded functions that may be present in the returned JSON data from executing as the JSON text is evaluated.

Listing 6.18 shows the details for a servlet that is used to receive AJAX requests from a browser client. The requests are processed and JSON data is returned. In this case two types of JSON data can be returned: a secured block of JSON data wrapped between comments and a block of JSON data containing an embedded function that demonstrates how destructive actions could be performed by a malicious function embedded in the data.

Listing 6.18   *AJAX Front-Controller Servlet*

```java
public class FrontController extends HttpServlet
{
  private static final String JSON_COMMENTED =
    "/*" +
    "[" +
    "  {" +
    "    \"name\": \"object 1\"," +
    "    \"message\": \"Hello from object 1\"" +
    "  }," +
    "  {" +
    "    \"name\": \"object 2\"," +
    "    \"message\": \"Hello from object 2\"" +
    "  }," +
    "  {" +
    "    \"name\": \"object 3\"," +
    "    \"message\": \"Hello from object 3\"" +
    "  }," +
    "  {" +
    "    \"name\": \"object 4\"," +
    "    \"message\": \"Hello from object 4\"" +
    "  }," +
    "  {" +
    "    \"name\": \"object 5\"," +
    "    \"message\": \"Hello from object 5\"" +
    "  }," +
    "  {" +
    "    \"name\": \"object 6\"," +
    "    \"message\": \"Hello from object 6\"" +
    "  }" +
    "]" +
    "*/";

  private static final String JSON_EMBEDDED_FUNCS =
    "[" +
    "  {" +
    "    name: \"object 1\"," +
    "    message: \"Hello from object 1\"," +
    "    evil: alert(\"You should not see this!\")" +
    "  }," +
    "  {" +
    "    name: \"object 2\"," +
    "    message: \"Hello from object 2\"" +
    "  }," +
    "  {" +
    "    name: \"object 3\"," +
    "    message: \"Hello from object 3\"" +
    "  }," +
```

```
"    {" +
"      name: \"object 4\"," +
"      message: \"Hello from object 4\"" +
"    }," +
"    {" +
"      name: \"object 5\"," +
"      message: \"Hello from object 5\"" +
"    }," +
"    {" +
"      name: \"object 6\"," +
"      message: \"Hello from object 6\"" +
"    }" +
"]";

protected void doGet(HttpServletRequest req,
                     HttpServletResponse res)
  throws ServletException, IOException
{
  String messageResult = "{\"result\": \"failed\"}";

  String resource = req.getPathInfo();
  if (null != resource &&
      resource.equalsIgnoreCase("/commented"))
  {
    messageResult = JSON_COMMENTED;
  }
  else if (null != resource &&
           resource.equalsIgnoreCase("/evilfuncs"))
  {
    messageResult = JSON_EMBEDDED_FUNCS;
  }

  res.setContentType("application/json");
  PrintWriter out = res.getWriter();
  out.println(messageResult);
}

protected void doPost(HttpServletRequest req,
                      HttpServletResponse res)
  throws ServletException, IOException
{
  res.setContentType("application/json");
  PrintWriter out = res.getWriter();
  out.println("{\"result\": \"success\"}");
}

protected void doPut(HttpServletRequest req,
                     HttpServletResponse res)
  throws ServletException, IOException
```

```
{
  res.setContentType("application/json");
  PrintWriter out = res.getWriter();
  out.println("{\"result\": \"success\"}");
}

protected void doDelete(HttpServletRequest req,
                        HttpServletResponse res)
  throws ServletException, IOException
{
  res.setContentType("application/json");
  PrintWriter out = res.getWriter();
  out.println("{\"result\": \"success\"}");
}
}
```

The front controller servlet shown in Listing 6.18 returns either the secured JSON data or the block of JSON data containing the potentially dangerous embedded function. The content type for the returned HTTP response is set to application/json and the data is passed as textual JSON data that is to be parsed or evaluated by the web browser client.

Validating input values and constraining JSON data are just two of the building blocks needed for a secured mashup infrastructure. The frameworks shown in the preceding sections provide a simple but effective means for validating data and protecting JSON data to be used in AJAX invocations.

Summary

This chapter discussed fundamental security issues that must be addressed when designing and implementing mashup components, processes, and artifacts. The open nature of the mashup development model causes security to be a primary concern for developers of a mashup infrastructure. They must be prepared to handle such security issues as cross-site request forgery (CSRF), AJAX security weaknesses, cross-site scripting, and secure sign-on across multiple domains.

Because a mashup is a page or application built typically using data combined from more than one site, security vulnerabilities can multiply quickly. In addition, external mashups can embed your components and UI artifacts, thereby combining your functionality and data with components and UI artifacts of unknown origin. It's your responsibility to protect your data and functionality from hackers and other intrusions.

External components must be included in a development team's testing process right alongside an organization's own components. External components should be tested individually and in aggregate with other components of a given mashup. And because hackers never rest, security testing should be performed on a continuous basis to guard against new exploits and to ensure that your application or infrastructure remains secure.

In the next chapter I discuss the concepts presented thus far as a step-by-step tour through the technologies and implementations for each high-level mashup category.

Chapter 7

Step-by-Step: A Tour through a Sample Mashup

To this point, I have discussed the importance of analyzing the specific programming entities that can be combined in a mashup along with the corresponding issues and solutions for each. This has been presented as three high-level categories of items—user interface artifacts (presentation), data (resources), and/or application functionality (processes). UI artifacts include such entities as HTML snippets, on-demand JavaScript, web service APIs, RSS feeds, and/or other sundry pieces of data. The implementation style, techniques, and technologies used for each category of mashup items present certain constraints and subtleties.

In this chapter I discuss the concepts presented thus far as a step-by-step tour through the technologies and implementations for each high-level mashup category.

Building the Mashup Presentation Layer

The presentation layer for a given mashup can pull from a local service platform, publicly available APIs, RSS data feeds, dynamic JavaScript snippets, widgets, and badges.

The presentation page shown in the following listings illustrates techniques for viewing disparate data in a portal-like manner. The page integrates business documents, a geocoded map, an RSS feed, a calendar gadget, a Twitter counter chicklet, and a Twitter archive list delivered as RSS.

Most third-party UI artifacts rely on an API key to be presented to the third-party site for a page to use the artifacts. Listing 7.1 illustrates the use of an API key to access the Google Maps UI artifacts APIs.

Listing 7.1   *Presenting an API Key to Access Google Maps UI Artifacts*

```
<html>
<head>
<!-- Include Google Maps Javascript Library -->
<script type="text/javascript" src="http://maps.google.com/maps?file=api&v=1&
key=ABQIAAAA01HpWF7mf2aW91RNaGDc7xTfGML3OZxtDDthfq-
aZ1uFtrk9MRS_VWEizymnfki_h891qU7A0ts2PA">
</script>
```

The code in Listing 7.1 relies on an API key that must be retrieved in a previously executed registration process. The registration site is located at http://code.google.com/apis/maps/signup.html. The key you receive is valid for a single web domain.

Listing 7.2 illustrates the body of a "load" function wherein a hard-coded Google map is retrieved and applied to a div element in the DOM to show a simple Google map.

Listing 7.2   *JavaScript and DOM Manipulation to Display a Google Map*

```
<script>
  function load()
  {
    if (GBrowserIsCompatible())
    {
      // create map component in div with the id = "map"
      var map = new GMap2(document.getElementById("map"));

      // create map components components
      map.addControl(new GSmallMapControl());
      map.addControl(new GMapTypeControl());

      // create center point when map is displayed
      map.setCenter(new GLatLng(37.4419, -122.1419), 13);

      // create information balloon for center point
      // when map is displayed
      map.openInfoWindow(map.getCenter(),
                         "<b>Your Company Here</b>");

      // create clickable point in the same place as
      // the center point, so the user can re-open the
      // info balloon if they close it
      var point = new GLatLng(37.395746, -121.952234);
      map.addOverlay(createMarker(point, 1));
    }
  }
```

```
function createMarker(point, number)
{
  var marker = new GMarker(point);

  // create clickable point with title for address
  GEvent.addListener(marker, "click", function()
  {
     marker.openInfoWindowHtml("<b>Your Company Here</b>");
  });
  return marker;
}

</script>
</head>
<body onload="load()">
```

The code in Listing 7.2 relies on DOM-manipulation techniques to apply a Google map to the page. The map is applied and a marker is shown on the map.

Listing 7.3 illustrates the div element that will hold the results from the Google map retrieval.

Listing 7.3 *DIV Element That Will Contain the Google Map*

```
<div id="map" style="border-style:ridge;
            position: absolute;
            left: 220px;
            top: 10px;
            width:400px;
            height:300px">
</div>
```

For retrieving a Google map using dynamic location information, AJAX techniques can be used to enable dynamic service requests and to reduce full page refreshes. In this scenario, location information such as city, state, and zip code can be passed to a mashup server where the location information is massaged and passed to the Google Maps API. The latitude and longitude for the given location are returned to the client and applied to the Google Maps JavaScript code to present the graphical map.

AJAX techniques rely on the use of the XMLHttpRequest JavaScript object. This object is used to send HTTP requests from a JavaScript client to a server and to receive responses from the server synchronously or asynchronously.

Listing 7.4 uses an instance of the XMLHttpRequest object in the ajaxGet method to pass a standard HTTP GET request to a server. The data retrieved from the server is in XML format and is accessed via the XMLHttpRequest where it is parsed and passed to the createMap method where the Google map is retrieved and applied to the DOM.

Listing 7.4   *Using AJAX Techniques to Dynamically Retrieve a Google Map*

```
<!DOCTYPE html PUBLIC "-//W3C//DTD XHTML 1.0 Strict//EN"
  "http://www.w3.org/TR/xhtml1/DTD/xhtml1-strict.dtd">

<html xmlns="http://www.w3.org/1999/xhtml"
      xmlns:v="urn:schemas-microsoft-com:vml">
<head>
  <meta http-equiv="content-type"
        content="text/html; charset=UTF-8"/>
  <title>Google Maps</title>

  <script type="text/javascript"
          src="http://maps.google.com/maps?file=api&" +
               "v=1&key=...">
</script>

  <script type="text/javascript">
    //<![CDATA[

    if (GBrowserIsCompatible())
    {
      // ============================================
      // createMarker function
      // ============================================
      function createMarker(point, html)
      {
        var marker = new GMarker(point);
        GEvent.addListener(marker, "click", function()
        {
          marker.openInfoWindowHtml(html);
        });
        return marker;
      }


      // ============================================
      // createMap function
      // ============================================
      function createMap(latitude, longitude, locationInfo)
      {
        // Display the map, with some controls and
        // set the initial location
        var map = new GMap2(document.getElementById("map"));
        map.addControl(new GLargeMapControl());
        map.addControl(new GMapTypeControl());
        map.setCenter(new GLatLng(latitude, longitude), 8);

        // Set up marker
```

```
    var point = new GLatLng(latitude, longitude);
    var marker = createMarker(point, locationInfo)
    map.addOverlay(marker);
}


//===================================================
// initializes the XMLHTTP object
//===================================================
function getHTTPObject()
{
  var xmlhttp = null;
  var success = false;

  // List of MS XMLHTTP versions - newest first
  var MSXML_XMLHTTP_PROGIDS = new Array(
      'MSXML2.XMLHTTP.5.0',
      'MSXML2.XMLHTTP.4.0',
      'MSXML2.XMLHTTP.3.0',
      'MSXML2.XMLHTTP',
      'Microsoft.XMLHTTP'
  );

  for (var i = 0;
       i < MSXML_XMLHTTP_PROGIDS.length && !success;
       i++)
  {
    try
    {
      xmlhttp =
        new ActiveXObject(MSXML_XMLHTTP_PROGIDS[i]);
      success = true;
      return xmlhttp;
    }
    catch (e)
    {
      xmlhttp = false;
    }
  }

  if (!xmlhttp && typeof XMLHttpRequest != 'undefined')
  {
    try
    {
      xmlhttp = new XMLHttpRequest();
    }
    catch (e)
    {
      xmlhttp = false;
    }
  }
```

```
    return xmlhttp;
  }


=========================================
    // ajaxGet function
    // =====================================
    function ajaxGet(apiURL)
    {
      var locationInfo =
       document.getMapForm.locationInfo.value;
      var xmlRequest = getHTTPObject();

      // The false param indicates a synchronous call
      //
      xmlRequest.open("GET",
                      apiURL + '?location=' + locationInfo,
                      false);
      xmlRequest.send(locationInfo);
      if (xmlRequest.status == 200)
      {
        if (xmlRequest.responseText)
        {
          var xmlDoc = xmlRequest.responseXML;

          var latitude =
          xmlDoc.getElementsByTagName('latitude')[0].
            firstChild.data;
          var longitude =
          xmlDoc.getElementsByTagName('longitude')[0].
            firstChild.data;

          createMap(latitude, longitude, locationInfo);
        }
      }
      else
      {
        alert("ajaxPost failed with status: "
          + xmlRequest.status);
      }
    }
  }
  else
  {
    // display a warning if the browser was not compatible
    alert("Sorry, Google Maps API is incompatible " +
         "with this browser");
  }
```

```
//]]>
  </script>
</head>
```

The code in Listing 7.4 retrieves latitude and longitude values for a given location string. The location string is passed to a mashup server where it is manipulated to pass to the Google Maps API. The Google Maps API returns the latitude and longitude information, and the mashup server then wraps this in XML format to be passed back to the AJAX client. The client then uses Java-Script to parse the XML to retrieve the latitude and longitude values. These values are passed to the Google Maps APIs to retrieve the actual map, which is then applied to the DOM of the page. Listing 7.5 illustrates sample code that can be used to retrieve location information from a user and then passed to the JavaScript function where it is sent to the server using the XMLHttpRequest object.

Listing 7.5 *Form to Receive Location Data from a User to Use to Dynamically Retrieve a Google Map*

```
<body onunload="GUnload()">

<p/>

<form method="POST"
  action=
    "javascript:ajaxGet('http://example.com/services/getMap')"
  name="getMapForm">
  Location: <input type="text" value="" name="locationInfo"/>
  <input type="submit" value="Get Map" name="submit"/>
</form>

<p/>

<div id="map" style="width: 550px; height: 450px"></div>
</body>
</html>
```

The code in Listing 7.5 passes the location specified by the user to the Java-Script ajaxGet method. The location is then passed to the server to retrieve latitude and longitude information. The latitude and longitude are then used by the client to retrieve a Google map, which is then applied to the "map" DIV element. In Listing 7.5, the XMLHttpRequest object is called indirectly through the JavaScript method, ajaxGet, which is invoked via the form's POST request.

Location data that is passed to the server should be encapsulated in a service API or resource API that can be reused in a number of different scenarios. The actual logic for passing the location data to the Google Maps API, parsing the

latitude and longitude from the response, and for wrapping the latitude and
longitude in XML is shown in Listing 7.6.

Listing 7.6   *Service Code for Retrieving Latitude and Longitude Data for a Given
Location String*

```
public void locationToLatLong(String locationStr,
                              LatitudeLongitude latLong)
  throws Exception
{
  String encodedLocationStr =
    URLEncoder.encode(locationStr, "UTF-8");

  String url = API_URL + "?q=" + encodedLocationStr +
             "&output=xml&key=" + API_KEY;

  // send the actual request using HTTP
  //
  String response = HTTPUtils.sendHTTPRequest(url, null);

  DocumentBuilder docBuilder =
    DocumentBuilderFactory.newInstance().newDocumentBuilder();
  Document doc =
    docBuilder.parse(new InputSource(
                        new StringReader(response)));
  if (null != doc)
  {
    // latitude/longitude is nested in a coordinates element
    //
    NodeList nodeList =
      doc.getElementsByTagName("coordinates");
    if (null != nodeList && nodeList.getLength() > 0)
    {
      Node locationNode = nodeList.item(0);
      if (null != locationNode)
      {
        String longLatAltStr = locationNode.getTextContent();
        StringTokenizer tokenizer =
          new StringTokenizer(longLatAltStr, ",");
        if (tokenizer.hasMoreTokens())
        {
          latLong.longitude = tokenizer.nextToken();
          latLong.latitude = tokenizer.nextToken();
          return;
        }
      }
    }
  }
}
```

```
    throw new Exception("Invalid data returned " +
                        "in locationToLatLong");
}
```

As shown in Listing 7.6, latitude and longitude values are returned to the service caller encapsulated within a LatitudeLongitude class instance. This is a simple data structure shown in Listing 7.7.

Listing 7.7 *Structure for Encapsulating Latitude and Longitude Values*
```
public final class LatitudeLongitude
{
  public String latitude = "";
  public String longitude = "";

  public LatitudeLongitude(String latitude, String longitude)
  {
    this.latitude = latitude;
    this.longitude = longitude;
  }

  public String toString()
  {
    return "Latitude=" + latitude + ", Longitude=" + longitude;
  }
}
```

Retrieving information from a remote service in Java involves sending an HTTP GET request using the HttpURLConnection class and parsing the response as needed. Listing 7.8 illustrates Java code for sending an HTTP GET request.

Listing 7.8 *HTTP Request/Response Handling in Java*
```
  public static String sendHTTPRequest(String url)
    throws Exception
{
  String res = null;

  try
  {
    HttpURLConnection con = null;
    InputStream inStream = null;
    OutputStream outputStream = null;

    try
    {
      con = (HttpURLConnection)new URL(url).openConnection();
      con.setDoInput(true);
      con.setRequestMethod("GET");
      inStream = con.getInputStream();
```

```
      res = parseHTTPResponse(inStream);
    }
    finally
    {
      try
      {
        inStream.close();
        outputStream.close();
        con.disconnect();
      }
      catch (Exception e)
      {
      }
    }
  }
  catch (IOException e)
  {
    e.printStackTrace();
  }
}

  return res;
}
```

Parsing a simple textual response of an HTTP GET request retrieved using the
HttpURLConnection class can be achieved using an instance of the BufferedReader
class and techniques similar to the code in Listing 7.9.

Listing 7.9 *Parsing an HTTP Response in Java*
```
  public static String parseHTTPResponse(InputStream inStream)
    throws IOException
{
  BufferedReader br = null;
  br = new BufferedReader(new InputStreamReader(inStream,
                                       "UTF-8"));
  StringBuffer buf = new StringBuffer();
  String line;
  while (null != (line = br.readLine()))
  {
    buf.append(line).append("\n");
  }
  return buf.toString();
}
```

In Listing 7.9, response data from an HTTP GET request is retrieved via an
InputStream that is read a line at a time.

The presentation layer for a flexible and powerful mashup application
depends on a modular and flexible infrastructure. The next section discusses

how this is achieved using an OSGi-based foundation for a service-oriented mashup infrastructure.

Building the Mashup Infrastructure Foundation

The foundation for an effective enterprise mashup infrastructure is structured around a multilayered platform. The layers for the mashup infrastructure are implemented as interconnected service bundles that are deployed to a kernel supporting the modular OSGi framework.

The service bundles in this infrastructure are deployed to the OSGi kernel, which manages service registrations, unregistrations, and lifecycles.

An OSGi infrastructure is ideally suited for a mashup infrastructure, since mashups are based on principles of modularity and service-orientated concepts. OSGi technology combines aspects of these principles to define a dynamic service deployment framework that is amenable to remote management.

The OSGi Service Platform provides functionality to Java that allows applications to be constructed from small, reusable, and collaborative components. These components can be composed and deployed as a service or application.

The service platform exposed by OSGi allows changes to be made to services and service bundles without requiring restarts. To minimize the coupling, as well as make these couplings managed, the OSGi technology provides a service-oriented architecture that enables these components to dynamically discover each other.

For the infrastructure implemented in the following examples, the OSGi implementation Apache Felix (http://felix.apache.org) is used. Felix can be easily embedded into other projects and used as a plug-in or dynamic extension mechanism. It is this capability that is used to construct the service-handling functionality within the service-oriented kernel of the mashup infrastructure. With this infrastructure in place, services can be installed, updated, and uninstalled as OSGi bundles.

The OSGi kernel operates around the concept of polling for service bundles that are placed in a specified directory from which they will be deployed. When a service bundle is deployed, the services contained within will be registered with the kernel and available for use by service consumers using local (in-VM) Java method calls.

Starting the OSGi Kernel

The OSGi kernel can be executed as a daemon thread in a stand-alone application or from another process. Once started, the kernel polls for new services, changed services, and removed services from a given directory.

The code in Listing 7.10 illustrates the instantiation, initialization, and startup of an OSGi-based kernel that operates embedded within the context of a servlet-based mashup infrastructure.

Listing 7.10   *Embedded OSGi Kernel*

```
System.setProperty("org.mashups4j.kernel",
                   "org.mashups4j.kernel.osgi.OSGiKernel");
String realPath = getServletContext().getRealPath("/");
File servicesLocationDir = new File(realPath, "services");
try
{
  kernel = KernelFactory.getKernel(servicesLocationDir);
  kernel.start();
}
catch (KernelException e)
{
  e.printStackTrace();
  throw new ServletException(e);
}
```

In Listing 7.10, a kernel is instantiated, initialized, and started. Once the kernel is started, service bundles can be dropped within the directory specified where they will be automatically deployed to the mashup infrastructure.

OSGi Kernel Initialization

The details for constructing and initializing the OSGi kernel are illustrated in Listing 7.11.

Listing 7.11   *Construction and Initialization of the OSGi Kernel*

```
public class OSGiKernel
  implements BundlePollerListener,
             Kernel
{
  private static final int POLL_MILLIS = 30000;
  private static final String API_PATH_PROP = "API_PATH";

  private KernelActivator m_activator = null;
  private Felix m_felix = null;
  private File m_cachedir = null;
  private BundlePoller m_bundlePoller = null;
  private File m_bundlesLocation = null;
  private HashMap<String, Object> serviceMap =
                          new HashMap<String, Object>();

  /**
   * Constructs an instance of this kernel
   */
```

```java
public OSGiKernel()
{
}

public void initialize()
  throws KernelException
{
  // Create a temporary bundle cache directory
  try
  {
    m_cachedir =
      File.createTempFile("osgikernel.cache", null);
  }
  catch (IOException e)
  {
    throw new
      KernelException("Unable to create cache directory: "
                            + e);
  }

  m_cachedir.delete();


  // Create a case-insensitive configuration property map.
  //
  Map configMap = new StringMap(false);

  // Configure the Felix runtime properties.
  //
  configMap.put(FelixConstants.EMBEDDED_EXECUTION_PROP,
              "true");
  configMap.put(FelixConstants.SERVICE_URLHANDLERS_PROP,
              "false");

  // Add core OSGi packages to be exported from the class path
  // via the system bundle.
  //
  configMap.put(Constants.FRAMEWORK_SYSTEMPACKAGES,
            "org.osgi.framework; version=1.3.0," +
            "org.osgi.service.packageadmin; version=1.2.0," +
            "org.osgi.service.startlevel; version=1.0.0," +
            "org.osgi.service.url; version=1.0.0," +
            "org.osgi.util.tracker; version=1.3.2," +
            "org.xml.sax; version=1.0.0," +
            "sun.misc; verion=1.0.0," +
            "javax.xml.parsers; version=1.0.0," +
            "org.w3c.dom; version=1.0.0");
```

```
// Explicitly specify the directory for caching bundles.
//
String cacheDir = m_cachedir.getAbsolutePath();
configMap.put(BundleCache.CACHE_PROFILE_DIR_PROP,
              cacheDir);
configMap.put(BundleCache.CACHE_PROFILE_PROP,
              "OSGiMashupKernel");

try
{
  // Create kernel activator;
  //
  m_activator = new KernelActivator();
  List list = new ArrayList();
  list.add(m_activator);

  // Now create an instance of the framework with
  // our configuration properties and activator.
  //
  m_felix = new Felix(configMap, list);

  // instantiate the service poller and designate
  // the time between polling cycles
  //
  m_bundlePoller =
    new OSGiBundlePoller(m_bundlesLocation, POLL_MILLIS);
  m_bundlePoller.addBundlePollerListener(this);
}
catch (Exception e)
{
  throw new KernelException("Could not create OSGi kernel: "
                            + e);
}
}
```

In Listing 7.11 an instance of the Felix framework is initialized with needed properties including needed packages and the directory for caching bundles that are deployed to the kernel. A bundle poller is instantiated that will poll for new bundles, changed bundles, and removed bundles so that they might be deployed automatically.

OSGi Kernel Lifecycle

The code in Listing 7.12 illustrates the methods within the OSGi kernel that start and stop the kernel.

Listing 7.12 *Starting and Stopping the OSGi Kernel*

```
/**
 * Starts this kernel
 *
 * @throws KernelException
 */
public void start()
  throws KernelException
{
  // Start the felix framework when starting the kernel.
  try
  {
    m_felix.start();
    m_bundlePoller.start();
  }
  catch (BundleException e)
  {
    throw new KernelException("Could not start OSGi kernel: "
                              + e);
  }
}

/**
 * Stops this kernel
 *
 * @throws KernelException
 */
public void stop()
  throws KernelException
{
  // Stop the felix framework when stopping the kernel.
  try
  {
    m_bundlePoller.stop();
    m_felix.stop();
    deleteFileOrDir(m_cachedir);
  }
  catch (BundleException e)
  {
    throw new KernelException("Could not stop OSGi kernel: "
                              + e);
  }
}
```

In Listing 7.12 the Felix framework and bundle poller are started and stopped when the kernel is started and stopped, respectively.

Building the Mashup Process Layer

Processes in the mashup infrastructure are embodied for the most part as independent services. Each service is defined and deployed within the constructs of an OSGi bundle. Bundles consist of one or more services that are deployed automatically to the OSGi kernel.

Services contained within an OSGi bundle are discovered as a bundle is placed in the path from which the bundle poller reads. As a bundle is discovered, the services contained therein are read and installed in the OSGi kernel.

The following section details the processes that are involved with managing services contained within bundles and deployed to the OSGi kernel.

OSGi Kernel Service Methods

The code in Listing 7.13 illustrates the methods within the OSGi kernel that expose functionality for resolving services contained in bundles, discovering the services available from the kernel, and retrieving an actual service mapped to a given web application relative path.

Listing 7.13 *Service Discovery and Access Methods within the OSGi Kernel*

```
private void resolveServiceMappings()
{
  serviceMap = new HashMap<String, Object>();

  // Use the system bundle activator to gain external
  // access to the set of installed bundles.
  //
  Bundle[] bundles = m_activator.getBundles();
  if (null != bundles && bundles.length > 0)
  {
    for (int i = 0; i < bundles.length; i++)
    {
      Bundle bundle = bundles[i];

      // get the ServiceReference list from each bundle
      //
      ServiceReference[] serviceRefs =
        bundle.getRegisteredServices();
      if (null != serviceRefs)
      {
        for (int j = 0; j < serviceRefs.length; j++)
        {
          ServiceReference serviceRef = serviceRefs[j];
          String path =
            (String)serviceRef.getProperty(API_PATH_PROP);
```

```
            if (null != path && path.length() > 0)
            {
              // Retrieve service object for service reference.
              //
              Object service =
                bundle.getBundleContext().
                  getService(serviceRef);

              // cache each service with a mapping to its
              // preferred path
              //
              serviceMap.put(path, service);
            }

            // unget the service object to decrement the use count
            //
            bundle.getBundleContext().ungetService(serviceRef);
        }
      }
    }
  }
}

/**
 * Retrieves a list of the paths for all installed services
 *
 * @return a list of names of all installed services
 */
public String[] getInstalledServicePaths()
{
  resolveServiceMappings();

  String[] paths = new String[serviceMap.keySet().size()];
  serviceMap.keySet().toArray(paths);

  return paths;
}

/**
 * Retrieves a service object by path
 *
 * @param servicePath - the path of the service to find
 * @return the service object or null
 */
public Object getServiceByPath(String servicePath)
{
  resolveServiceMappings();
```

```
Iterator<String> iter = serviceMap.keySet().iterator();
while (iter.hasNext())
{
  String path = iter.next();
  if (servicePath.equalsIgnoreCase(path))
  {
    return serviceMap.get(path);
  }
}

return null;
}
```

In Listing 7.13 services contained within bundles are added to the kernel's cache and exposed to interested service consumers.

Listing 7.14 illustrates the methods within the OSGi kernel that are called by the bundle poller when bundles are added, changed, or removed. Also illustrated are methods for installing the bundles within the Felix framework.

Listing 7.14   *Service Discovery and Access Methods within the OSGi Kernel*

```
/**
 * Installs a bundle in this kernel
 *
 * @param bundleLocation
 * @return Object - the newly install bundle
 * @throws KernelException
 */
public Object installBundle(String bundleLocation)
  throws KernelException
{
  String tmpBundleLocation = bundleLocation;
  if (tmpBundleLocation.startsWith("file:/") == false)
  {
    tmpBundleLocation = "file:/" + tmpBundleLocation;
  }
  Bundle installedBundle =
    m_activator.installBundle(tmpBundleLocation);

  return installedBundle;
}

/**
 * Uninstalls a bundle from this kernel
 *
 * @param bundleLocation
 * @throws KernelException
 */
```

```java
public void uninstallBundle(String bundleLocation)
  throws KernelException
{
  String tmpBundleLocation = bundleLocation;
  if (tmpBundleLocation.startsWith("file:/") == false)
  {
    tmpBundleLocation = "file:/" + tmpBundleLocation;
  }
  m_activator.uninstallBundle(tmpBundleLocation);
}


/**
 * BundlePoller method
 *
 * @param evt
 */
public void bundleAdded(BundlePollerEvent evt)
{
  try
  {
    String bundleLocation = evt.getBundleLocation();
    installBundle(bundleLocation);
  }
  catch (KernelException e)
  {
    e.printStackTrace();
  }
}


/**
 * BundlePoller method
 *
 * @param evt
 */
public void bundleChanged(BundlePollerEvent evt)
{
  try
  {
    String bundleLocation = evt.getBundleLocation();
    uninstallBundle(bundleLocation);
    installBundle(bundleLocation);
  }
  catch (KernelException e)
  {
    e.printStackTrace();
  }
}
```

```
/**
 * BundlePoller method
 *
 * @param evt
 */
public void bundleRemoved(BundlePollerEvent evt)
{
  try
  {
    String bundleLocation = evt.getBundleLocation();
    uninstallBundle(bundleLocation);
  }
  catch (KernelException e)
  {
    e.printStackTrace();
  }
}
}
```

In Listing 7.14 added, changed, or removed bundles within the Felix framework are retrieved from a specified file system location.

The OSGi kernel registers itself with the service poller to receive notifications when service bundles are added, updated, and removed from the services directory. This allows the kernel to register and unregister bundles with the underlying Felix framework.

Front Controller Servlet and the Service Cache

In the mashup infrastructure described in this chapter, HTTP requests are handled by a front controller servlet where they are dispatched to service APIs and/or resource requests. A service cache is provided as the intermediary between the front controller servlet and the OSGi kernel. The service cache retrieves services from the kernel and uses them to handle service requests received by the front controller servlet.

Listing 7.15 illustrates the interactions between the front controller servlet's doGet method and the service cache.

Listing 7.15 *Interactions between the Front Controller and the Service Cache*
```
protected void doGet(HttpServletRequest request,
                     HttpServletResponse response)
  throws ServletException, IOException
{
  Object service = null;
  Model model = null;
```

```
try
{
  service = ServiceCache.get(getKernel(),
                                request.getPathInfo());
  if (service instanceof Service)
  {
    model = ((Service)service).read(request.getPathInfo(),
                                request.getParameterMap(),
                                getServletContext());
  }
  else
  {
    model = ServiceHelper.dynamicallyInvokeService(service,
                                                request);
  }
}
catch (ServiceException e)
{
  e.printStackTrace();
  throw new ServletException(e.getMessage());
}

serializeModel(response, model);
}
```

In Listing 7.15 HTTP GET requests are handled by the front controller's doGet
method. Services are retrieved from the service cache based on path information
passed in each HTTP GET request. The services are then invoked and the results
are serialized back to the client as HTTP responses. Notice that services that
implement the Service interface are invoked directly. Services that do not implement the Service interface are invoked dynamically using reflection. This is discussed later in this chapter.

Listing 7.16 illustrates the process of serializing results returned from service
requests back to the HTTP client.

Listing 7.16 *Method for Serializing Service Results Back to an HTTP Client*

```
private void serializeModel(HttpServletResponse response,
                                Model model)
  throws IOException
{
  response.setContentType(model.getMimeType());
  response.setContentLength(model.getContentLength());

  if (model.canBeStringified())
  {
    response.getWriter().write(model.toString());
  }
```

```
 else
  {
    ServletOutputStream outStream =
      response.getOutputStream();
    outStream.write(model.getBytes());
    outStream.flush();
  }
}
```

In Listing 7.16 service results are serialized back to the client using either the response's `PrintWriter` object or the response's `OutputStream` object depending on the type of response data.

Listing 7.17 illustrates the service cache implementation.

Listing 7.17   *Implementation for the Service Cache*

```
public class ServiceCache
{
  private static ServiceCache instance = null;

  private static ServiceCache getInstance(Kernel kernel)
  {
    if (null == instance)
    {
      instance = new ServiceCache(kernel);
    }

    return instance;
  }

  public static Object get(Kernel kernel, String servicePath)
    throws ServiceException
  {
    return getInstance(kernel).getService(servicePath);
  }

  private Kernel kernel = null;

  public ServiceCache(Kernel kernel)
  {
    this.kernel = kernel;
  }

  private Object getService(String servicePath)
    throws ServiceException
  {
    if (servicePath == null || servicePath.length() <= 0)
    {
```

```
            throw new ServiceException("Service path is empty in "
                            + getClass().getName()
                            + ".getService()");
    }

    Object service = kernel.getServiceByPath(servicePath);
    if (null != service)
    {
      return service;
    }

    throw new ServiceException("Service [" + servicePath +
                        "] not found in "
                        + getClass().getName()
                        + ".getService()");
  }
}
```

Notice in Listing 7.17 service instances are retrieved from the kernel by relative paths. The kernel is the actual cache and the service cache simply acts as a façade between service consumer and service.

Service Implementations

Each service that is deployed to the mashup infrastructure defines a public interface and an implementation class. The code shown in Listing 7.18 illustrates the interface for the Google Maps service alluded to earlier in this chapter.

Listing 7.18 *Interface for the Google Maps Service*
```
public interface GoogleMapsService
{
  /**
  * Converts a location string to latitude/longitude coordinates
  *
  * @param locationStr - the location string to convert
  * @param latLong - structure to hold the latitude/longitude
  * @throws Exception
  **/
  void locationToLatLong(String locationStr,
                        LatitudeLongitude latLong)
    throws Exception;
}
```

The interface in Listing 7.18 defines one method, locationToLatLong, which should convert a given location string to a latitude and longitude pair.

Listing 7.19 illustrates the Google Maps service implementation.

Listing 7.19 *Implementation for the Google Maps Service*

```
public class GoogleMapsImpl
  implements GoogleMapsService
{
  private static final String API_KEY = "...";
  private static final String API_URL =
      "http://maps.google.com/maps/geo";

  /**
   * Converts a . string to latitude/longitude coordinates.
   * The response is in the following format:
   * <pre>
   * <?xml version="1.0" encoding="UTF-8"?>
   * <kml xmlns="http://earth.google.com/kml/2.0">
   *   <Response>
   *     <name>Salt Lake City, UT</name>
   *     <Status>
   *       <code>200</code>
   *       <request>geocode</request>
   *     </Status>
   *     <Placemark id="p1">
   *       ...
   *       <Point>
   *         <coordinates>-111.888189,40.771592,0</coordinates>
   *       </Point>
   *     </Placemark>
   *   </Response>
   * </kml>
   * </pre>
   *
   * @param locationStr - the location string to convert
   * @param latLong - holds the latitude and longitude
   * @throws Exception
   */
  public void locationToLatLong(String locationStr,
                                LatitudeLongitude latLong)
    throws Exception
  {
    String encodedLocationStr =
      URLEncoder.encode(locationStr, "UTF-8");
    String url = API_URL + "?q=" +
                 encodedLocationStr + "&output=xml&key=" +
                 API_KEY;
    String response = HTTPUtils.sendHTTPRequest(url, null);

    DocumentBuilder docBuilder =
      DocumentBuilderFactory.newInstance().newDocumentBuilder();
```

```
      Document doc =
        docBuilder.parse(new InputSource(
                           new StringReader(response)));
      if (null != doc)
      {
        NodeList nodeList =
          doc.getElementsByTagName("coordinates");
        if (null != nodeList && nodeList.getLength() > 0)
        {
          Node locationNode = nodeList.item(0);
          if (null != locationNode)
          {
            String longLatAltStr = locationNode.getTextContent();
            StringTokenizer tokenizer =
              new StringTokenizer(longLatAltStr, ",");
            if (tokenizer.hasMoreTokens())
            {
              latLong.longitude = tokenizer.nextToken();
              latLong.latitude = tokenizer.nextToken();
              return;
            }
          }
        }
      }

      throw new Exception("Invalid data returned.");
    }

    public Object execute(Properties props)
    {
      System.out.println(getClass().getName() + ".execute()");

      Object locationObj = props.get("location");
      LatitudeLongitude latLong = new LatitudeLongitude("", "");

      try
      {
        locationToLatLong((String)locationObj, latLong);
      }
      catch(Exception e)
      {
        e.printStackTrace();
      }

      return latLong;
    }
}
```

Notice in Listing 7.19 that an execute method is provided as a generic invocation entry point. This enables the service cache to invoke the functionality of each service in a generic manner. This process is discussed later.

To further illustrate the concepts surrounding service deployment within the OSGi bundle framework, another service is illustrated in Listing 7.20. This service retrieves location information about a given user profile exposed by the Twitter microfeed web site.

Listing 7.20   *Interface of a Twitter Location Retrieval Service*
```
public interface TwitterService
{
  /**
  * Retrieves the location of a given user.
  *
  * @param targetUserID - the ID of the user
  * @throws Exception
  **/
  String getUserLocation(String targetUserID)
    throws Exception;
}
```

The interface in Listing 7.20 defines one method, getUserLocation, which should retrieve the location information for a given user of the Twitter microfeed service.

Listing 7.21 illustrates the Twitter location-retrieval service implementation.

Listing 7.21   *Implementation of a Twitter Location Retrieval Service*
```
public class TwitterImpl
  implements TwitterService
{
  private static final String API_URL =
    "http://twitter.com/users/show/";

  /**
  * Retrieves the location of a given user.
  *
  * @param targetUserID - the ID of the user
  * @throws Exception
  */
  public String getUserLocation(String targetUserID)
    throws Exception
  {
    String response =
      HTTPUtils.sendHTTPRequest(API_URL +
                                targetUserID + ".xml", null);
    DocumentBuilder docBuilder =
      DocumentBuilderFactory.newInstance().newDocumentBuilder();
    Document doc =
```

```
      docBuilder.parse(new InputSource(
                       new StringReader(response))));
  if (null != doc)
  {
    NodeList nodeList = doc.getElementsByTagName("location");
    if (null != nodeList && nodeList.getLength() > 0)
    {
      Node locationNode = nodeList.item(0);
      if (null != locationNode)
      {
        return locationNode.getTextContent();
      }
    }
  }

  throw new Exception("Invalid HTTP response " +
                      "content encountered");
}

public Object execute(Properties props)
{
  Object targetUserIDObj = props.get("targetUserID");
  String retStr = "";
  try
  {
    retStr = getUserLocation((String)targetUserIDObj);
  }
  catch(Throwable t)
  {
    t.printStackTrace();
  }

  return retStr;
}
}
```

As with the Google Maps service, Listing 7.21 illustrates an execute method provided as a generic invocation entry point.

Each service to be deployed to the OSGi-based mashup infrastructure is registered using an implementation of the BundleActivator interface. This implementation class is designated in the .jar file and contains the resources and classes that embody a given bundle. The ServiceProvider class shown in Listing 7.22 illustrates the implementation details for the Google Maps service-provider class.

Listing 7.22 *Implementation of the BundleActivator Interface*
```
public class ServiceProvider
  implements BundleActivator,
            ServiceListener
```

```
{
  /**
   * Implements BundleActivator.start().
   * Registers a number of services using the bundle context;
   * Attaches properties to the services that can be queried
   * when performing a service look-up.
   *
   * @param context the framework context for the bundle.
   */
  public void start(BundleContext context)
  {
    System.out.println(getClass().getName() + ".start()");
    context.addServiceListener(this);

    Properties twitterProps = new Properties();

    // specify the relative web app path for this service
    //
    twitterProps.put("API_PATH", "/twitter");

    // register the Twitter service
    //
    context.registerService(TwitterService.class.getName(),
                          new TwitterImpl(), twitterProps);

    Properties googleMapsProps = new Properties();

    // specify the relative web app path for this service
    //
    googleMapsProps.put("API_PATH", "/googlemaps");

    // register the Google Maps service
    //
    context.registerService(GoogleMapsService.class.getName(),
                          new GoogleMapsImpl(), googleMapsProps);

    System.out.println(getClass().getName() + " started");
  }

  /**
   * Implements BundleActivator.stop().
   *
   * @param context the framework context for the bundle.
   */
  public void stop(BundleContext context)
  {
    System.out.println(getClass().getName() + ".stop()");
    context.removeServiceListener(this);
```

```
    System.out.println(getClass().getName() + " stopped");
}

public void serviceChanged(ServiceEvent event)
{
  String[] objectClass =
    (String[])event.getServiceReference().
      getProperty("objectClass");

  if (event.getType() == ServiceEvent.REGISTERED)
  {
    System.out.println(getClass().getName() +
                      ": Service of type " +
                      objectClass[0] + " registered.");
  }
  else if (event.getType() == ServiceEvent.UNREGISTERING)
  {
    System.out.println(getClass().getName() +
                      ": Service of type " +
                      objectClass[0] + " unregistered.");
  }
  else if (event.getType() == ServiceEvent.MODIFIED)
  {
    System.out.println(getClass().getName() +
                      ": Service of type " +
                      objectClass[0] + " modified.");
  }
  else
  {
    System.out.println(getClass().getName() +
                      ": Service of unknown type " +
                      event.getType());
  }
}
}
```

In Listing 7.22 the registerService method on the BundleContext instance is called to register the Twitter service and the Google Maps service. The implementation of the BundleActivator interface must be designated within the bundle itself for the OSGi framework to know which class will register the bundle's services. This leads us to the discussion of compiling and packaging the service bundle.

Bundling Services

Service bundles are compiled and packaged using the Maven build tool and a plug-in specifically designed for OSGi bundles. The Maven POM file is shown in Listing 7.23.

Listing 7.23   *Maven POM File for Compiling and Packaging a Bundle*

```
<project>
  <modelVersion>4.0.0</modelVersion>
  <packaging>bundle</packaging>
  <name>A bunch of services</name>
  <description>Miscellaneous services.</description>
  <groupId>org.mashups4j</groupId>
  <artifactId>MiscServices</artifactId>
  <version>1.0.0</version>

  <dependencies>
    <dependency>
      <groupId>org.apache.felix</groupId>
      <artifactId>org.apache.felix.main</artifactId>
      <version>1.0.3</version>
    </dependency>
  </dependencies>

  <build>
    <plugins>
      <plugin>
        <groupId>org.apache.felix</groupId>
        <artifactId>maven-bundle-plugin</artifactId>
        <version>1.4.0</version>
        <extensions>true</extensions>
        <configuration>
          <instructions>
            <Import-Package>
              org.mashups4j.services.*,
              javax.xml.*,
              org.xml.sax.*,
              org.w3c.dom.*,
              org.osgi.framework,
              *
            </Import-Package>

            <Export-Package>
              org.mashups4j.services.utils.*,
              org.mashups4j.services.registry.*,
              org.mashups4j.services.google.*,
              org.mashups4j.services.twitter.*
            </Export-Package>

            <Bundle-Activator>
              org.mashups4j.services.registry.ServiceProvider
            </Bundle-Activator>
            <Bundle-Vendor>Mashups4J</Bundle-Vendor>
          </instructions>
```

```
        </configuration>
      </plugin>
    </plugins>
  </build>
</project>
```

Notice in Listing 7.23 how a plug-in is specified with an artifactID of maven-bundle-plugin. This plug-in is where the details of the bundle are specified. These details include packages to be imported by the bundle, packages to be exported by the bundle, and the BundleActivator implementation. In this specific case, the classes contained within the org.mashups4j.services.google and org.mashups4j.services.twitter packages are exported and the org.mashups4j.services.registry.ServiceProvider class is designated as the BundleActivator implementation.

When the POM file shown in Listing 7.23 is processed by the Maven build tool, a .jar file is produced containing all the classes for the bundle along with a manifest declaring information used by the OSGi framework when the bundle is deployed. This manifest information includes some of the same information shown in the POM, such as imported and exported bundle information and the BundleActivator implementation. Also included in the manifest are the bundle's symbolic name and the bundle version. The .jar file can then be placed in the directory polled by the bundle poller described previously where the .jar file will be loaded and its contained services deployed to the OSGi framework and, therefore, to the mashup infrastructure.

Dynamically Invoking Service Logic

As discussed previously, an execute method is provided by each service to act as a generic invocation entry point. This enables the service cache to invoke the functionality of each service in a generic manner. This process is illustrated in Listing 7.24.

Listing 7.24 *Helper Class for Dynamically Invoking Service Calls*
```
public class ServiceHelper
{
  public static Model dynamicallyInvokeService(Object service,
                               HttpServletRequest request)
  {
    Properties paramProps = new Properties();
    Enumeration enumer = request.getParameterNames();
    while (enumer.hasMoreElements())
    {
      String paramName = (String)enumer.nextElement();
      paramProps.put(paramName,
                     request.getParameter(paramName));
    }
```

```java
    return dynamicallyInvokeService(service, paramProps);
}

public static Model dynamicallyInvokeService(Object service,
                                    final Properties props)
{
  // we are looking for this method:
  //   public Object execute(Properties props)

  Method method = null;

  try
  {
    method = service.getClass().getMethod("execute",
                                    Properties.class);

    try
    {
      final Object retObj = method.invoke(service, props);
      Model model = null;
      if (retObj instanceof Model)
      {
        model = (Model)retObj;
      }
      else
      {
        model = new Model()
        {
          public Object contents = retObj;

          public String getMimeType()
          {
            String outputtype =
              (String)props.get("outputtype");
            if (outputtype != null)
            {
              if (outputtype.equalsIgnoreCase("xml"))
              {
                return "application/xml";
              }
            }

            return "text/plain";
          }

          public int getContentLength()
          {
            return contents.toString().length();
          }
```

```
          public boolean canBeStringified()
          {
            return true;
          }

          public byte[] getBytes()
          {
            return contents.toString().getBytes();
          }

          public void setContents(Object contents)
          {
            this.contents = contents;
          }

          public String toString()
          {
            return contents.toString();
          }
        };
      }

      return model;
    }
    catch (IllegalAccessException e)
    {
      e.printStackTrace();
    }
    catch (InvocationTargetException e)
    {
      e.printStackTrace();
    }
  }
  catch (NoSuchMethodException e)
  {
    e.printStackTrace();
  }

  return null;
  }
}
```

Listing 7.24 illustrates two dynamicallyInvokeService methods—a method that takes a service object and an HttpServletRequest instance. This method simply redirects to a method that takes a service object and a list of properties. The latter method uses reflection to try to locate an execute method on the service object that takes a list of properties. If this method is found it is invoked and the list of properties is passed to it. The result returned from the execute method is wrapped in a Model object and passed back to the caller.

The properties passed to the dynamicallyInvokeService are queried to see if an outputtype property is defined. If it is defined and XML is specified as the output type, the Model object is configured as an XML-based model. The caller can then serialize it as XML, and an AJAX client can parse it using JavaScript XML parsing techniques.

An instance of the OSGiKernel will dispatch service invocations through services registered with the kernel. The kernel relies on a bundle polling mechanism that monitors a given directory. The bundle poller registers new bundles and contained services as they are found, unregisters bundles and services as they are removed, and updates existing bundles and services as they are changed.

The Bundle Poller

The bundle polling process allows hot deployment of bundles and the services contained within a bundle at runtime without stopping and restarting the kernel.

Listing 7.25 illustrates the polling process of the bundle poller.

Listing 7.25 *Bundle Polling Method*

```
private void poll()
{
  File[] files = m_bundlesLocation.listFiles();
  if (m_cachedFiles == null)
  {
    // add all new
    if (null != files && files.length > 0)
    {
      m_cachedFiles = new ArrayList<CachedFile>();
      m_cachedFiles.addAll(fileArrayToCachedList(files));
      fireBundleAddedForAll();
    }
  }
  else if (files.length <= 0)
  {
    // remove all
    fireBundleRemovedForAll();
  }
  else
  {
    // pick and choose
    List<File> newFileList = Arrays.asList(files);
```

```
      // find deleted files
      ArrayList<File> deletedFiles = new ArrayList<File>();
      Iterator<CachedFile> cachedFileIter =
        m_cachedFiles.iterator();
      while (cachedFileIter.hasNext())
      {
        CachedFile cachedFile = cachedFileIter.next();
        if (null == isFileInList(cachedFile.m_file, newFileList))
        {
          deletedFiles.add(cachedFile.m_file);
        }
      }

      // Remove deleted files from cache
      Iterator<File> deletedFileIter = deletedFiles.iterator();
      while (deletedFileIter.hasNext())
      {
        CachedFile cachedFile = cachedFileIter.next();
        removeFileFromCache(cachedFile.m_file);
      }

      // remove deleted files from new list
      newFileList.removeAll(deletedFiles);

      // find new and changed files
      Iterator<File> newFileIter = newFileList.iterator();
      while (newFileIter.hasNext())
      {
        File newFile = newFileIter.next();
        CachedFile cachedFile =
          isCachedFileInList(newFile, m_cachedFiles);
        if (null != cachedFile)
        {
          // test modified date
          if (newFile.lastModified() >
              cachedFile.m_lastModified)
          {
            fireBundleChanged(newFile);
          }
        }
        else
        {
          m_cachedFiles.add(new CachedFile(newFile));
          fireBundleAdded(newFile);
        }
      }
    }
  }
}
```

As a bundle is discovered to be added, changed, or removed from the services directory, the bundle poller will add it to its private cache and fire an event to all registered listeners conveying information about the bundle.

Event-Firing Mechanisms

The fireBundleRemoved method, the fireBundleAdded method, and the fireBundleChanged method iterate through the list of listeners and invoke the appropriate method on each listener, passing a BundlePollerEvent object that contains information about the event and the bundle.

The methods in Listing 7.26 illustrate the implementation details for firing events from the bundle poller as bundles are added, removed, and modified.

Listing 7.26 *Event Firing Methods*

```
private void fireBundleRemoved(File aFile)
{
  BundlePollerEvent evt =
    new BundlePollerEvent(this, aFile.getAbsolutePath());
  Iterator<BundlePollerListener> listenerIter =
    m_listeners.iterator();
  while (listenerIter.hasNext())
  {
    BundlePollerListener listener = listenerIter.next();
    listener.bundleRemoved(evt);
  }
}

private void fireBundleAdded(File aFile)
{
  BundlePollerEvent evt =
    new BundlePollerEvent(this, aFile.getAbsolutePath());
  Iterator<BundlePollerListener> listenerIter =
    m_listeners.iterator();
  while (listenerIter.hasNext())
  {
    BundlePollerListener listener = listenerIter.next();
    listener.bundleAdded(evt);
  }
}

private void fireBundleChanged(File aFile)
{
  BundlePollerEvent evt =
    new BundlePollerEvent(this, aFile.getAbsolutePath());
  Iterator<BundlePollerListener> listenerIter =
    m_listeners.iterator();
  while (listenerIter.hasNext())
```

```
  {
    BundlePollerListener listener = listenerIter.next();
    listener.bundleChanged(evt);
  }
}
```

The lifecycle methods, start and stop, on the ServicePoller object start and stop the necessary tasks and processes that a ServicePoller instance needs to effectively load and unload services as they are added and removed from the services directory.

Lifecycle Methods

The start method ensures that the services directory is created and then starts a timer that runs at intervals specified by the host component of the ServicePoller instance. The task associated with the timer is responsible for instigating the polling process that will check the services directory for service changes.

The methods in Listing 7.27 illustrate the implementation details of the lifecycle methods for the service poller.

Listing 7.27 *Bundle Poller Lifecycle Methods*

```
public void start()
  throws KernelException
{
  if (m_bundlesLocation.exists() == false)
  {
    m_bundlesLocation.mkdir();
  }
  else if (!m_bundlesLocation.isDirectory())
  {
    throw new KernelException(getClass().getName()
                    + ".start() invalid bundles location: "
                    + m_bundlesLocation.getAbsolutePath());
  }

  TimerTask timerTask = new TimerTask()
  {
    public void run()
    {
      poll();
    }
  };
  m_timer = new Timer();
  m_timer.scheduleAtFixedRate(timerTask, 0, m_pollMillis);
}

public void stop()
  throws KernelException
```

```
{
  m_timer.cancel();
  m_timer = null;
}
```

Listing 7.27 illustrates how a `Timer` instance is used to schedule service polling at regular intervals.

Event Listener Support Methods

The `addBundlePollerListener` method and the `removeBundlePollerListener` method are responsible for respectively adding and removing listeners to the `BundlePoller` instance.

Listing 7.28 illustrates the implementation details of the event listener methods for the bundle poller.

Listing 7.28 *Bundle Poller Event Listener Methods*
```
public void
addBundlePollerListener(BundlePollerListener listener)
{
  m_listeners.add(listener);
}

public void
removeBundlePollerListener(BundlePollerListener listener)
{
  m_listeners.remove(listener);
}
```

Once a listener is added to the bundle poller the listener will receive notifications as bundles are added, removed, and modified.

Processes and UI artifacts within a mashup infrastructure depend on data from many different sources. Concepts and implementation techniques for a generic mashup data layer are discussed in the following sections.

Building the Mashup Data Layer

UI artifacts and processes for a mashup infrastructure rely on content and data from multiple sources. Content and data are modeled as resources. Resources are retrieved using a REST-based invocation model; in other words, resources are created, retrieved, updated, and deleted using a simple syntax that relies on URIs to define the location of each resource.

This section defines a generic mashup data layer that can access data from multiple sources using a REST-based invocation model. The resources can then be serialized to a mashup application or page in different semantic formats.

The following section discusses the main access point for resources—the resource cache.

The Resource Cache

Resources are retrieved from a resource cache using path information supplied by the resource consumer. In the cache defined here, simple file system paths are used to access resources; however, this can be easily enhanced to support database paths, remote service API paths, and others.

Listing 7.29 illustrates the public interface for the resource cache.

Listing 7.29 *Resource Cache Interface Definition*
```
public interface ResourceCache
{
  void createResource(String resourcePath,
                      Object context,
                      Object data)
    throws ResourceException;

  Resource readResource(String resourcePath,
                        Object context,
                        boolean getCurrentCopy)
    throws ResourceException;

  void updateResource(String resourcePath,
                      Object context,
                      Object data)
    throws ResourceException;

  void deleteResource(String resourcePath,
                      Object context)
    throws ResourceException;

  long getResourceLastModified(String resourcePath,
                               Object context)
    throws ResourceException;
}
```

Notice how the methods defined by the resource cache interface follow the simple CRUD (create, read, update, and delete) pattern.

Listing 7.30 illustrates the static/global fields and methods exposed by the resource cache.

Listing 7.30 *Resource Cache Static/Global Fields and Methods*
```
public class FileSystemResourceCache
{
  private static final String RESOURCE_PREFIX =
    "WEB-INF/classes";
```

```java
private static ResourceCache instance = null;

// ====================================================
// public static methods
// ====================================================

public static ResourceCache getInstance(boolean saveInstances)
{
  if (null == instance)
  {
    instance = new FileSystemResourceCache(saveInstances);
  }

  return instance;
}
```

Listing 7.30 illustrates one main global entry point into the resource cache—the getInstance method. The getInstance method creates the instance of the resource cache, if needed, and returns it to the caller. A boolean parameter passed to the method specifies whether to save instances in the cache as they are retrieved. If this parameter is false, the resource caches acts simply as a façade between the resource consumer and the resource.

Listing 7.31 illustrates the instance fields and methods exposed by an instance of the resource cache.

Listing 7.31 *Resource Cache Instance Fields and Methods*
```java
// ====================================================
// member fields
// ====================================================

private boolean saveInstances = false;
private HashMap<String, Resource> resources =
  new HashMap<String, Resource>();

// ====================================================
// constructors
// ====================================================

public FileSystemResourceCache(boolean saveInstances)
{
  this.saveInstances = saveInstances;
}

// ====================================================
// non-public instance methods
// ====================================================
```

```
protected String
filePathFromRequest(ServletContext servletContext,
                    String resourcePath)
{
  return servletContext.getRealPath("") + resourcePath;
}


protected void writeToFile(HttpServletRequest request,
                           File file,
                           boolean append)
    throws IOException
{
  String value = request.getParameter("value");
  if (null == value)
  {
    throw new IOException("Parameter 'value' not found.");
  }

  FileOutputStream outStream =
    new FileOutputStream(file, append);
  outStream.write(value.getBytes(), 0,
                  value.getBytes().length);
  outStream.flush();
  outStream.close();
}


// =====================================================
// public instance methods
// =====================================================

/**
 * Creates a resource
 *
 * @param resourcePath
 * @param context
 * @param data
 * @throws ResourceException
 */
public void createResource(String resourcePath,
                           Object context,
                           Object data)
    throws ResourceException
{
  String filePath =
    filePathFromRequest((ServletContext)context, "/"
                        + RESOURCE_PREFIX
                        + resourcePath);
  File file = new File(filePath);
```

```java
    try
    {
      boolean append = false;
      writeToFile((HttpServletRequest)data, file, append);
    }
    catch (Exception e)
    {
      e.printStackTrace();
      throw new ResourceException(e);
    }
  }

  /**
   * Retrieves a resource
   *
   * @param resourcePath
   * @param context
   * @param getCurrentCopy
   * @return the resource
   * @throws ResourceException
   */
  public Resource readResource(String resourcePath,
                               Object context,
                               boolean getCurrentCopy)
    throws ResourceException
  {
    if (resourcePath == null || resourcePath.length() == 0)
    {
      throw new ResourceException("Resource path is empty in "
                                  + getClass().getName()
                                  + ".readResource()");
    }

    String filePath =
      filePathFromRequest((ServletContext)context,
                          resourcePath);

    // look for cached copy, if possible
    //
    if (!getCurrentCopy)
    {
      Resource resource = resources.get(filePath);
      if (null != resource)
      {
        return resource;
      }
    }
```

```java
// get the contents of the resource file
//
InputStream inStream =
  ((ServletContext)context).
    getResourceAsStream(RESOURCE_PREFIX
                        + resourcePath);
if (null == inStream)
{
  throw new ResourceException("Resource [" + resourcePath
                              + "] not found in "
                              + getClass().getName()
                              + ".readResource()");
}

ByteArrayOutputStream outStream =
  new ByteArrayOutputStream();
try
{
  byte[] bytes = new byte[4096];
  int bytesRead = 0;
  while ((bytesRead = inStream.read(bytes)) > 0)
  {
    outStream.write(bytes, 0, bytesRead);
  }
}
catch (IOException e)
{
  throw new ResourceException("Error retrieving resource ["
                              + resourcePath + "] in "
                              + getClass().getName()
                              + ".readResource()");
}

byte[] resourceBytes = outStream.toByteArray();

Resource resource =
  new SimpleResource(resourcePath, resourceBytes);

// store copy in cache
//
if (saveInstances == true)
{
  resources.put(filePath, resource);
}

return resource;
}
```

```java
/**
 * Modifies a resource
 *
 * @param resourcePath
 * @param context
 * @param data
 * @throws ResourceException
 */
public void updateResource(String resourcePath,
                           Object context,
                           Object data)
  throws ResourceException
{
  String filePath =
    filePathFromRequest((ServletContext)context, "/"
                        + RESOURCE_PREFIX + resourcePath);
  File file = new File(filePath);

  try
  {
    boolean append = (file.exists() ? true : false);
    writeToFile((HttpServletRequest)data, file, append);
  }
  catch (Exception e)
  {
    e.printStackTrace();
    throw new ResourceException(e);
  }
}


/**
 * Deletes a resource
 *
 * @param resourcePath
 * @param context
 * @throws ResourceException
 */
public void deleteResource(String resourcePath,
                           Object context)
  throws ResourceException
{
  String filePath =
    filePathFromRequest((ServletContext)context, "/"
                        + RESOURCE_PREFIX + resourcePath);
  File file = new File(filePath);

  if (file.exists())
  {
```

```java
    if (file.delete() == false)
    {
      throw new ResourceException("Error deleting resource ["
                                + filePath + "]");
    }
  }
}


/**
 * Retrieves the last-modified date for a resource
 *
 * @param resourcePath
 * @param context
 * @return the last modified date of the resource
 * @throws ResourceException
 */
public long getResourceLastModified(String resourcePath,
                                    Object context)
  throws ResourceException
{
  if (resourcePath == null || resourcePath.length() == 0)
  {
    throw new ResourceException("Resource path is empty in "
                        + getClass().getName()
                        + ".getResourceLastModified()");
  }

  // check that the resource exists
  //
  URL resourceURL = null;

  try
  {
    resourceURL =
      ((ServletContext)context).getResource(resourcePath);
  }
  catch (MalformedURLException e)
  {
    throw new ResourceException(e);
  }

  if (resourceURL == null)
  {
    throw new ResourceException("Resource [" + resourcePath
                        + "] not found in "
                        + getClass().getName()
                        + ".getResourceLastModified()");
  }
```

```
    long lastModified = 0;

    try
    {
      URLConnection urlConn = resourceURL.openConnection();
      lastModified = urlConn.getLastModified();
    }
    catch (IOException e)
    {
      e.printStackTrace();
    }

    return lastModified;
  }
}
```

Listing 7.31 illustrates utility methods for manipulating the resources on disk and for converting a web context and resource path to a file system path. Important to note is the implementation of the CRUD interface methods.

Resource consumers can use the file system resource cache to store and retrieve resources from a file system. In the following section a resource consumer that also acts as an HTTP request adapter is shown.

The Resource Cache HTTP Adapter

Requests received by a web application are handled by the ResourceAdapter servlet. This servlet converts HTTP requests to resource manipulation (create, read, update, and delete) requests and dispatches the converted requests to the resource cache.

Listing 7.32 illustrates the implementation of the ResourceAdapter servlet.

Listing 7.32 *Resource Adapter Implementation*
```
public class ResourceAdapter
  extends HttpServlet
{
  protected void doGet(HttpServletRequest req,
                       HttpServletResponse res)
    throws ServletException, IOException
  {
    try
    {
      Resource resource =
        FileSystemResourceCache.getInstance(true).
          readResource(req.getPathInfo(),
                       getServletContext(),
                       false);
```

```
      serializeResource(res, resource);
    }
    catch (ResourceException e)
    {
      e.printStackTrace();
      throw new ServletException(e);
    }
  }

  protected void doPost(HttpServletRequest req,
                        HttpServletResponse res)
    throws ServletException, IOException
  {
    try
    {
      FileSystemResourceCache.getInstance(true).
          updateResource(req.getPathInfo(),
          getServletContext(),
          req);
      PrintWriter out = res.getWriter();
      out.println("success");
    }
    catch (ResourceException e)
    {
      e.printStackTrace();
      throw new ServletException(e);
    }
  }

  protected void doPut(HttpServletRequest req,
                       HttpServletResponse res)
    throws ServletException, IOException
  {
    try
    {
      FileSystemResourceCache.getInstance(true).
          createResource(req.getPathInfo(),
          getServletContext(),
          req);
      PrintWriter out = res.getWriter();
      out.println("success");
    }
    catch (ResourceException e)
    {
      e.printStackTrace();
      throw new ServletException(e);
    }
  }
```

```java
protected void doDelete(HttpServletRequest req,
                        HttpServletResponse res)
  throws ServletException, IOException
{
  try
  {
    FileSystemResourceCache.getInstance(true).
        deleteResource(req.getPathInfo(),
                        getServletContext());
    PrintWriter out = res.getWriter();
    out.println("success");
  }
  catch (ResourceException e)
  {
    e.printStackTrace();
    throw new ServletException(e);
  }
}

protected long getLastModified(HttpServletRequest req)
{
  try
  {
    return FileSystemResourceCache.getInstance(true).
            getResourceLastModified(req.getPathInfo()
                                    getServletContext());
  }
  catch (ResourceException e)
  {
    e.printStackTrace();
  }

  return 0;
}
```

Notice in Listing 7.32 how the `FileSystemResourceCache` is used as the access point to resource. A complete solution would offer a factory or configuration model where the type of cache (file system, database, and so on) could be specified dynamically.

In Listing 7.33 a method of the `ResourceAdapter` class is shown that serializes a given `Resource` instance to the servlet output stream.

Listing 7.33 *Resource Serialization Method*
```java
private void serializeResource(HttpServletResponse response,
                               Resource resource)
  throws IOException
{
```

```
response.setContentType(resource.getMimeType());
response.setContentLength(resource.getContentLength());

if (resource.canBeStringified())
{
  response.getWriter().write(resource.toString());
}
else
{
  ServletOutputStream outStream = response.getOutputStream();
  outStream.write(resource.getBytes());
  outStream.flush();
}
  }
}
```

The method in Listing 7.33 uses information supplied by the `Resource` instance to specify the content type and content length of the HTTP response. The contents of the `Resource` instance are then serialized out to the HTTP response as either a string or a stream of bytes.

Listing 7.34 illustrates a simple implementation of the `Resource` interface. This implementation supports resources that can be represented as a stream of bytes.

Listing 7.34 *Simple Resource Implementation*
```
public class SimpleResource
  implements Resource
{
  private String resourceFileName = "";
  private byte[] resourceBytes = null;

  public SimpleResource(String resourceFileName,
                        byte[] resourceBytes)
  {
    this.resourceFileName = resourceFileName;
    this.resourceBytes = resourceBytes;
  }

  public String getMimeType()
  {
    if (resourceFileName.toLowerCase().endsWith(".txt"))
    {
      return("text/plain");
    }
    else if (resourceFileName.toLowerCase().endsWith(".xml"))
    {
      return("text/xml");
    }
```

```java
else if (resourceFileName.toLowerCase().endsWith(".html"))
{
  return("text/html");
}
else if (resourceFileName.toLowerCase().endsWith(".rss"))
{
  return("application/rss+xml");
}
else if (resourceFileName.toLowerCase().endsWith(".rdf"))
{
  return("application/rdf+xml");
}
else if (resourceFileName.toLowerCase().endsWith(".atom"))
{
  return("application/atom+xml");
}
else if (resourceFileName.toLowerCase().endsWith(".xls"))
{
  return("application/vnd.ms-excel");
}
else if (resourceFileName.toLowerCase().endsWith(".doc"))
{
  return("application/msword");
}

return "text/plain";
}

public int getContentLength()
{
  System.out.println(getClass().getName() +
                ".getContentLength returning: " +
                resourceBytes.length);
  return resourceBytes.length;
}

public byte[] getBytes()
{
  return resourceBytes;
}

public boolean canBeStringified()
{
  if (resourceFileName.toLowerCase().endsWith(".txt"))
  {
    return true;
  }
  else if (resourceFileName.toLowerCase().endsWith(".xml"))
  {
```

```
      return true;
    }
    else if (resourceFileName.toLowerCase().endsWith(".html"))
    {
      return true;
    }
    else if (resourceFileName.toLowerCase().endsWith(".rss"))
    {
      return true;
    }
    else if (resourceFileName.toLowerCase().endsWith(".rdf"))
    {
      return true;
    }
    else if (resourceFileName.toLowerCase().endsWith(".atom"))
    {
      return true;
    }

    return false;
  }

  public String toString()
  {
    return new String(resourceBytes);
  }
}
```

The SimpleResource class shown in Listing 7.34 uses the file extension to determine the MIME type for the resource. In a more robust implementation the MIME type would be specified by the object that creates the resource to ensure accuracy and flexibility.

Summary

A mashup infrastructure must expose and support programming entities that can be combined in a mashup. The infrastructure must also address the corresponding issues and solutions for each type of entity. This is modeled as three high-level categories of items—user interface artifacts (presentation), data (resources), and/or application functionality (processes). UI artifacts include such entities as HTML snippets, on-demand JavaScript, web service APIs, RSS feeds, and/or other sundry pieces of data. The implementation style, techniques, and technologies used for each category of mashup items present certain constraints and subtleties.

Mashup infrastructures provide components, services, and UI artifacts for building mashups from the point of view of the presentation layer, process layer, and data layer. This chapter showed some techniques for achieving a simple implementation of this model. I also discussed the concepts presented thus far as a step-by-step tour through the technologies and implementations for each high-level mashup category.

In the next chapter I discuss some real-life scenarios involving a variety of mashup tools and commercial mashups, focusing on the different implementation considerations and challenges for each one.

Chapter 8

Commercial Mashups and Tools for Building Mashups

Enterprise mashups have entered many different vertical domain applications and services. This includes, for example, reports that employ mashups of web traffic, maps, and other analytical data; mashups that give employees access to repair, order, and service history for aircraft engine parts, mashups that consolidate data from multiple sources; and mashups that integrate client data with email content to provide alerts containing reports of property matches.

In this chapter I discuss some real-life scenarios involving a variety of mashup tools and commercial mashups, focusing on the different implementation considerations and challenges for each one.

Tools for Building Mashups

Mashup tools and environments use facilities for integrating content and UI artifacts. These tools seek to simplify the process of building mashups in graphical drag-and-drop editors, configuration management tools, and other mechanisms. The following sections discuss some of the more prominent mashup tools and environments currently available.

JackBe Presto Enterprise Mashup Platform

The Presto Enterprise Mashup platform (http://www.jackbe.com) builds on the Presto enterprise mashup server to provide users with access to disparate data from such sources as internal services, external services, and application relational databases.

To build a mashup with the Presto Enterprise Mashup platform, perform the steps in the following sections.

Download and Install Presto Enterprise Mashup Platform

1. Download the Presto Enterprise Mashup platform from http://www.jackbe.com.

2. Extract the contents of the zip file into a directory of your choosing.

3. Run the startup script (setup.bat or setup.sh) from the same directory to set up the Presto configuration. Press Enter for all questions to accept the defaults or specify your own values.

Run Presto Enterprise Mashup Platform

1. Start the Presto Repository by running the startup script (server.bat or server.sh) from the /prestorepository/hsqldb directory of your Presto installation.

2. Start the Presto Mashup Server by running the startup script (start-Presto.bat or startPresto.sh) from the /mashupserver directory of your Presto installation.

3. Go to the Presto home page at http://<hostname>:<port>/presto. Choose Upgrade and copy and paste the license key from the email sent to you from JackBe.

4. Go to the Presto home page at http://<hostname>:<port>/presto/home and log in using admin/adminadmin as the username and password. You will be presented with a page that looks similar to that shown in Figure 8.1.

Publish Sample Services and Mashups

JackBe supplies some sample services and mashups that you can use to get acquainted with the platform. These are registered by running the script (registersamples.bat or registersamples.sh) found at /prestocli of your Presto installa-

Figure 8.1   *The JackBe Presto Enterprise Mashup platform home page*

tion. Once the samples are registered, you must publish them by running the script (publish-mashups.bat or publish-mashups.sh) found at /mashupclient/bin of your Presto installation.

After the samples are registered and published, refresh the Presto Enterprise Mashup platform home page. The home page now appears similar to Figure 8.2.

Click the Create Mashups button to start the Presto Wires environment. You are now presented with a page similar to Figure 8.3.

The Wires environment exposes a canvas containing a required output icon or "block." The output block represents the ultimate results of the mashup. You build your mashup by adding blocks to the Wires canvas and connecting the blocks. It is important to note that the order in which blocks are added determines the order the blocks are executed.

Figure 8.4 illustrates the Wires canvas with a YahooWeatherREST block and another block to its left. The block to the left represents the zip code that will be used as parameterized input for the weather block. The weather block will

Figure 8.2   *The JackBe Presto Enterprise Mashup platform home page with sample services and mashups*

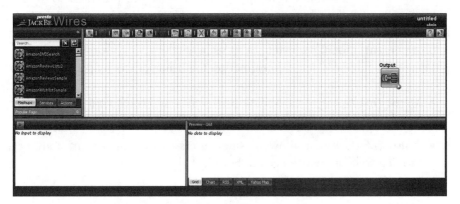

Figure 8.3   *The JackBe Presto Wires environment*

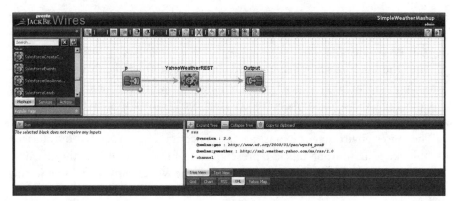

Figure 8.4 *The two blocks added to the Wires environment*

use the zip code, retrieve weather information for the location represented by the zip code, and send the weather information to the output block.

The mashup created from the blocks shown in Figure 8.4 produces RSS containing the weather for the input specified.

Once you have specified the blocks, parameterized them as you want, and connected them, connect the final block to the output block. Now, click the Save icon at the top of the Wires page. Enter a name, description, information provider, and tags for the mashup and click the OK button. When a mashup is saved, it is saved in a sandbox area. You must publish the mashup for others to use it. To publish the mashup, click the Publish icon at the top of the Wires page. The mashup can then be used on its own or by others to create additional mashups.

Pentaho Google Maps Dashboard

Pentaho dashboards (http://www.pentaho.com/products/dashboards/) is a mashup tool that delivers information using a visual interface to provide a view into individual, departmental, or enterprise performance metrics. Pentaho dashboards deliver information to business users to allow them to understand and improve organizational performance by using vital metrics information.

Pentaho dashboards deliver information to business users by providing

- Metrics-management capabilities that define and track vital metrics at the individual, departmental, or enterprise level

- A user interface that allows business users to see which metrics are performing well and which need to be adjusted

- Reports and analysis showing which factors are contributing to poor performance and to the most favorable performance

- Delivery of business metrics to large numbers of users, integrated into portal applications

- Notifications alerting users of exceptions

Pentaho has integrated with Google Maps in a mashup environment to provide geographical functionality to Pentaho reports and analyses.

This capability is made possible via a content and data mashup between Google Maps and Pentaho's business intelligence framework. To implement this, you use a series of Pentaho action sequences, which are instructions to Pentaho's solution engine, to retrieve address information for geographical regions of customers. You then use Google's GClientGeocoder class to change the address information into latitude and longitude coordinates. These coordinates are then passed to the Google Maps API as the browser's onload() event is fired. The coordinates are then plotted on the map.

Points on the map are color-coded to represent the location for each customer. When you change the threshold limits, the points on the map are updated.

Figure 8.5 illustrates an example of a Pentaho dashboard.

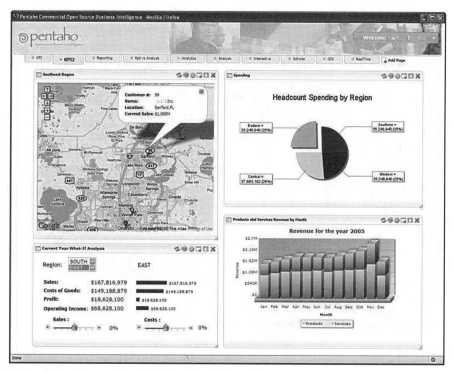

Figure 8.5 *An example of a Pentaho dashboard*

One of the primary features of the Pentaho dashboard is its ability to display detailed sales data, as a report or as a chart, for each customer plotted on a map. This is accomplished using Pentaho's action sequences, which are combinations of AJAX functionality and data from the Google Maps API. When a point on a map is selected by a user, the Pentaho engine retrieves the data for the customer, builds a chart or report representing the data, and transmits the result to the browser to be displayed in the dashboard.

Serena's Business Mashups for Oracle

Unitask Software offers solutions for the Oracle E-Business Application Suite. These solutions enable clients to solve issues relating to deployment, use, and maintainability for an on-demand Oracle E-Business Application environment. The Serena Business Mashup foundation enables a productive boost to the Oracle environment via coordination, automation, and collaboration. The integration of the Unitask Object Migration Manager (OMM) with Serena Business Mashups automates the transition of Oracle E-Business Suite components through development, testing, and production.

Serena Business Mashups provide traceability and auditing within a mashup, providing a powerful solution for auditing internal and external processes.

Serena Business Mashups allow you to control mashups, deploy mashups, version mashups, and report on the history of mashup deployments. This provides visibility into a mashup infrastructure allowing you to monitor critical systems.

The OMM mashup integrates multiple frameworks, components, and objects including profiles, PL/SQL packages, forms definitions, reports, tables, views, and others.

OMM provides a solution for moving objects and components between Oracle E-Business Suite instances. The security architecture of Unitask's OMM enables organizations to ensure that only authorized individuals can commit approved changes. OMM's user interface enables users to migrate work from one instance to another in a manageable and secure way.

OMM integrates with Oracle E-Business Suite as follows:

- Via the Oracle E-Business Suite security infrastructure

- Using the standard Oracle UI

- As an internal component of the Oracle E-Business Suite

The OMM mashup records migration of components within the Serena Business Mashup repository. By centralizing the migration process, the OMM and

Serena Business Mashups integration provides a central location from which to audit change control processes.

Figure 8.6 illustrates the relationships between clients, Oracle E-Business Suite components, Serena's Business Mashup, and Unitask's Object Migration Manager.

Figure 8.6 illustrates how Unitask's OMM acts as the primary integration point between Oracle's E-Business Suite source and target components in a mashup development scenario.

Automated migration of components in the Serena Business Mashup can be performed by a diverse group of talent including developers, business experts, and others without requiring expert knowledge as to the components being migrated.

By adopting the Serena Business Mashup platform, an organization enjoys a solution that solves common business problems involving the transfer of control from Oracle to other applications and data sources.

The Serena Business Mashup platform is complemented by a powerful development environment, the Serena Mashup Composer. To get started building mashups with the Serena Mashup Composer, perform the steps in the following sections.

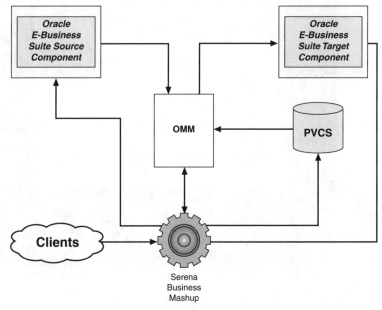

Figure 8.6 *Relationships between clients, Oracle E-Business Suite components, Serena's Business Mashup, and Unitask's OMM*

Building a Mashup with Serena Mashup Composer

1. Download Mashup Composer from http://www.serena.com.

2. Register for a Serena Business Mashups account. After you register for a Serena Business Mashups account, you receive an email message confirming that your account has been activated.

3. Install Serena Mashup Composer by executing the installation program from the downloaded location.

4. Launch Mashup Composer from the Windows Start menu and click Connect Mashup Composer to Your On Demand Account to connect to the Mashup Repository. Provide the information from the confirmation email you received, including machine name, port, username, and password. Mashup Composer now presents a screen similar to Figure 8.7.

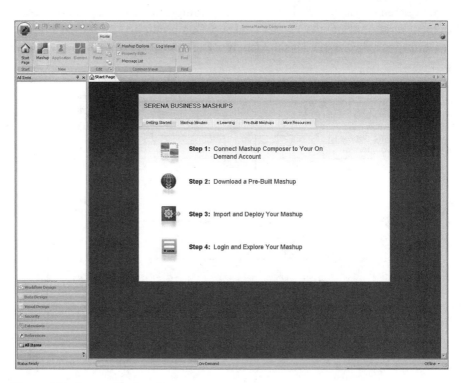

Figure 8.7   *Serena Mashup Composer startup screen*

Create a new mashup by following these steps:

1. From the top toolbar, select the Mashup button, choose the Blank Mashup type, and then type a name and category for your mashup. Click OK.

2. Click the Application button from the top toolbar and then enter a unique name for your application. Click OK. And then click OK on the next dialog.

3. Right-click the Forms node in the All Items pane on the left. Select Add New > State Form from the pop-up menu.

4. Scroll to the bottom of the Form Palette on the right of the screen. Drag the RSS Widget onto the new State Form.

5. Enter a URL for an RSS feed such as http://feedproxy.google.com/ ProgrammableWeb. Now, drag the Google Gadget Widget from the Form Palette to the State Form.

6. Click the Search for Google Gadget link to the right of the Content field in the Property Editor. This loads the Google Gadgets web page in a browser.

7. Choose a Google Gadget, such as TheStreet.com Ratings gadget. Copy the code for this gadget and paste it into the Content field of the Property Editor in Serena Mashup Composer.

8. Click the Preview button from the top toolbar to preview the mashup.

9. Click the Save icon from the top-left of the screen to save the mashup locally.

10. Select the Home tab at the top of the page, and then select Deploy. Follow the steps for deploying your mashup to the Business Mashups server.

Your mashup is now complete and ready to be used.

Salesforce AppExchange

Salesforce's AppExchange provides an on-demand application-sharing Platform-as-a-Service (PaaS) that enables a way to browse, try, install, and publish applications developed on the Force.com platform. Users can build and publish applications to the AppExchange directory, allowing other Salesforce users an easy way to find, install, and use the applications.

Web Service APIs

The Force.com platform provides web services APIs that enable programmatic access to an organization's information using a mashup API.

The Force.com platform allows users to customize, integrate, and extend an organization's applications and services using multiple languages by

- Customizing the applications with custom fields, links, objects, layouts, buttons, record types, s-controls, and tabs

- Integrating Salesforce with the organization's internal systems

- Delivering real-time information to company portals

- Populating business systems with customer information

- Extending the application's UI, business logic, and data services with new functionality to meet the business requirements of the organization

The Force.com API complies with the SOAP (Simple Object Access Protocol) 1.1 specification, the WSDL (Web Service Description Language) 1.1 specification, and WS-I Basic Profile 1.1.

To access the Force.com web services APIs, you need a WSDL file that defines the web service. The WSDL can be used to generate an API to access the Force.com web service it defines.

There are two Force.com web services APIs for which you can obtain WSDL files:

- **Enterprise Web Services API**—This API is typically used by enterprise users who are developing client applications for their organization. The enterprise WSDL file is a strongly typed representation of an organization's data. It provides information about an organization's schema, data types, and fields, allowing a tight integration between the organization and the Force.com web service

- **Partner Web Services API**—This API is typically used by Salesforce.com partners who are developing client applications for multiple organizations.

Once users have access to a WSDL file, it can be imported into a development environment to generate programming objects to use in building web service client applications for a given programming language. Web service client applications use standard web service protocols to perform such functionality as

- Log in to the server and receive authentication information.

- Query an organization's information.

- Perform text queries against an organization's data.

- Create, update, and delete data.

- Perform administrative tasks, such as retrieving user information, changing passwords, and so on.

- Replicate data locally.

All Force.com web services API calls are

- **Service requests and responses**—A client application prepares and submits a service request to a Force.com web service API and receives a response.

- **Synchronous**—Once an API call is invoked, a client application waits until it receives a response from the service. A failed invocation results in an error being returned.

- **Automatic**—Every operation that writes to a Salesforce object is committed automatically to storage. Attempts to write to multiple records in an object are treated as separate transactions.

Figure 8.8 illustrates the Force.com API stack.

Security

Client applications that access an organization's Salesforce data are subject to the same security protections that are used in the Salesforce user interface. Additional protection is available for organizations that install AppExchange managed packages if those packages contain components that access Salesforce via the API.

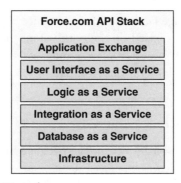

Figure 8.8 *Force.com API stack*

User Authentication   Calling applications must log in using valid credentials for an organization. The server authenticates the credentials and, if found to be valid, provides the calling application with

- **A session ID**—This can be used by all subsequent web service calls during the session.

- **A URL address**—This is used for the client application's web service requests.

An organization's administrator to Salesforce controls the availability of given functionality by configuring profiles and assigning users to them. To access an API, a user must be granted the proper profile permissions. Client applications can query or update only objects and fields to which they have access as configured in their profile.

When users log in to Salesforce, either via the Salesforce UI, programmatic API, or a desktop client, Salesforce confirms that the login is authorized in such ways as the following:

1. Salesforce checks whether the user's profile has time restrictions. If time restrictions are specified, any login outside the specified hours is denied.

2. Salesforce checks whether the user's profile has IP address restrictions. If IP address restrictions are defined for the user's profile, any login from an undesignated IP address is denied.

3. If the login is directed from a browser that includes a Salesforce cookie, the login is allowed.

4. If the user's login is from an IP address in an organization's trusted IP address list, the login is allowed.

API Access in AppExchange Packages   The Salesforce AppExchange API allows access to objects and calls based on the permissions of a user who is accessing API. To prevent security issues from emerging when installed packages have components that access data via the API, Salesforce provides additional security, including

- Restricting access to component APIs

- Restricting access to an AppExchange package by an administrator when the package is installed

- Restricting outbound ports to any feature where a port is specified, such as outbound messages, AJAX proxy calls, and so forth

Outbound Messaging

SOAP messages can be sent by Salesforce's outbound messaging to a designated endpoint when a workflow rule change is triggered.

An outbound messaging listener operates under the following conditions:

- The listener must be reachable from the public Internet.

- The message must be transported from ports 80, 443, or 7000-10000 (inclusive).

- The common name (CN) of the certificate must match the domain name for your endpoint's server, and the certificate must be issued by a trusted certificate authority.

Kapow Mashup Server

Kapow Technologies offers a group of software products providing business solutions for content migration, portal facilitation, web service support, and on-demand harvesting of web content.

The Kapow Mashup Server product family provides solutions for the following areas:

- Web data collection and content migration

- Creation of web services and data feeds via REST, WADL, RSS, and ATOM

- On-demand mining of web-based information that can be imported directly into Excel

- Clip and deploy of web content to portals

Kapow Mashup Server offers three editions, discussed in the following sections.

Data Collection Edition

The Data Collection Edition allows you to access multiple data types, using a visual scripting environment. Web content and data collected can then be written to a database, published as a web service, or transformed for use by other applications. Java and C# APIs are provided to drive the execution of robots.

Figure 8.9 illustrates the components and interactions of the Kapow Data Collection Edition.

The Data Collection Edition allows you to access multiple data types, using a visual scripting environment. Collected data within the Data Collection Edition can be manipulated using a set of provided C# and Java APIs.

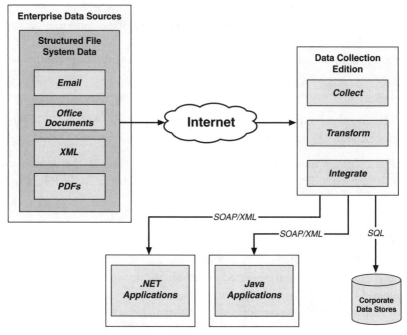

Figure 8.9   *Kapow Data Collection Edition*

Web 2.0 Edition

The Web 2.0 Edition allows you to create an RSS feed from ordinary web sites and to add the feed to an RSS reader.

Figure 8.10 illustrates the components and interactions of the Kapow Web 2.0 Edition.

As shown in Figure 8.10, Kapow Web 2.0 Edition provides a strong relationship between web content, SDKs, and other mashup development environments.

The Web 2.0 Edition uses REST and RSS as the mechanisms for collecting data from web sites.

Portal Content Edition

The Portal Content Edition is a development environment that interacts with portals via the web interface. This edition does not require a proprietary portlet development container or environment.

Figure 8.11 illustrates the components and interactions of the Kapow Portal Content Edition.

As shown in Figure 8.11, Kapow Portal Content Edition provides an integration point between web content, portals, and mashup development environments.

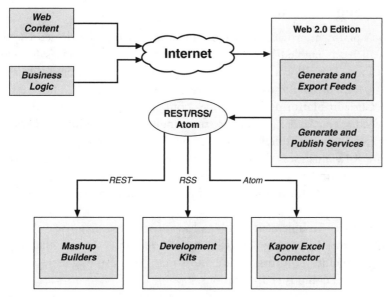

Figure 8.10 *Kapow Web 2.0 Edition*

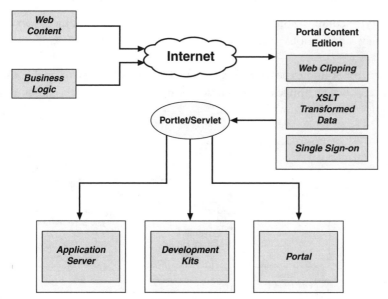

Figure 8.11 *Kapow Portal Content Edition*

Systemation Corizon

Corizon's platform provides an environment in which prefabricated UI components can be assembled to create new composite user interfaces for mashup applications. This allows business logic to be mashed into composite applications targeting different business scenarios or user groups.

The Corizon platform also provides configuration tools and a deployment infrastructure that uses functionality from multiple applications and systems to deliver solutions that address disparate and dynamic needs.

Figure 8.12 illustrates the relationships of components operating within the Corizon platform.

The Corizon platform provides the following functionality:

- **UI service enablement**—This allows users to noninvasively refactor unstructured, existing UI artifacts into reusable services that represent pages, windows, forms, tables, and so on. The resulting services can then be used in composite applications.

- **UI service library**—UI services can be deployed to a service provider as a library of reusable, machine-readable application resources.

- **UI service composition**—The platform allows users to combine UI services into new applications and services.

The Corizon Studio exposes and uses the UI Services Library to enable users to design composite applications. These composite applications can then be deployed using the Corizon Composer.

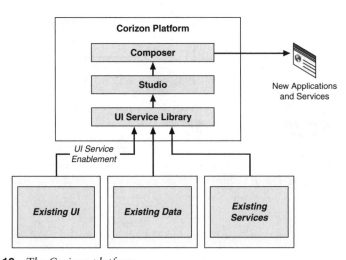

Figure 8.12 *The Corizon platform*

The Corizon Studio seeks to provide the following benefits:

- Remove the burden of complex composite application development.

- Work with organizations to create solutions collaboratively and iteratively.

- Deploy composite applications securely to large user communities.

- Leverage SOA and legacy applications.

- Monitor and understand user activity and system activity.

Attensa Managed RSS Platform

The Attensa Managed RSS platform is a mashup environment facilitating a managed, RSS/XML, publish/subscribe network that streamlines communication and collaboration in an organization.

Attensa's Managed RSS platform and FeedServer connect to blogs, wikis, and other Web 2.0 platforms allowing information to be shared by groups of associated users no matter where they are located.

Figure 8.13 illustrates the relationships of components operating within the Attensa Managed RSS platform.

Attensa FeedServer

The Attensa FeedServer exposes a scalable, publish/subscribe environment that integrates into IT network environments. The FeedServer is a Java/PHP/JavaScript-based system that operates on a LAMP stack. Using the FeedServer as an RSS platform enables groups or organizations to receive and publish RSS information securely. Attensa's publish/subscribe environment supports Confluence,

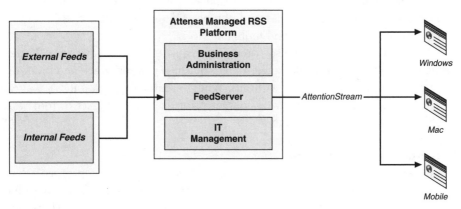

Figure 8.13 *The Attensa Managed RSS platform*

Roller, WordPress, Jive Clearspace and Forums, SharePoint, TypePad, Moveable Type, and others.

The Attensa FeedServer allows users to create custom feeds, edit and publish content, and channel custom feeds to targeted users and groups.

Users can use the Attensa FeedServer to create an email-to-RSS feed by adding an email address generated by FeedServer to the To: field in an email client. Content can then be published by sending an email to this address.

The Attensa FeedServer provides users with a central location to discover applicable feeds that can be organized in a taxonomy-based library using categories and subcategories. Users can create folders and subfolders, name them, and move feeds between folders. Users can browse and search through the feed library to create custom reading lists of relevant feed subscriptions.

Feeds can be added to the Attensa FeedServer using Attensa browser toolbars. Attensa toolbars support Internet Explorer and Firefox. These toolbars can automatically discover RSS feeds on web pages and provide a preview of the discovered feed content. Custom lists of feeds can be created, imported, and exported using OPML files.

Users and groups can be configured on the FeedServer locally or by synchronizing with an LDAP directory. The Attensa FeedServer stores all user data in a database that mirrors and synchronizes with an LDAP directory. This allows FeedServer to remain current as to organization changes, users, and groups. FeedServer users can authenticate against an LDAP directory.

The FeedServer uses a tiered architecture with a clustered design to manage and direct workload demands to specific servers.

Attensa Managed Clients

Attensa offers an assortment of managed client applications for a variety of environments and platforms. Attensa Managed Clients can direct feeds to web-based readers, Windows and Mac desktops, Microsoft Outlook, IBM Lotus Sametime instant messaging, and mobile devices.

Attensa RSS feed readers use AttentionStream technology (discussed in the following section) and are designed to help business workers track and monitor dynamic business information without having to search or request it.

Attensa desktop clients provide content prioritization and a set of tools for publishing, tagging, and collaboration.

Attensa AttentionStream

Attensa's AttentionStream technology is a predictive ranking protocol that automatically discovers the most relevant information for users based on behavior it observes as users read and process articles and feeds. AttentionStream continuously analyzes data for a user such as the time and frequency that feeds and articles are read, deleted, and/or ignored. This allows Attention-Stream to display feeds and articles in a prioritized list according to the user's interests. This prioritization is continuously refined as future data is processed.

The Attensa FeedServer and Attensa Managed Clients use the Attensa Attention-Stream protocol to route information to different reader clients throughout the Attensa platform. This keeps a user's clients synchronized. AttentionStream analyzes a user's reading behavior and data access patterns to provide reporting and analytics that can be used by organizations to identify the most efficient communication channels for a user.

Denodo Platform

Denodo offers a data integration platform that seeks to enable organizations with the ability to create composite, SOA-based, data services for enterprise mashups that can access, extract, and merge data across multiple data sources.

The Denodo platform is designed around a three-layered architecture to provide the following features:

- **Access, extract, and update**—Three data engines search, gather, and index data from unstructured data sources, semistructured data sources, and structured data sources.

- **Transform and relate**—This layer transforms, normalizes, cleanses, and combines disparate data using semantic tools, metadata, and a visual query builder.

- **Application integration**—Composite data is integrated with applications and processes using data services, events, feeds, Java APIs, queries, and/or search interfaces.

Denodo's enterprise mashup platform provides automation technology that uses example-based learning to update itself when web sites change.

Figure 8.14 illustrates the relationships of components operating within the Denodo platform.

As shown in Figure 8.14 the Denodo platform integrates structured, semistructured, and unstructured data with disparate web and enterprise applications.

The Denodo enterprise mashup platform allows you to access disparate data sources, internal and external in many different formats, as follows:

- **Introspect**—Introspect and access relational databases using JDBC and ODBC, XML, SOAP and REST web services, flat files, Excel files, feeds using RSS and ATOM, and more.

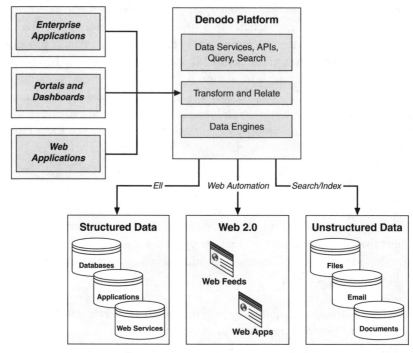

Figure 8.14   *Denodo platform*

- **Navigate**—Navigate and extract content from non-AJAX and AJAX-based web sites, blogs, and wikis.

- **Connect**—Connect to content management systems, file systems, email systems, and search engines. Also, develop custom connectors to read and write from data sources via a plug-in architecture.

- **Native support**—Native parsing, crawling, and indexing support for Microsoft Word and Adobe PDF file formats.

- **Index**—Index unstructured data from web sites, flat files, Word documents, PDFs, email systems, RSS feeds, and relational databases.

Denodo's enterprise platform provides component-based automation for accessing disparate web content using

- **Component library**—Prebuilt components provided for browsing, extracting, and structuring web-based information

- **Data handling operators**—Operators such as iterators, conditions, and for data handling

- **Automation**—Component wizards to simplify process generation

- **Native support**—Native support for building and reusing JavaScript UI artifacts

- **Automated maintenance**—An automatic maintenance mechanism with the ability to build self-maintaining web extractions

- **Workflow modeling**—Workflow process modeling for automation of web and data integration processes

The enterprise platform offered by Denodo allows you to mashup web data with enterprise databases, applications, and unstructured information, as follows:

- **Graphically**—Transform and combine different data types using graphical tools.

- **Hierarchically**—Manage hierarchical information natively.

- **Structurally**—Combine structured data with unstructured data using text mining mechanisms, taxonomy filters, and semantic tools.

- **Flexibly**—Data transformation GUI and programmatic tools and data cleansing mechanisms that can be extended with plug-in tools.

- **Semantically**—Metadata visualization and exchange.

The platform allows you to integrate Denodo with other enterprise or web architectures in the following ways:

- Integrates with systems via JDBC, Java APIs, SOAP and REST web services, message buses, search interfaces, RSS feeds, and others

- Supports queries of XML data using XPath

Denodo's enterprise platform provides a data integration engine that provides

- Delivery of data asynchronously

- Query processing delegation that intelligently uses the most capable data source

- A configurable cache system that enables tuning to serve queries directly from a cache

- Session transfer among IE/Firefox browsers and other HTTP/JavaScript clients

The Denodo enterprise platform provides security features such as

- Granular authentication to databases and data views using LDAP or built-in security

- Firewall support to distributed components to different network segments

- SSL encryption and authentication for communication between modules

The platform enables scalability and reliability as follows:

- Support for third-party load balancers

- Transactional catalog storage, automated swapping, support for XA-compliant endpoints

- System management via JMX

- View and source query execution plan trace

FlowUI RIA Enterprise Mashup Framework

The FlowUI RIA Enterprise Mashup Framework is an open source software development framework for building Rich Internet Applications (RIAs). FlowUI can mashup data and services exposed by an enterprise or from external sources. FlowUI is implemented using Adobe Flex and can, therefore, run in a browser-based environment across all major OS platforms including Windows, Macintosh, and Linux.

The FlowUI framework is designed around the concepts of the Model-View-Controller-Service (MVCS) architecture with enhancements to facilitate the development of enterprise applications.

An application built on FlowUI is divided into four logical components representing state, presentation, business logic, and communication. These components are defined as follows:

- **Model**—The state of the application. The model is composed of value objects for an application. Updates to the model are made known to components in the view via data binding.

- **View**—Composed of the visual components that embody the UI including Adobe Flex interface components, FlowUI interface components, and application-specific pages and components.

- **Business Logic**—Contains the business logic for an application.

- **Service**—Contains service proxies that communicate with remote services to provide data and functionality to an application. Data returned from services is used to update the model. Service proxies can be autogenerated by the Adobe Flex Builder Import Web Service utility.

Figure 8.15 illustrates the logical application architecture of the FlowUI RIA Enterprise Mashup Framework.

The FlowUI RIA Enterprise Mashup Framework requires the Adobe Flex Framework, and using Adobe Flex Builder is recommended.

The FlowUI RIA framework uses a data dictionary to store all the attributes about an application's value objects, including their properties and interrelationships. FlowUI uses the information in the data dictionary to automate the generation of UI artifacts that display and edit an application's data. These generated UI artifacts manage data conversion, formatting, validation, data management in value objects, and interrelationships between value objects.

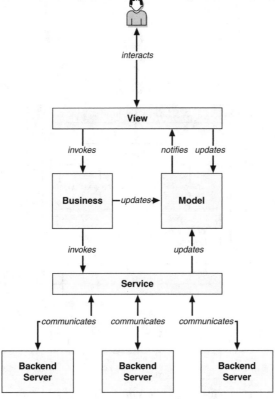

Figure 8.15 *The logical application architecture of the FlowUI RIA Enterprise Mashup Framework*

The FlowUI framework pages are implemented as self-contained components built around the MVC design pattern.

The logical page components of the FlowUI framework are as follows:

- **Model**—The model is composed of data that is specific to a page. When
  data in the model is updated it notifies the components in the view via
  data binding.

- **View**—The view is composed of the MXML file for a page and the page's
  visual components. The components are bound to the model.

- **Controller**—The controller is embodied within a Page Command Handler
  object that can invoke business logic in the application's business layer.

Figure 8.16 illustrates the logical page components of the FlowUI RIA Enterprise Mashup Framework.

FlowUI forms are designed to simplify common user interface tasks in an
enterprise application. FlowUI forms are configuration driven and retrieve

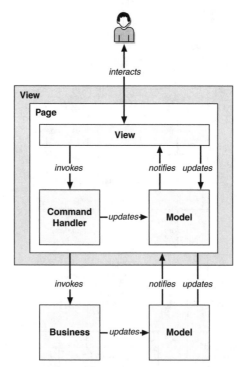

Figure 8.16   *The logical page components of the FlowUI RIA Enterprise Mashup
Framework*

attributes about the data to be displayed and edited from the application data dictionary.

Commercial Mashups

Many commercial mashups are becoming available every day. The following sections discuss a few of the more prominent commercial mashups currently available.

Arrowpointe Maps

Arrowpointe Maps is an on-demand mashup that facilitates communications between Salesforce.com and MapQuest, enabling a simple means for users to map Salesforce data.

Three approaches can be used to plot data on a map using Arrowpointe Maps:

1. **Map pages**—These are configurable query pages that an administrator configures for users. It provides end users a user interface for using specific fields to view data on maps. Map Pages support mapping of items on Salesforce.com such as Leads, Accounts, Contacts, Cases, and custom objects.

2. **Map from views**—Custom buttons for Leads, Accounts, Contacts, Opportunities, and Cases are downloaded in an AppExchange application that can be placed on Salesforce Views. This lets users map records in a view.

3. **Map from reports**—This lets users apply a map to any report data that has an address or a portion of an address.

Zmanda Internet Backup to Amazon S3

Zmanda is the commercial division of Amanda, an Open Source backup and recovery application with partners that include Red Hat, MySQL, and Oracle.

Zmanda's primary product is Amanda Enterprise, a network-based backup and recovery mashup solution designed to back up and recover files from multiple hosts across a network and store data on Amazon's S3 online storage service, disk, tape, or other devices. Also offered is Recovery Manager (ZRM) for MySQL, which is aimed specifically at MySQL-based databases and applications. Amanda Enterprise's support for Amazon S3 is configurable for each Amanda Enterprise Server.

To use Amanda Enterprise's support for Amazon S3, users must purchase the Zmanda Internet Backup to Amazon S3 option and sign up to use Amazon S3 via Zmanda. S3 users are charged using a pricing model that involves both data transfer and storage capacity usage.

The Amanda Enterprise's support for Amazon S3 offers the following benefits:

- **Optimized**—Offsite backup storage and recovery with layered security and bandwidth optimization

- **On-demand**—Anytime, anywhere data retrieval that is faster than restoring from offsite tape storage

- **ROI**—Pay-as-you-go usage

- **Management**—A browser-based management console that makes it easy to configure Amazon S3 as a target for backup and archiving

Recovery from Amazon S3 allows you to find files or directories using click Restore from the management console.

Big Contacts

Big Contacts is a web-hosted contact management and sales force automation mashup that integrates with technologies from Skype, S3, and Alexa Thumbnail.

Big Contacts includes a group calendar designed to track meetings as well as events for members of a team. A calendar can be viewed four different ways:

- As a One-Day view

- As a Seven-Day view

- As a 31-Day view

- As a 31-Day Group

Big Contacts comes with a number of built-in reports, including contact reports, activity reports, and calendar reports. Each report can be downloaded as an Excel file or viewed in a browser.

Any web-enabled device can be used to access Big Contacts. Mobile access is enabled via an optimized, dedicated, low-bandwidth version of Big Contacts. It includes the most commonly used features of Big Contacts. For example, you can

- Search for contacts.

- See contact details.

- Schedule meetings.

- Assign tasks.

- View team activity.

Big Contacts has an import wizard to enable importing of all existing contact data in CSV format. Contacts, meetings, tasks, and contact history can be exported, as well.

Big Contacts has a search facility providing several ways to find a contact or group of contacts:

- **Standard Search**—This involves a single search box that allows users to enter the name of a contact or company to search for. As a user types, a list of matching contacts is displayed below the search box. This search provides the option to search your entire database to locate contact records that contain a given name anywhere including notes, calls, meetings, attachments, and emails.

- **Advanced Search**—This search facility allows users to search on multiple data fields such as city, contact type, or lead source. A result is returned with all the matching contacts. Users have the option of downloading results as an Excel spreadsheet or viewing them in a browser window.

- **Contact Browser**—This allows users to search for a contact by selecting which data fields to browse for.

- **Tag Browser**—This uses preselected tags as the fields on which to search and operates much like the Contact Browser.

- **Contact Table**—This allows users to view, edit, merge, delete, and assign tasks to multiple contacts at once. After loading the Contact Table, users can select how many contacts to display and can filter them based on contact type and team member.

- **Contact Cloud**—This presents a page with all contacts' last names listed. The contact names will vary in size and color depending on the amount of activity a contact has seen. Contact activity includes meetings held, tasks assigned, notes written, and others.

Redfin

Redfin is an online real estate brokerage that employs satellite maps to display information about homes for sale. The mashup combines real estate listings, tax records, and analytics to show given homes on a map. Sellers and buyers can use Redfin's service to present a home for sale or to negotiate offers on a home.

Buyers can search for homes on Redfin's site, arrange home tours with Redfin, and initiate an offer on a home listed on the site. Each given transaction (negotiations, contingencies, and paperwork) is handled by the same Redfin agent team.

Sellers can use Redfin's site to present a home for sale. A local Redfin team works with sellers to get a home ready to sell and to set the price. Once an offer is received, Redfin negotiates on behalf of the seller and manages all the paperwork.

Redfin's business model is based on handling transactions partially online and partially face-to-face. The Redfin technology mashes real estate listings with third-party data, including maps, property outlines, third-party appraisals, and tax records. Redfin employs agents directly and compensates them based on customer satisfaction.

The platform exposed by Redfin uses Microsoft Virtual Earth as the underlying map infrastructure. Microsoft Virtual Earth provides features such as

- Address/location lookup

- Geocoding and batch geocoding

- Business/Yellow Page listings

- Driving directions

- Real-time traffic incidents/congestion

- Points of interest near a location

- Direct integration into Redfin site

- Lists of geographic entities for a particular geographic latitude/longitude

Summary

Enterprise mashups can be found in many different applications and services. Mashups are used in real-life situations such as web traffic reports, maps, and other analytical data; repair, order, and service history reports for the aircraft industry; and real estate reports integrating client data to match a buyer's need with a seller's property.

This chapter presented content and examples to help bring together many of the threads and concepts introduced throughout the book.

In the next chapter I discuss some of these trends and possibilities that enterprise mashups are likely to follow, and I propose forecasts for the future of enterprise mashups.

Chapter 9

Mashup Forecasts and Trends

An enterprise mashup environment offers enterprises many opportunities to integrate data and systems that prove useful in daily business operations. Using this integration in an intelligent manner can make a huge difference in an organization's bottom line. Exploiting the dynamic nature of an enterprise mashup infrastructure to achieve strategic objectives can prove profitable for an organization over time. Aside from helping domain experts for a business meet market needs responsively, a mashup infrastructure enables an enterprise to realize reduced costs in application development and maintenance. In a mashup environment, services and applications can be created by non-IT people, therefore reducing typical bottlenecks encountered when technical talent is needed. Mashup artifacts such as widgets, semantic data, and business services can be reused by developers and domain experts within an organization as well as by business partners.

The trends and possibilities for enterprise mashups look promising. In this chapter I discuss some of these trends and possibilities that enterprise mashups are likely to follow and propose forecasts for the future of enterprise mashups.

Solving Problems with Enterprise Mashups

Enterprise applications and services largely depend on structured data from relational databases and email servers. Business organizations use proprietary office suites and content management systems to use unstructured data that is stored in documents and on file systems. Semantic technologies are helping to add structure to much of the content used today via RSS and Atom feeds. Similarly, previously unstructured data found in web pages is slowly becoming structured with semantic technologies. Enterprise mashup infrastructures are beginning to emerge and are offering integration solutions within organizations for structured and unstructured information.

Businesses are realizing the value hidden in the vast amount of data that is stored in their information systems. This information, enabled with semantic meaning, offers a competitive edge and a productivity boon to organizations in ways that up to this point have been prohibitive to consider. The introduction of mashup techniques and technologies is a point of integration for data, processes, and UI artifacts that is enabling organizations with a form of agility that has not been available up to now.

Enterprise mashup infrastructures and semantic technologies automate the extraction of content from web pages, disparate data stores, heterogeneous information systems, and other structured and unstructured information sources. Extracted information is then repurposed in a mashup environment to be used by other applications and services in insightful ways that prove useful as markets demand. The dynamic nature of an enterprise mashup environment enables a business to provide a level of service that in the past has been completely reliant on the availability of software engineering resources. No longer will businesses be restricted by this reliance. On the contrary, businesses will soon be able to respond to market demands using very high-level tools and techniques in the hands of domain-savvy users.

Enterprise mashups are beginning to be applied in many different ways. Database management personnel are using mashup techniques and technologies to create frameworks of reusable data components and services from structured and unstructured data sources. These components and services can be orchestrated to form composite applications and services to solve real-time business problems. In this environment, domain experts can integrate data components and services to create location-specific, effectively targeted sales campaigns based on information gleaned from call centers, CRM systems, and product lists. Similarly, organizations can extract information from semantically rich data components and services to intelligently identify potential customers, garner feedback about current products and services, and draw comparisons with competitors. In this respect, enterprise mashups are being used to dynamically and effectively solve integration problems. Enterprise mashups can provide artifacts and components to the financial services industry to enable precise investing and marketing efforts.

For example, analyzing sales data for a given time period can be intelligently facilitated using artifacts and time-series data integrated from CRM systems, sales reports, and online maps services. This integrated mashup can be embodied as a dashboard that can be viewed and manipulated by marketing and sales professionals to enable them to direct future efforts towards strategic goals offering the most ROI.

Another area that is sure to benefit from the mashup world is business intelligence (BI) analysis. BI offers support to organizations to enable them to make predictive business decisions based on historical data gathered from sales reports, production systems, accounting numbers, and others. Exposing historical data as semantic artifacts permits a mechanism that can be used to build tools that organizations can use to respond to market trends and user patterns proactively rather than reactively.

Figure 9.1 illustrates the integration possibilities provided by an enterprise mashup infrastructure.

Figure 9.1 illustrates how a mashup infrastructure acts as the primary integration point for disparate data found in various business systems.

As semantic technologies propagate across the web, the Internet itself will become collectively more intelligent and will thereby provide information that can be used reliably to build analytical business tools.

Marketing will use semantic technologies to target potential customers in a contextual manner. Using semantic data collected from web sites, an organization will be able to publish ads that fit the context of the web site more accurately. Organizations will also be able to publish ads based on behavioral patterns with confidence rather than attempting to guess the context of a given web site or search result based on the vague meanings of groups of phrases found on the page.

Enterprise mashups arrive at a time when solving the problem of integrating disparate data sources and content has reached a critical point. The promise of simplified transformations, integration, and management that enterprise mash-

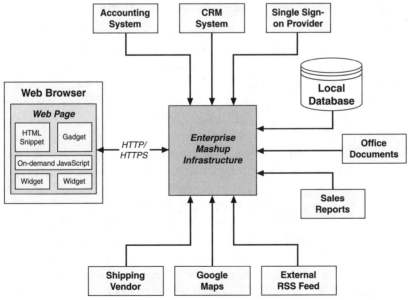

Figure 9.1 *The integration possibilities provided by an enterprise mashup infrastructure*

ups offers is timely indeed. This simplification is due to the ability of mashups to be created and maintained by nontechnical or semitechnical users.

The generation of users entering the workforce today is well acquainted with the Internet and basic computing concepts. This trend will certainly continue to grow with emerging generations of users to the point that creating applications and services from reusable mashup artifacts will be second nature. However, this trend will only equate with productivity if organizations expose infrastructures of mashup artifacts that hide the more complex issues surrounding enterprise integration, such as governance, security, and management.

Building an Open, Agile Mashup Environment

For an organization to realize the benefits that mashups promise, the organization needs to equip itself with a mashup infrastructure that will provide users and domain experts with the proper tools. Specifically, an enterprise mashup infrastructure must provide flexible, dynamic mashup artifacts and services that are enabled with the intelligence specific to the particular vertical domain of the organization. The mashup infrastructure must be comprehensive enough to provide a secure environment in which internal users can operate safely and in which partners can operate without worrying about data privacy, compliance violations, and other issues.

Enterprise Mashup Environment Considerations

Mashup builders are beginning to emerge that provide intelligent tools, services, and artifacts to domain experts, enabling them with the power to create new applications and services without assistance from an IT department. This will eventually evolve to the point where the mashup environment will be considered an unseen IT group, providing the resources to create new data integration components, UI artifacts, and business services.

Within an effective enterprise mashup environment, IT personnel are released to focus on critical engineering projects, leaving on-demand business needs such as UI changes, service orchestration, and data integration up to domain experts and business analysts. This will enable organizations to solve pressing business problems and exploit new business opportunities more effectively.

Realizing the benefits provided by a dynamic mashup infrastructure in an enterprise environment depends on how effectively the mashup infrastructure operates within the constraints that control all enterprise IT systems, such as security, governance, and compliance. The openness enjoyed by the consumer mashup model must be tempered to operate behind firewalls and security barriers.

The following list outlines some of the guidelines that organizations should follow when provisioning themselves with an enterprise mashup infrastructure:

- Choose techniques and technologies that can be used to build UI artifacts, data components, and services to ease information access for your domain experts.

- Decide which applications, services, and data currently available to your organization will provide the most ROI when exposed as reusable mashup components. Pay particular attention to data and services that might have been overlooked when using traditional software engineering methods. This will include any unique datasets and services that are individually small in number but significant when viewed as a group. This is often referred to as "The Long Tail" of a sales graph.

- Apply proper restrictions to data and services. Ensure that a comprehensive permissions framework is in place to provide the proper flexibility to all forms of data access throughout the infrastructure.

- Be sure to design and create UI artifacts, data components, and services that will provide a positive ROI most quickly.

- Think long term. The infrastructure should be viewed as a living organism that will evolve to adapt to business demands for years to come.

Securing information in a mashup model is a tricky proposition when trying to create a flexible, agile infrastructure. Information needs to be accessed from multiple sources and must be available to multiple receiving parties. Securing information in this open environment is complex and must be implemented with great care to keep unwanted eyes from viewing sensitive data.

An essential part of a mashup security strategy is the understanding of where data will be integrated before it is presented to a user or to an application. If you have a firm grasp on this process, the proper constraints and technologies can be applied and restricting access becomes much easier. The goal for applying security in an enterprise mashup infrastructure is creating an environment where corporate guidelines are enforced and creativity is encouraged. This encourages users to embrace your mashup model and promotes a positive, cooperative, replication environment among mashup users, applications, and services.

Another primary ingredient of a successful mashup security strategy is presenting an authentication and authorization framework to users and applications where multiple protocols and methods are supported without too much additional work by users of the framework. A comprehensive framework must support methods such as username/password, PKI, OAuth, SAML tokens, Kerberos, and others.

Performance and availability are other considerations that must be accounted for in a successful enterprise mashup infrastructure. Performance and availability in a normal web application environment can be a formidable task in itself. Adding the complexity of reliance on third-party services and components makes this task much more difficult. Extensive testing models and processes must be in place to continually monitor access to third-party services to address any bottlenecks that may occur at any time. Service level agreements (SLAs) become much harder to support in an environment where performance is reliant on many third-party services and artifacts. Therefore, you must ensure that all third-party components offer the same degree of assurance that you are charged with according to any SLAs in place. Caching and out-of-process updates are mechanisms that can be applied to third-party data to help meet performance requirements.

An enterprise mashup infrastructure must above all promote extensibility through customization. This implies that your architecture presents a public interface that remains constant across revisions so that users might be able to confidently build upon your infrastructure without concern that future upgrades and updates will negatively impact their efforts. This can be solved with intelligent and effective management tools and frameworks that provide the ability to update individual modules within the infrastructure without affecting other modules.

Finally, an effective and agile enterprise mashup infrastructure should encourage and support industry standards pertaining to the business domain of your organization. Standards for data integration, content aggregation, inter-component communication, service APIs, and so on should be adhered to and supported to promote reuse of your mashup services and artifacts as well as enabling your infrastructure with the ability to support as many third-party services and artifacts as possible.

OpenSocial, Facebook, MySpace, and Other Social Platforms

The climate that has led to the popularity of the mashup model owes a lot to the social trends and technologies that have permeated the web. Social interactions on the web have emerged from simple search-and-bookmark activities to a model comprised of comprehensive semantic discovery and linking with tags and notifications. This semantically enabled discovery/tag/notification model has enabled semitechnical users to create interest-based social sites and services using high-level artifacts and languages. Social sites and platforms are now some of the most popular stops on the web.

For IT departments, supporting social platforms and technologies is no longer a question of "if" but "when." Organizations stand to gain substantial rewards by proper support of a mashup platform that is, by nature, social. Since most organizations rely on social interaction—for example, word-of-mouth—to promote products and services, it stands to reason that technologically based social interactions that can reach vast numbers of potential customers should be a top priority for marketing and sales efforts.

Many different social platform sites and services have already emerged and are enjoying great success. These include LinkedIn, Plaxo, Facebook, MySpace, FriendFeed, and others. Many of these sites are in themselves incarnations of mashup integration technologies and techniques.

Figure 9.2 illustrates the integration possibilities provided by social platforms and an enterprise mashup infrastructure.

In Figure 9.2 data from various social platforms feeds into a mashup infrastructure to be integrated with data from internal business systems.

Social networking already reaches into the pockets of users in many ways. Paid services and applications on social sites, ad networks targeting social site profiles and bloggers, and music sites sharing information between users are examples of this. This model will be exploited by enterprises that adapt to social platforms with necessary constraints and preparations in place.

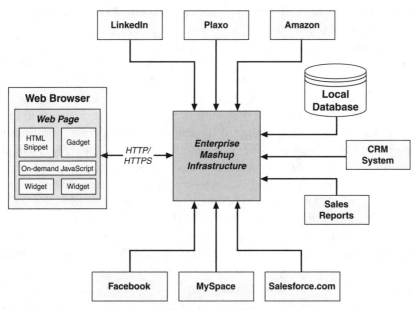

Figure 9.2 *The integration possibilities provided by social platforms and an enterprise mashup infrastructure*

An example of a useful implementation of social techniques used in an enterprise environment might include tracking prospects by monitoring community sites to determine potential customers or clients. Another example might use sites such as LinkedIn or Plaxo to determine the highest-profile clients to design marketing and sales efforts around enticing and keeping such clients. Certainly customer care will improve as a result of using semantic technologies to track user comments and competitors' activities.

Realizing social platform success at the enterprise level entails using social technologies and techniques to build relationships with individuals and groups instead of simply gathering information about potential customers.

Some of the social platforms currently in use are discussed in the following sections.

OpenSocial Platform

OpenSocial presents a unified API for building social applications with services and artifacts served from multiple sites. The OpenSocial API relies on standard JavaScript and HTML as the platform languages developers can use to create applications and services that interconnect common social connections.

An extensive community of partners is developing OpenSocial. This community partnership is leading to a platform that exposes a common framework by which sites can become socially enabled. Some of the sites currently supporting OpenSocial include iGoogle, Friendster, LinkedIn, MySpace, Ning, Plaxo, Salesforce.com, and others.

OpenSocial presents functionality and content as Google Gadgets. This allows developers to exploit the toolset that Google presents for building and deploying gadgets, such as the Google Gadget Editor, XML-based user preferences, the Google remote content retrieval API, and the gadget sandbox.

APIs for OpenSocial rely on transmitting requests and responses within the context of an OpenSocial container. A site can host OpenSocial applications if it supports the OpenSocial container requirements defined in the OpenSocial API specification. An OpenSocial container is a component running as a server that adheres to a few restrictions and requirements such as implementing all methods of the JavaScript API reference; handling all request types defined in the Gadgets API specification; and supporting JSON, XML, and AtomPub data formats.

Applications written to OpenSocial can communicate with an OpenSocial container using the OpenSocial RESTful API. This API enables servers, mobile devices, and browsers to update information, send messages, and retrieve information from an OpenSocial container without requiring user participation. Information is exchanged via AtomPub or as a JSON-enabled service defined in the OpenSocial REST Protocol specification and the OpenSocial RPC Protocol specification.

To host OpenSocial applications, a site must implement the methods, data formats, and request/response patterns defined in the OpenSocial API Specification. This can be facilitated easily using the Apache Shindig project (http://incubator.apache.org/shindig/), which provides an open source implementation of the OpenSocial API specification and the Google Gadgets API specification.

Portable Contacts Specification

The Portable Contacts specification is targeted at creating a standard, secure way to access address books and contact lists using web technologies. It seeks to do this by specifying an API defining authentication and access rules, along with a schema and a common access model that a compliant site provides to contact list consumers.

The Portable Contacts specification defines a language-neutral and platform-neutral protocol whereby contact list consumers can query contact lists, address books, and profiles from providers. The protocol defined by the specification outlines constraints and requirements for consumers and providers of the specification. The specification enables a model that can be used to create an abstraction of almost any group of online friends or user profiles that can then be presented to consumers as a contact list formatted as XML or JSON data.

In contrast with other standards relating to contacts and contact information, the Portable Contacts specification seeks to define a comprehensive set of methods and mechanisms for discovering, reading, and modifying the contact information.

The current version of the Portable Contacts specification (v1.0 Draft C) is wire-compatible with version 0.8.1 of the OpenSocial RESTful Protocol specification; therefore, any provider compliant with OpenSocial RESTful Protocol 0.8.1 is also a compliant Portable Contacts provider. The Portable Contacts specification is intended to continue this compatibility with future revisions.

OAuth and Basic Authorization are the two authorization methods currently supported by the Portable Contacts specification. Service providers of the Portable Contacts specification must support OAuth Core and OAuth Discovery if they want to provide delegated authorization to consumers.

Friendster Developer Platforms

Friendster presents two developer platforms providing APIs to access Friendster data, integrate with components and services exposed within the Friendster web site environment, and create applications for the Friendster application framework. Response data is returned from either platform as XML or JSON.

The first platform, referred to as the OpenSocial Platform, is based on the OpenSocial standard to allow you to write applications for Friendster. Friendster installs your OpenSocial-developed application by uploading your application's OpenSocial XML file and registering it with Friendster's application framework.

The second platform, referred to as Platform V1, leverages a REST-based interface to allow access to Friendster data and resources. Platform V1 relies on a previously issued API key and shared secret key. Platform V1 can be tested in a Friendster-provided test tool. An application installed in the Friendster environment using Platform V1 uses a concept referred to as the "canvas page" of the Friendster application framework. The canvas page is where the UI for your application resides when it is activated by a user.

Facebook Platform

Facebook presents an API that embodies a platform for building applications that execute in the Facebook web site environment for members of the Facebook social network. The Facebook API permits applications to use the connections and profile data for Facebook users. This information facilitates applications that are, in context with the Facebook platform, socially aware. The Facebook API enables applications to use profile information and connections as a conduit for publishing to Facebook news feeds and Facebook profile pages. Access to an individual's profile information and connections is contingent on the approval of a profile owner's permission specified in the individual's privacy settings.

Facebook relies on an API key and application secret key to identify an application to Facebook and to authenticate requests made within the Facebook environment.

As with the Friendster platform, Facebook presents the concept of a canvas page URL in which an application's UI resides within Facebook and a callback URL that is used to specify the location of a host containing the application's logic.

Client libraries for building Facebook applications in many different programming languages are available from Facebook and third-party sites.

MySpace Platform

MySpace presents an application platform that enables you to build applications that can access and operate on MySpace user information within the context of MySpace site pages. The MySpace platform supports development of applications based on the OpenSocial model, in regards to accessing data and interacting with participating sites. The MySpace platform also builds on the OpenSocial extensions model to enable nonstandard concepts embedded within photo albums and other page scenarios.

The following are some of the primary aspects of the MySpace application platform:

- **New message types**—New types of messages unique to applications within MySpace are supported by the Application Communications Channel (ACC) within the MySpace platform.

- **Access delegation and request signing**—The OAuth standard is supported by the MySpace platform for HTTP request signing and access delegation.

- **Server-to-server communication**—Server-to-server HTTP requests are supported by the MySpace platform via a RESTful API that responds with either XML or JSON data.

- **Canvas page**—The MySpace platform also presents the concept of a canvas page in which the user interface for applications is contained.

The MySpace application platform provides a test harness in which applications can be tested using a limited number of profiles.

Developers working within the MySpace application platform can link certain bits of a MySpace account outside MySpace using the MySpace Data Availability framework. This framework relies on the OpenSocial REST APIs and MySpace's REST APIs to communicate profile information, media snippets, and social connection graphs within a standards-based model that uses delegated authentication to ensure access privacy via access tokens, partner keys, and shared secrets as defined by the OAuth protocol to provide delegated authentication.

Mobile and SDK-Related Mashups

Mobile device usage has escalated to the point that it would be harder for many people to give up their mobile phone or PDA than it would be for them to give up any other communication device. This trend coupled with increased mobile bandwidth and the power that modern mobile devices offer makes the mobile device landscape a fertile environment for applications and services. This landscape is being exploited at an astounding rate by applications exposing location-based content, games, collaboration, and so on. The possibilities for mashup-based applications and services are enormous.

Mobile devices are being equipped with powerful web browsers in which HTML, JavaScript, and CSS are enabled. This facilitates a prime environment for widget/gadget technologies. While some mobile-specific techniques and SDKs are needed for enhanced mobile application development, most standard web widgets will work fine. This point will ring even more true as mobile technologies advance.

The advent of such devices as Apple's iPhone and Google's G1 demonstrated that the experience presented by mobile devices can be equal to or greater than the experience presented by a personal computer. The freedom that mobile devices offer along with location-based services creates a unique environment for application developers.

Mashups are showing that simplified integration of data, UI artifacts, and processes create refreshingly new applications that serve to satisfy specific needs. This trend is already spilling over into the realm of mobile devices along with unique mobile functionality such as the ability to expose content based on the location of the mobile device. Other uses unique to a mobile device environment will soon emerge, such as

- Scanning bar codes and comparing prices at competing merchants on demand

- Receiving notification when a client or coworker is nearby

- Receiving alerts about new real estate properties immediately as they become available

- Recording pictures and/or videos of crime or accident scenes and transmitting them in real-time

Creating an enterprise mashup infrastructure for unique mobile device capabilities must facilitate dynamic data transformation, enrichment, and integration suitable for mobile platforms. Equally important is the need for UI artifacts tailored to fit the small display footprint offered by mobile devices.

Another aspect of mobile-device aware mashup infrastructures is the need to provide APIs that support the semantic nature of the latest web technologies. This includes APIs supporting Atom, RSS, REST, AtomPub, and RDF.

Other considerations that should be addressed by an enterprise mashup infrastructure that is mobile-device friendly are

- Location-based access and services

- Open, yet secure enterprise-based connections or graphs

- Support for standards such as OpenSocial, microformats, and DataPortability

- Taxonomies providing contextual services enabling intelligent location-based services and/or client-aware, preference-based services

- Sophisticated authentication and authorization frameworks supporting mobile-device platforms

- Integration with functionality such as calendar events and contact management

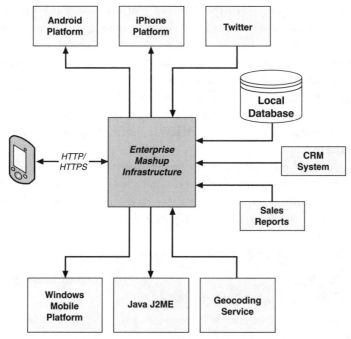

Figure 9.3 *The integration possibilities provided by mobile platforms and an enterprise mashup infrastructure*

The diagram in Figure 9.3 illustrates some of the possible integration points for a system operating within a mashup infrastructure that exploits mobile platform APIs.

As shown in Figure 9.3 mobile platform APIs within a mashup infrastructure present just as many and most likely more possibilities than a browser-aware infrastructure.

The following sections discuss a few of the most widely used mobile platforms and how they can be applied to a mashup infrastructure.

Android Platform

The Android platform is based on the Linux kernel and includes a collection of mobile device software components including SDKs, a virtual machine, support for audio and video media, a scaled-down implementation of SQL, and others. The Android platform is actively developed by a group of technology and mobile companies, specifically, the Open Handset Alliance, which includes Google, Intel, Motorola, Samsung, T-Mobile, and others. The goal of this alliance is to create a complete, free, and open mobile platform. The alliance provides a software development kit (SDK) to be used to develop applications.

Applications are written to the Android platform using the Java programming language and run on the Android virtual machine, which sits atop a Linux kernel.

The diagram in Figure 9.4 illustrates the architectural stack of components and frameworks of the Android platform.

As shown in Figure 9.4 the components and frameworks that embody the architectural stack of the Android platform are similar to any well-designed, decoupled platform with one or more layers between application development code and the machine.

Building a mashup application or service on top of the Android platform stack will most likely materialize as an aggregate of services and components from the Applications layer and the Applications Framework layer of the Android platform stack, as shown in Figure 9.4.

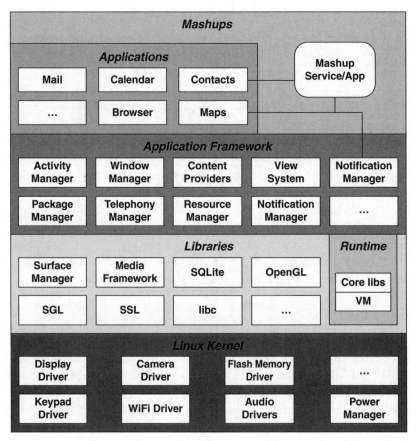

Figure 9.4   *The architectural stack of components and frameworks of the Android platform*

The Android SDK includes the Android framework, application libraries, sample applications, a device emulator, a debugger, and monitoring tools.

All Android applications are based on an assortment of frameworks and services, including

- An extensible collection of UI artifacts called Views that includes an embeddable browser, text boxes, lists, grids, and buttons

- Data hosting components called Content Providers that enable applications to access data from other applications (such as Contacts), or to share their own data

- A resource manager that facilitates access to external files containing data and content such as XML files, images, and layout templates used by application code

- A notification manager for displaying status bar alerts

- A lifecycle management component called the Activity Manager that manages application lifecycle and navigation backstack

The currently available Android-powered phone comes with several preloaded Google applications including Gmail, Gmail contact management, Google Search, Google Maps, Google Calendar, YouTube, and Google Talk.

Many of the Google applications preloaded on the phone such as Google Talk, Gmail, and Google Calendar are synchronized to a high degree with corresponding web browser applications from Google. This enables items updated on a web browser application to be pushed to the phone in real-time and items updated on the phone to be made immediately available to web applications.

In addition to features and functionality typically found in a Google application environment, several enhancements have been added to take advantage of the integrated environment in which Android applications execute. For example, Google Search can be invoked instantly to find information about data contained in many applications as they are running.

iPhone OS

The iPhone from Apple is a mobile device enabled with web browsing capabilities, an application execution environment, and mobile phone functionality. The iPhone is built on an operating system and technologies run natively on the iPhone and other compatible devices. The iPhone operating system shares many foundational concepts and technologies with Mac OS X, although the iPhone OS is optimized for a mobile environment. This similarity with Max OS X makes developing applications for the iPhone familiar to existing Mac OS X developers. Some concepts are unique to the iPhone environment, such as a multitouch interface, a smaller graphical display, autorotation, and the iPhone accelerometer (iPhone's technology for measuring acceleration and gravity-induced forces), which need to be addressed when developing for the iPhone.

Figure 9.5 illustrates the architectural stack of components and frameworks of the iPhone OS platform.

As shown in Figure 9.5 the architectural stack of the iPhone platform is abstracted in several layers allowing development tasks to be targeted at only the specific level providing the functionality needed for a given application or service.

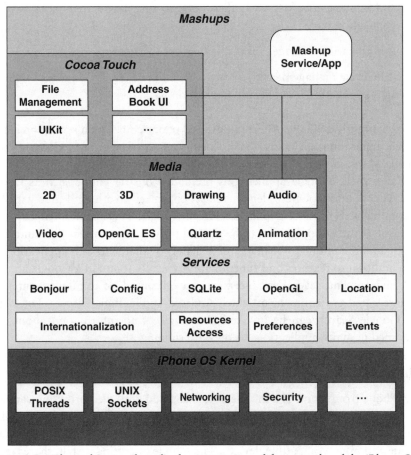

Figure 9.5 *The architectural stack of components and frameworks of the iPhone OS platform*

Building a mashup application or service on top of the iPhone platform will most likely emerge as a combination of services and components from the Cocoa Touch layer, the Media layer, and the Services layer of the iPhone platform stack, as shown in Figure 9.5.

The iPhone SDK includes sample code as well as tools for building, testing, executing, and debugging applications for the iPhone.

Currently you must develop applications for iPhone within the Xcode environment on a Mac OS X computer using C or Objective-C. Xcode is Apple's integrated development environment shipped with every copy of Max OS X. A graphical workbench is included with Xcode. This workbench includes a text editor, an integrated build system, a debugger, and a PowerPC compiler. A tool called Interface Builder where you can assemble and connect UI components for an application is also provided.

The Xcode environment now includes support for developing and testing iPhone applications. An iPhone simulator that works in conjunction with an iPhone or compliant device to test such items as multitouch and accelerometer functionality is presented with Xcode.

Windows Mobile

The Windows Mobile operating system includes a number of applications for mobile devices. Devices such as Pocket PCs and Smartphones can run the Windows Mobile OS. The development platform is based on Microsoft's Win32 API. The operating environment for Windows Mobile includes many of the same concepts as desktop environments built on the Win32 API. The current version of Windows Mobile is Windows Mobile 6.1.

A number of options exist for developing a Windows Mobile application or service. These options include writing to native code with Visual C++, writing to the Common Language Runtime environment using managed code within the .NET Compact Framework, or writing browser-based code that operates within Internet Explorer Mobile.

A subset of the .NET Framework, the .NET Compact Framework shares several concepts and components with the .NET Framework and, therefore, many of the features of a Windows desktop application environment.

Along with the .NET Compact Framework, you can also develop managed applications for Windows Mobile-based Pocket PC and Smartphone devices using the Windows Mobile SDK. The SDK includes managed classes giving you access to a device's system configuration and management services.

You can write to the Windows Mobile native APIs when you want high performance. Development at this layer is facilitated using Visual C++ to access the Win32 libraries and the MFC and ATL frameworks.

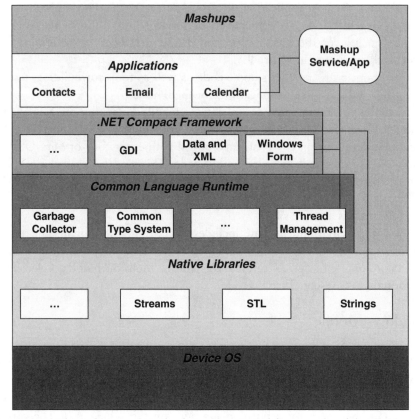

Figure 9.6   *The architectural stack of components and frameworks of the Windows Mobile platform*

Visual Studio is the typical development environment for Windows Mobile application and service development. Visual Studio includes the Windows Mobile SDKs and emulators.

The diagram in Figure 9.6 illustrates the architectural stack of components and frameworks of the Windows Mobile platform.

As shown in Figure 9.6 the architectural stack of the Windows Mobile platform is abstracted in several layers allowing development to target specific functionality to meet the needs of each application or service.

Java J2ME

Java 2 Micro Edition (J2ME or Java ME) is an environment for running applications on mobile devices and embedded devices. Java ME includes support for standard network protocols and for building secure, graphical applications that can be installed to a device on demand. Applications built with Java ME can be installed and executed on many different devices.

Java ME technologies are designed to operate within environments that have limited display space, memory, and capacity for power. The Java ME development platform provides a set of technologies and standards specifically created for building applications and services to operate on such devices.

The Java ME platform directs application development towards building on a configuration layer providing a virtual machine with a core set of libraries, a profile layer providing more specific APIs, and an application layer providing more specific APIs.

The diagram in Figure 9.7 illustrates the architectural stack of components and frameworks of the Java ME platform.

As shown in Figure 9.7 the architectural stack of the Java ME platform is abstracted in several layers that allow an application, service, or mashup to take advantage of each layer as needed.

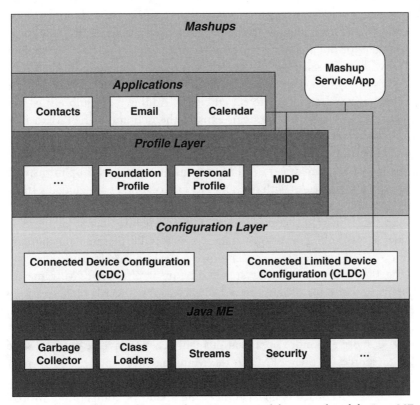

Figure 9.7 *The architectural stack of components and frameworks of the Java ME platform*

The Connected Limited Device Configuration (CLDC) shown in Figure 9.7 is provided for building applications for small, limited devices, and the Connected Device Configuration (CDC) shown in Figure 9.7 is provided for building applications on more powerful devices.

Business Process Management for Mashups

Business process management (BPM) typically defines a set of processes that direct organizations towards optimizing business execution. BPM helps to analyze, organize, and automate business processes, practices, and systems towards success.

Current business operations must be ready to deal with multiple standards, increased automation, and more complex technologies delivering large assortments of data from disparate sources. BPM deals with integration of data from these disparate sources using various access mechanisms where the data can then be analyzed and operated on. Adding service-oriented techniques based on semantically rich technologies to this data-intensive atmosphere creates a prime environment for building data and process-driven mashups. The very definition of BPM within this setting might even be considered a mashup by itself.

BPM typically exposes key performance indicators (KPIs) that organizations use to manage and monitor project efficiency. Adding a mashup infrastructure to today's BPM state of affairs can expand the definition of BPM to include processes that were prohibitive in the past.

Many mashups already facilitate ad hoc integration practices with data sources, processes, and systems. BPM systems built on a mashup infrastructure can direct these processes with tools and technologies that are guided within the constraints and governance rules for a given industry or organization.

Figure 9.8 illustrates how a mashup infrastructure might facilitate BPM activities across an organization's many systems and disparate data sources.

Figure 9.8 illustrates how an enterprise mashup infrastructure can act to bind together data sources and systems to create an effective BPM framework.

Enterprise mashups promise to aid BPM systems towards orchestrating systems and processes by integrating data and services with semantic technologies and interactive tools. As modern security standards are embraced across the enterprise, more and more organizations will begin to involve external services and data sources in their BPM efforts. Mapping sites will be used to provide location-specific content to BPM dashboards. RSS feeds can be accessed to provide up-to-date feedback from customers and about the competition. More uses will be found on an exponential basis as aggregate services emerge.

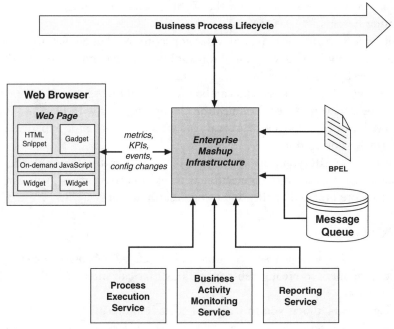

Figure 9.8 *Business process management operating within an enterprise mashup infrastructure*

Desktop/Web Hybrid Mashups

While mashups are conventionally thought of in terms of a web browser, other environments are starting to appear. Mobile phones, talked about earlier, are ripe for mashup applications. The desktop is another area that mashups will surely begin to play.

The following sections discuss some of the technologies and platforms available for building applications that lend themselves to a mashup application development environment for the desktop.

Adobe AIR

Adobe AIR is a runtime environment that includes the open source web browser engine, WebKit, and the Adobe Flash engine. This environment enables developers to use web technologies such as HTML, JavaScript, Flash, or Flex to build rich Internet applications that run on the desktop.

The Adobe AIR runtime provides AJAX technologies to allow AJAX developers to build rich Internet applications (RIAs) that can be delivered with a single installation file to execute within the WebKit browser engine across multiple operating systems.

Adobe AIR's runtime also allows developers to use Adobe Flex to use existing tools and code to build rich desktop applications that expand on the experience of a web browser by adding access to local resources.

Adobe Flash CS3 Professional can be used to build RIAs that execute within the Adobe AIR runtime environment on the desktop. As with Flex and Adobe AIR, Flash can be used to access local resources to enhance the experience of a web browser application.

With Adobe AIR, you can expand your mashup infrastructure to the desktop to establish a more direct connection with existing customers. You can also deliver a more branded application using desktop features.

Google Gears

Google Gears is an open source project that acts as a browser extension to enable developers to create web applications that can interact with a desktop via JavaScript APIs.

Google Gears allows you to store and access data locally from within a web browser. A local server that acts as a mechanism to serve cached web resources is provided by Google Gears as well as a worker-thread pool that enables background processing. A geolocation API is also provided by Google Gears to provide access to the geographical location of the host device.

The underlying security model of Google Gears is based on the same-origin policy to restrict a Gears application to accessing resources based on a given scheme, host, and port. This security model constrains a Gears application to storing and accessing data within a database created for a given site's origin.

Windows Gadgets

Windows Gadgets are small programs that are installed and executed in a Windows environment. Windows Gadgets can execute in undocked mode or docked within the context of a Windows Sidebar. Windows Sidebar is a tool provided by the Vista operating system as a means to organize gadgets.

Gadgets enable developers to write mini applications using web technologies such as HTML and JavaScript to receive notifications, access web resources, show photo albums, and perform other tasks.

Windows Gadgets installed on a given Windows system can be selected from a palette and placed on the Windows Sidebar in drag-and-drop fashion.

Summary

Mashup environments offer enterprises powerful opportunities and tools for integrating data and systems in daily business operations. Using this power and functionality intelligently as a tool for integration can be cost effective for an organization. Exploiting the agile and dynamic nature of a mashup infrastructure to achieve strategic objectives can increase ROI and prove to be profitable for an organization over time. A mashup infrastructure enables an organization to realize reduced development and maintenance costs for applications and systems. A mashup environment enables services and applications to be created by business-savvy users who may lack low-level technical skills. Mashup artifacts such as widgets, semantic data, and business services can be reused by business users and domain experts within an organization as well as by strategic partners.

Enterprise mashups are proving useful in many everyday business situations. In this chapter I discussed some of the trends that enterprise mashups are likely to follow as well as some of the scenarios in which mashups are currently being used, such as social networks, and some in which mashups are likely to emerge, such as mobile devices.

This book discussed some of the concepts of mashups as applied to an enterprise environment. Discussions throughout the book expanded on these concepts to guide you through the design and implementation of enterprise mashups and enterprise mashup infrastructures.

Appendix

Mashup Servers, Technologies, APIs, and Tools

Tools and APIs for mashups are emerging at an astounding rate. Most programming languages are being supported in some form in the mashup arena.

The following sections discuss some of the current servers, technologies, APIs, and editors available today for mashup development and deployment.

Mashup Servers

The definition of a mashup server can mean different things depending on the context. A server can be deemed a mashup server simply by offering an environment in which UI artifacts can be combined to form aggregate user interfaces. See Chapter 1 for a more complete definition of a mashup server.

Mashup servers in this context are technologies offering an environment that enables users to build mashup applications, services, and artifacts from disparate data sources and service providers.

The following discusses some of the more prominent mashup server environments available at the time of this writing.

Presto Mashup Server

The Presto Mashup Server (http://www.jackbe.com) is an enterprise mashup server that provides users with access to disparate data from such sources as internal and external services and relational databases.

Presto's Mashup Server converts services into "virtual services" that are mashup-ready and easy for end users to use in mashup applications. While providing access to these virtual services, the Presto Mashup Server also attempts to allow IT to govern, secure, and manage enterprise infrastructure and data assets.

Specifically, features reportedly enabled by Presto Server's service virtualization include

- **Easy information access**—The Presto Mashup Server is touted as empowering business users with easy access to vital information.

- **Real-time decision making**—The server attempts to help users locate, access, and integrate data according to changing business needs.

- **Collaboration and information sharing**—Sharing of mashups through trusted collaboration between users and partners is another primary feature exposed.

- **Governance and security**—Presto's server seeks to ensure that mashups meet enterprise governance and security requirements.

The Presto Mashup Server attempts to shift control of the business use of IT assets towards business experts while maintaining centralized governance of the assets.

All the Presto mashup products are enabled with the Enterprise Mashup Markup Language (EMML). EMML is a JackBe-specific, XML-based domain specific language intended for creating mashup applications and artifacts.

Presto Mashup Server relies on three implementation environments:

- Presto Mashlets enable mashup building using widgets. Once a mashlet is created it can be used anywhere typical widgets are used, including a desktop.

- Presto Wires, a web browser-based visual mashup composition tool allows users to consume and combine data from disparate data sources.

- Presto Mashup Studio is an Eclipse plug-in that enables Java programmers to design, test, debug, and deploy mashups. Developers use Presto Studio to write mashups with EMML and debug using Eclipse.

WSO2 Mashup Server

The WSO2 Mashup Server (http://wso2.org/projects/mashup) is a mashup platform for creating, deploying, and consuming mashup applications and services. The WSO2 Mashup Server provides support for

- Consuming and deploying services using dynamic scripting languages

- Simple deployment and redeployment; automatic and UI-based generation of web services artifacts (for example, WSDL, schema, policy)

- A set of gateways into a variety of information sources, including SOAP and POX/REST web services, and web pages

- Easily orchestrated UI artifacts via a variety of user interfaces including web pages, portals, email, Instant Messenger service, and Short Message Service (SMS)

The WSO2 Mashup Server lists the following features:

- Hosting of mashup services written using JavaScript with E4X XML extension

- Simple file-based deployment model

- JavaScript annotations to configure deployed services

- Autogeneration of metadata and runtime resources for deployed mashups

- JavaScript stubs that enable client access to the mashup service

- TryIt feature to invoke the mashup service through a web browser

- WSDL 1.1/WSDL 2.0/XSD documents to describe mashup services

- Ability to provide a custom user interface for mashups

- Many JavaScript Host objects that can be used when writing mashups, including:

  o **WSRequest**—Invokes web services from mashup services

  o **File**—File storage/manipulation functionality

  o **System**—A set of system specific utility functions

  o **Session**—Provides the ability to share objects across different service invocations

  o **Scraper**—Enables extracting data from HTML pages and presenting in XML format

  o **APPClient**—Atom Publishing Protocol client to retrieve/publish Atom feeds with APP servers

  o **Feed**—A generic set of host objects to read Atom and RSS feeds

- Support for recurring and longer running tasks

- Management console to manage mashups

- Sharing of deployed mashups with other WSO2 Mashup Servers

- Mashup sharing community portal (http://mashups.wso2.org) to share and host your mashups

The WSO2 Mashup Server supports the creation of web services written in JavaScript. The Mashup Server takes JavaScript files, placed in a local directory, and exposes the functions as web service operations. Web services can also be created using a provided wizard.

Kapow Mashup Server

The Kapow (http://www.kapowtech.com) product offering falls into two sub-scription-based categories: on-demand and on-premise. Determining which product fits your needs depends largely on the type of issues you are dealing with, what data sources you need to integrate with, and what the target application is for the data that you collect.

The following sections discuss the Kapow offerings.

On-Demand Service

Kapow OnDemand is a web-hosted, subscription-based service that enables automated collection of web-based information and data. The web content that you harvest can be integrated into existing applications and/or infrastructures.

This service is particularly well-suited for business experts who have a need to integrate web-based data into business processes and analyses in real-time. Using the Kapow Connector for Excel, web data can be collected and integrated, on-demand into a spreadsheet.

Kapow OnDemand provides ancillary utilities, which includes a Kapow-specific, Robot Development Environment to construct custom feeds and services, a role-based execution runtime, and an environment to monitor and manage your portfolio of services and feeds.

On-Premise Enterprise Server Environment

There are several editions of the Kapow Mashup Server, each of which is designed to support a different style of web data harvesting and use. However, all editions of the Kapow Mashup Server provide the same environment for execution, management, and monitoring of users' service robots.

Offerings other than the hosted Kapow OnDemand product are collectively referred to as Enterprise products. Enterprise products are installed and managed by Kapow customers at the customers' sites. The Enterprise Server environment supports multiple user communities and is typically installed on a single server.

A Kapow Enterprise Server can be configured as a stand-alone execution environment, or as multiple concurrent robot execution instances.

The following is a breakdown of the Kapow Enterprise Server editions:

- **Data Collection Edition**—Allows you to access multiple data types, using a visual scripting environment. Web content and data collected can then be written to a database, published as a web service, or transformed for use by other applications. Java and C# APIs are provided to drive the execution of robots.

- **Web 2.0 Edition**—Allows you to create an RSS feed from ordinary web sites and to add the feed to an RSS reader.

- **Portal Content Edition**—A development environment that interacts with portals via the web interface. This edition does not require a proprietary portlet development container or environment.

Control Center

Management and monitoring of a Kapow Enterprise Server are facilitated by the Kapow Control Center, which provides the following capabilities:

- Monitoring and stopping the robot execution environment

- Starting, stopping, and monitoring of one or more robots

- Performing various administrative tasks and gathering of runtime performance statistics

The Kapow Control Center allows you to monitor components and other resources running on a server, manage performance bottlenecks, and start or stop robot instances.

Robot Development Environment

The robot development environment for Kapow Enterprise products allows robots to be designed using a visual scripting model. The robot designer enables you to build robots that automatically harvest web content delivered to a desktop or application.

The robot development environment in the Enterprise products supports a wider range of styles of web harvesting and different ways to use the data once it's been harvested.

Examples of product-specific additional functionality supported in the robot development environment for Enterprise products include the following:

- Ability to clip one or more partial or full pages to harvest content that can be deployed as a portlet to portal servers such as IBM, BEA, and Oracle

- Directly read and write to SQL databases

- APIs for invoking robots as SOAP services from Java or .NET applications

- Creation of complex name/value pair data models and the ability to create composite data objects by combining data harvested from databases and other web data sources

While robots used in the OnDemand product can be designed by less technical individuals, robots designed for use with the Enterprise product typically require an individual with a more technical level of skills.

Choosing a Kapow Product
Table A.1 shows a comparison of Kapow products.

Table A.1 *Kapow Product Comparison*

	Portal Content Edition	Data Collection Edition	Web 2.0 Edition	Kapow OnDemand
Data sources	Public or private web	Public or private web, internal databases	Public or private web	Public web
Data consumers	Portals	Databases, web applications, Java & .NET tools, mashup modelers	Excel, web applications, mashup modelers	Excel, web applications, mashup modelers
Portal consolidation/ extension	X			
Mobile enablement	X	X		
Harvesting to a database		X		
Large-scale batch collection		X		
Desktop web harvesting to Excel			X	X
Syndicating data as a service			X	X
Data or content migration		X		
Hosting environment	On-premise	On-premise	On-premise	Kapow hosted

Table A.1 *Kapow Product Comparison (Continued)*

	Portal Content Edition	Data Collection Edition	Web 2.0 Edition	Kapow OnDemand
Software infrastructure & administration	Customer provided runtime environment	Customer provided runtime environment	Customer provided runtime environment	Kapow provided (failover, backup, restore, restart, web UI)
Data model complexity	This is a web clipping product. Data models not applicable.	Very complex data modeling. No limitation on number of name/value pairs.	Moderately complex data modeling. Limit of 25 name/value pairs.	Moderately complex data modeling. Limit of 25 name/value pairs.
Robot types	Clipping, integration	Data collection, integration	REST/RSS/Atom	REST/RSS/Atom
APIs supported	HTTP(S)	Java, .NET, SOAP, HTTP(S)	HTTP(S)	HTTP(S)
Robot execution styles	Real-time	Batch or real-time	Real-time	Real-time

Noting the preceding product comparison, the OnDemand service is the applicable choice when you need to collect data from the public web on a real-time basis that you intend to integrate directly into environments and applications capable of consuming XML. This is also the right choice for organizations that have limited IT proficiency and infrastructure and want to focus on the harvesting of web data without having to deal with the implementation and maintenance of an underlying software infrastructure.

Enterprise Products are a better choice when you're collecting large volumes of data from the web that is to be written to a database, published to a portal, or combined with other data sources.

Mashup Technologies and Techniques

Mashup development encompasses a wide range of languages, data formats, techniques, and technologies. The following sections discuss some of the most used within the current mashup arena.

HTML/XHTML

XHTML (eXtensible HyperText Markup Language) is a standard introduced in 2000 to form an integration of XML and HTML. XHTML embodies a web development language with a stricter set of constraints than traditional HTML.

An XHTML document must be structured as a well-formed XML document. This means that the document must have one and only one root element (the <html> element), and all elements within an XHTML document must be closed, named with all lowercase characters, and properly nested. All attributes within the document must be in lowercase as well. An XHTML document must have a <!DOCTYPE ...> declaration.

The example in Listing A.1 illustrates a simple, valid XHTML document.

Listing A.1   *A Simple XHTML Document*

```
<!DOCTYPE html
PUBLIC "-//W3C//DTD XHTML 1.0 Transitional//EN"
"http://www.w3.org/TR/xhtml1/DTD/xhtml1-transitional.dtd">
<html>
  <head>
    <title>Hello World</title>
  </head>
  <body>
    <p>Hello world!</p>
  </body>
</html>
```

The example in Listing A.1 is a typical HTML document. However, it is also a valid XHTML document since the DOCTYPE declaration is present and all elements are closed, as shown.

The importance of XHTML to a mashup environment is seen most significantly in the XHTML extension model defined by the XHTML Modularization specification. The XHTML Modularization specification provides definitions for such things as forms modules, iframe modules, scripting modules, and others. This enables efficient use of profiles to create subsets of XHTML for such things as mobile devices and semantically robust web pages and applications.

XML

XML is a general-purpose markup language for representing data. Data formatted as XML is easy for humans to read and understand. XML data is easy to transform into other formats using tools available in nearly every programming language. XML supports schema-based validation and is supported by many formal enterprise data format standards. Internationalization is supported explicitly with XML, and XML is platform and language independent and extensible.

XML is strictly a data markup specification and is verbose. It does not seek to integrate with any one programming language intrinsically via support for primitives, arrays, objects, and so on. Therefore, a distinctly separate process typically occurs between serializing XML data to and from the programming language.

XML is great for describing data in a human-readable manner and is a great format for serializing and transporting entire documents, and many specifications for business have mandated some dialect of XML as the payload format. Since XML was gaining such popularity as a universal document model, it seemed natural to design serialization techniques and technologies for it. XML begins to approach semantic meaning within data and documents using namespace context and metadata. For XML data to effectively embody semantic meaning, additional context must be applied in the form of such technologies as XSLT.

Even though XML is great for applying semantics to data and documents, it is not easily applied to programming language constructs. Mashups deal with data in smaller chunks, primarily from scripting languages running in a browser, and as such, XML was found to be a difficult fit at times.

Plain old XML (POX) is the name often given to XML when referring to it as a data-serialization format. POX was the original data format for which AJAX was developed. However, it was soon discovered that there was a need to reduce the size of payloads transported from browser to server and back. It was also apparent that more efficient techniques were needed to integrate payload data with scripting languages. JSON was developed to meet this need and is gaining widespread use and popularity.

AJAX

Asynchronous JavaScript and XML (AJAX) is a set of technologies and techniques that enable two primary web development functions: handling client/server requests and responses from within a browser page and manipulating the browser DOM to create dynamic user interfaces with a responsive look-and-feel, such as updating a UI artifact on a web page without refreshing the entire page.

AJAX is built on an HTTP communication mechanism from browser-to-server and back again that operates outside the normal user-instigated request/response process. This ability coupled with dynamic DOM manipulation techniques enables you to build richer web pages than traditional methods because it allows you to place a higher degree of application logic in the web page.

AJAX techniques enable a UI experience that can be much more responsive than typical HTML. However, AJAX presents a number of advantages and disadvantages for which you must be prepared.

Following are some advantages of using AJAX:

- Enables a communication model with a server using XML as the primary payload.

- Enables a more responsive UI due to being able to process small units of data at a time.

- Content can be retrieved via multiple connections, thereby possibly speeding up the retrieval process.

- Parts of a page can be updated in isolation to other parts, thereby reducing entire page problems due to an error in one section of the page.

- Bandwidth usage can be decreased since only small chunks of data from specific parts of a page can be transferred at any given time.

Following are some disadvantages of using AJAX:

- AJAX frameworks, technologies, and techniques are not yet as mature as traditional methods.

- Browser support for AJAX is not quite as secure as traditional methods.

- AJAX requires a more technical programming mindset than traditional web development methods, thereby raising personnel costs and reducing the size of the possible talent pool.

- The AJAX UI model conflicts with the browser's random Back button and Forward button navigation style, often leading to a confused user experience.

- Since AJAX depends on dynamic data retrieval and UI construction, search engines cannot process the content as effectively.

- The XMLHttpRequest object that AJAX depends on for its browser-to-server communication is subject to the browser security sandbox. Therefore, communication to a host other than the originating host is restricted.

- AJAX typically uses DOM-manipulation techniques to create dynamic UI effects. Although DOM-manipulation is becoming more consistent across browsers, there are still inconsistencies. You must be sure that the techniques you use in your mashup are consistent across all your targeted client execution environments.

- Request and response messages passing between client and server via the XMLHttpRequest object are obtained using different JavaScript methods depending on whether the browser is Microsoft-based (Internet Explorer). However, most AJAX libraries address this difference already.

- The use of the XMLHttpRequest object implies the need for JavaScript being enabled by the client execution environment. While this is generally the case, some execution environments and/or companies do not or will not allow JavaScript. Also, some search engine technologies will not pick up content semantics effectively if they are embedded within JavaScript code.

- The dynamic UI effects created by the use of DOM manipulation techniques can also wreak havoc on bookmarking and use of the Back or Forward button in a web browser. One of the effects enjoyed by the use of AJAX is a more desktop-like look-and-feel. However, the fundamental paradigm of the web browser is to allow unstructured browsing with the ability to go forward and backward with regards to your browsing history. Browsing history and AJAX execution history are usually unsynchronized, leading to confused users if not handled effectively.

- Since AJAX can execute requests asynchronously in the background, it is important to keep the user engaged and updated as background processes execute. This typically involves the use of UI controls such as progress bars and status dialogs to inform the user of the progress of these processes.

Even though the AJAX disadvantages in the preceding list are more numerous than the advantages, each advantage can be vitally important to an organization and, therefore, outweigh all the disadvantages on its own. For example, a UI that is more responsive and mimics a desktop application can mean the difference between success and failure for a site.

Screen Scraping

Screen scraping is the process of manually parsing the content of a site page, extracting the desired data from the page, and applying the data to your page or process. Once the data has been parsed and extracted, it is refactored into data structures that fit the semantics of your business and development environment. An example would be a mashup that uses publicly available data from government sites in concert with geographical or geopolitical data to create a site exposing high crime areas or to show trends in housing prices.

Screen scraping is usually used on a temporary basis, since there is no contract relating to programmatic access in place to ensure the prolonged consistency of the site. As a result, it is a fragile mechanism and must be constantly monitored to address changes that are bound to occur in the structure and/or availability of the page or site.

REST

REST (Representational State Transfer) is a model for interaction with resources based on a common, finite set of methods. For the HTTP protocol, this is embodied by the methods GET, POST, PUT, DELETE, and sometimes HEAD. In a REST-based application or interaction, resources are identified by a URI. The response for REST-based invocation is referred to as a representation of the resource.

REST is often realized using HTTP methods in the following manner:

1. Create the resource (PUT).

2. Retrieve a representation of the resource (GET).

3. Delete the resource (DELETE); modify the resource (POST).

4. Retrieve metadata about the resource (HEAD).

A resource in REST is regarded as any entity that can be directly referenced with a URI. Using this definition, anything that can be retrieved using a URI can be considered a resource. What an underlying infrastructure does to create the resource representation is of no concern to the resource consumer as long as the interface depicts a discrete and concrete chunk of data.

RDF

The Resource Description Framework (RDF) standard is built on the notion that all resources are to be referenced using URIs. RDF also attempts to promote semantic meaning to data. This idea is central to the mashup environment, where data is a collection of loosely coupled resources. With respect to this knowledge, RDF makes a great fit as a universal data model for the data layer of your mashup infrastructure.

RDF describes data as a graph of semantically related sets of resources. RDF describes data as subject-predicate-object triples, where a resource is the subject and the object shares some relation to the subject. The predicate uses properties in the form of links to describe the relationship between the subject and object. This interconnecting network of resources and links forms the graph of data that RDF seeks to define.

Using URIs to expose access to your resources and using RDF to create the graph of relationships between resources makes RDF a natural choice for a universal data format.

RSS and Atom

RSS and Atom are XML-based data formats for representing web feeds such as blogs and podcasts. RSS and Atom are ideally suited for representing data that can be categorized and described using channels, titles, items, and resource links. An RSS or Atom document contains descriptive information about a feed such as a summary, a description, the author, and the published date.

The same disadvantages are shared with RSS, Atom, and XML. RSS and Atom are primarily focused on representing resources and feed data. However, both formats are being adopted for more general purpose needs. RSS and Atom address semantic meaning by describing resources and other entities using standard tags that explicitly define the purpose of each particular element, for example, title, creator, and published date.

Feed readers that consume RSS and Atom are used to enable a model in which users subscribe to feeds/blogs that will be periodically queried by the readers. The readers then display a brief summary of the feed/blog content to the user. This makes an effective means for receiving updates for content of interest to a user.

Mashups often use RSS feed data as content and as a means for obtaining summary information about a given topic or entity to add value to the content. This process requires the ability to parse the feed data using XML-parsing code, often in JavaScript. Mashups also embed RSS and Atom readers in the page as a widget, gadget, badge, or other small component.

RSS is a good format for representing simple, categorized, dated textual data. RSS data is easily consumable using standard XML tools. Also, many specific RSS libraries and tools are available in most programming languages.

RSS has a number of benefits including the ability to aggregate content easily from multiple RSS data sources.

JSON

JSON (JavaScript Object Notation) is a JavaScript data format that is a subset of the JavaScript programming language and offers the advantage of easy accessibility and parsing from within a JavaScript environment. JSON supports a limited number of simple primitive types allowing complex data structures to be represented and consumed easily from standard programming languages.

Namespaces and schema-based validation are not supported by JSON, and JSON is not accepted by nearly as many formal enterprise data format standards as XML. JSON is a semantically challenged approach to data exchange, relying on tight couplings between data producer and data consumer to form an understanding of the data. However, where JSON lacks in semantic richness, it makes up for it in data terseness.

One can embody simple data structures with a limited set of primitives using JSON. Objects can also be represented with JSON as associative arrays.

JSON supports a limited number of simple primitive types allowing complex data structures to be represented and consumed easily from standard programming languages.

On-Demand JavaScript

On-demand JavaScript is a technique in which a <script> tag and its accompanying JavaScript source are embedded in an HTML page. When the <script> tag is encountered, it is evaluated, and the JavaScript source is executed. This mechanism is typically exploited by mashups by retrieving <script> snippets from a server after the page has been loaded, thereby only updating the portion of the page affected by the JavaScript source.

One reason for using on-demand JavaScript is to bypass the same-origin policy and retrieve content from multiple sites.

Listing A.2 illustrates an example of three instances of on-demand JavaScript embedded in an HTML page.

Listing A.2 *JavaScript Include Examples*
```
<html>
  <head>
    ...
  </head>
  <body>
    <script type="text/javascript" src="snippet1.js"></script>
    <script type="text/javascript" src="snippet2.js"></script>
    <script type="text/javascript" src="snippet3.js"></script>
  </body>
</html>
```

In this example, all three instances will be evaluated and executed when the HTML page is loaded.

On-demand JavaScript is often employed using AJAX and calls to a server via the XMLHttpRequest object. In this scenario, a response from the server is formatted as JavaScript. When the browser receives the response, it evaluates it, and the JavaScript is executed. Any actions specified in the JavaScript affecting UI components are seen as the JavaScript is executed.

Flash

Like AJAX, Flash objects can offer similar functionality in that once downloaded they can communicate asynchronously with a server. Consequently, YouTube videos can begin playing before the whole movie has been received: The user downloads a compact flash object, which downloads a small prefix of the video and begins playing it out while asynchronously fetching the remainder of the video. Supporting Flash requires an appropriate Adobe plug-in to be installed, although user penetration of this plug-in is more than 90%.

Toolkits exist allowing Internet applications to be written in a high level language and then rendered either as Flash objects or pages with AJAX components, meaning that it may be helpful to sometimes think of Flash and AJAX merely as object code. AJAX apps are typically easier for the researcher to reverse-engineer and understand for measurement purposes than the Shockwave Flash (SWF) format. Currently, Flash is mostly used for rendering rich embedded objects (video, audio, games): Few entire applications that store and recall data are implemented in Flash.

Widgets and Gadgets

Widgets are small UI components such as snippets of HTML, dynamic Java-Script, and embeddable widgets accessed from various sites. Metadata describing widgets and other UI components are stored within a repository or catalog of a mashup administration framework. The metadata can then be queried and accessed by mashup tools and developers to compose and orchestrate mashup pages and applications.

Mashup APIs

Many APIs are emerging from which mashups are being constructed. Many social sites use mashup techniques as models for their API offerings.

The following sections define some of the most prominent APIs in use for mashup development today.

OpenSocial API

OpenSocial presents a unified API for building social applications with services and artifacts served from multiple sites. The OpenSocial API relies on standard JavaScript and HTML as the platform languages developers can use to create applications and services that interconnect common social connections.

An extensive community of development partners is developing OpenSocial. This community partnership is leading to a platform that exposes a common framework by which sites can become socially enabled. Some of the sites currently supporting OpenSocial include iGoogle, Friendster, LinkedIn, MySpace, Ning, Plaxo, Salesforce.com, and others.

Functionality and content for OpenSocial are presented as Google Gadgets. This allows developers to exploit the toolset that Google presents for building and deploying gadgets, such as the Google Gadget Editor, XML-based user preferences, the Google remote content retrieval API, and the gadget sandbox.

Facebook APIs

Facebook exposes an API that embodies a platform for building applications that execute in the Facebook web site environment for members of the Facebook social network. The Facebook API permits applications to use the connections and profile data for Facebook users. This information enables application developers to build applications that are, in context with the Facebook platform, socially aware. The Facebook API enables applications to use profile information and connections as a conduit for publishing to Facebook news feeds and Facebook profile pages. Access to an individual's profile information and connections is contingent on the approval of a profile owner's permission specified in the individual's privacy settings.

Facebook relies on an API key and application secret key to identify an application to Facebook and to authenticate requests made within the Facebook environment.

Amazon Associates Web Service APIs

Amazon Associates Web Service facilitates access to Amazon's databases allowing developers to take advantage of Amazon's powerful e-commerce content and functionality. This enables you to build your own web store to sell items from Amazon or from your own store.

Amazon Associates Web Service provides the following primary features:

- **Product catalog**—Provides access to Amazon's product database

- **Customer and seller reviews**—Provides access to Amazon's customer and seller review database

- **Product images**—Allows you to display product images used on www.amazon.com

- **Latest offerings**—Allows access to the latest Amazon offerings, including digital media

Flickr APIs

The API exposed by Flickr consists of a group of methods and API endpoints. To execute functionality using the Flickr API, you need to select a request format (REST, XML-RPC, or SOAP), send a request to an endpoint specifying a method and arguments, and handle the formatted response.

All Flickr API request formats take a list of named parameters including method, api_key, and format.

The Flickr API methods encompass CRUD-styled (create, read, update, and delete) functionality for accessing and manipulating such things as user photos, authentication, blogs, contacts, favorites, groups, and others.

Available Flickr API response formats are REST (simple XML), XML-RPC, SOAP, JSON, and PHP serialized format.

Flickr API kits are available from third parties for many different languages including ActionScript, C, Java, .NET, Perl, PHP, Python, and Ruby.

eBay APIs

eBay provides a number of APIs to interact with its product and service offerings. The following briefly discusses each API:

- **eBay API**—Enables you to communicate directly with the eBay database in XML format. By using the API, an application can provide a custom interface, custom functionality, and other custom operations. Using the API, you can create programs that

  - Submit items for listing on eBay.

  - Get the current list of eBay categories.

  - View information about items listed on eBay.

  - Get high bidder information for items you are selling.

  - Retrieve lists of items a particular user is currently selling through eBay.

  - Retrieve lists of items a particular user has bid on.

  - Display eBay listings on other sites.

  - Leave feedback about other users at the conclusion of a commerce transaction.

- **eBay Shopping API**—Makes it easy to search for things on eBay.

- **eBay Merchandising API**—Provides item and product recommendations that can be used to cross-sell and up-sell eBay items to buyers.

- **eBay Trading API**—Provides web service access to the eBay marketplace. It enables third-party applications to build custom applications, tools, and services that leverage the eBay marketplace.

- **eBay Client Alerts API**—Makes it easy to receive near real-time seller and buyer alerts about events on the eBay site.

- **eBay Platform Notifications**—Allows an application to request that eBay send notifications to URLs or email addresses. Notifications are triggered by events such as the ending of a listing or the creation of a transaction.

- **Research API for eBay**—An API provided by a third party that allows an application to retrieve historical eBay data.

Libraries for the eBay APIs are available for .NET, C#, ASP, VB, Java JSP, PHP, Perl, Python, JavaScript, and Flash.

YouTube APIs

The YouTube APIs and tools enable you to integrate YouTube's video content and functionality into your web site, software application, or device.

Data API

The Data API lets you incorporate YouTube functionality into your own application or web site. The Data API allows a program to perform a large subset of the operations available on the YouTube web site. This API makes it possible to search for videos and retrieve standard feeds. A program can also authenticate as a user to upload videos, modify user playlists, and more.

The Data API targets developers who are accustomed to programming in server-side languages. It is useful for developing sites or applications that have a need for a tighter integration with YouTube. This integration could be a web application that uploads videos to YouTube or a device or application that embeds YouTube functionality inside another platform or application. The Data API gives you programmatic access to videos and user information residing on the YouTube web site. This allows you to personalize your site or application with the YouTube user's information as well as perform actions on their behalf, providing you have the needed authorization.

YouTube provides a group of client libraries that abstract the API into language-specific object models.

Player APIs

The YouTube Player APIs allow you to control YouTube video playback on your web site. The API allows you to configure settings, drive the player's interface, or build your own player controls.

The YouTube player APIs let you control how YouTube videos look. There are two kinds of YouTube players:

- **Embedded player**—Can be customized and annotated with controls that allow you to configure the player to find videos, show playlists, listen for events, pause videos, and perform other functions.

- **Chromeless player**—A video container without controls. The chromeless player is intended for developers who want to design their own video player. Both players have the same JavaScript and ActionScript APIs.

Widgets

Widgets are UI artifacts you can embed in your web site to give it YouTube functionality. YouTube widgets are JavaScript components that you can place in a web page to enhance it with YouTube's content. Widgets are well-suited for users who are familiar with HTML and JavaScript, but may not be skilled at server-side programming. Currently, YouTube offers two widgets:

- **Video Bar**—Allows you to add a strip of video thumbnails to a site. After clicking on a thumbnail in the widget, a floating player opens to play the video on your site. YouTube offers a wizard to get you started and a programming guide to help you along the way.

- **Video Search Control**—Allows you to use the Google AJAX Search API to search through YouTube's content. The widget presents a search box that is preconfigured with a set of tags defined by you. The search box also displays thumbnails for the video results. These videos can then be played on the same page.

Mashup Editors

A number of powerful mashup editor environments are available in which data and UI artifacts can be integrated (see http://blogs.zdnet.com/Hinchcliffe/?p=174).

The following sections discuss some of the more prominent mashup editor environments currently available.

Yahoo! Pipes

Yahoo! Pipes (http://pipes.yahoo.com/pipes/) is a mashup composition environment presented as a free online service that allows you to integrate RSS and Atom feeds and create data mashups in a visual editor without writing code. Yahoo! Pipes can be used to aggregate, manipulate, and integrate content from the web.

Simple data and feed sources can be combined via commands in a manner similar to using UNIX pipes to create filtered and transformed results. Here are a few ways Yahoo! Pipes can be used:

- Create a custom feed by combining many feeds into one and then sorting, filtering, and translating them.

- Geocode feeds and browse the items on an interactive map.

- Remix data sources and use the Pipe to power a new application.

- Build custom vertical search pages.

- Power widgets/badges on a web site.

- Consume the output of any Pipe as RSS, JSON, KML, and other formats.

You can use Pipes to create web projects or publish web services without writing any actual code. You make a Pipe by dragging preconfigured modules onto the Pipe editor's canvas and wiring the modules together in the editor. Each Pipe consists of multiple modules, which perform a single, specific task. Each module has one or more input and output terminals, represented by small circles in the editor. You wire modules together by dragging a "wire" from one module to another module. Once the modules are wired together, the output from one module will serve as input to another module.

Yahoo! Pipes allows you to add user-input fields to connected modules in addition to data sources and feeds. User input fields are exposed at runtime as form fields in which users of the Pipe can enter data.

Google Mashup Editor

Google Mashup Editor is an AJAX-based development framework and environment that allows you to edit, compile, test, and manage mashup applications. Google Mashup Editor provides a set of tools that enable developers to create simple web applications and mashups with Google services such as Google Maps and Google Base.

Creating applications with Google Mashup Editor is enabled via declarative XML tags, JavaScript, CSS, and HTML. A proprietary JavaScript API is also available. The Google Mashup Editor allows you to create and deploy a mashup with one tool. Debugging is provided using JavaScript debugging tools such as Firebug.

Google Mashup Editor includes a built-in reference guide to all tags and attributes. You can publish a finished mashup application to Google's servers.

The primary components and functions of Google Mashup Editor are

- **Editing**—The editor is a browser-based text area that contains the main `<gm:page>` tags. You create an application by placing HTML, CSS, JavaScript, and GME tags between the `<gm:page>` tags. Any standard HTML, CSS, or JavaScript that can be placed between the `<body>` and `</body>` tags in an HTML document can go between the `<gm:page>` tags. Google Mashup Editor provides syntax checking and highlighting. When an application is compiled, all GME tags are transformed into JavaScript.

- **Testing**—A Test button is provided at the top of the Google Mashup Editor page to test an application.

- **Publishing**—When an application is ready to be published, you use the Publish Project menu item to deploy the application to Google's servers. When you publish your application, Google Mashup Editor presents to you a URL where your application is hosted. You can also deploy an application as a Google Gadget using the Submit Gadget option in Google Mashup Editor. This creates a Google Gadget and a gadget.xml file containing settings for the gadget. You can edit the gadget.xml file directly in the Editor.

- **Hosting**—Applications created with Google Mashup Editor are hosted by Google. The source code and uploaded resource files are stored using the open source project hosting feature of Google Code. When you start a new project, Google Mashup Editor creates a new, open source repository on Google Code to store the source files and other resources associated with the project. The source code is created under the Apache 2.0 open source license. You can change the license as you wish.

- **Project source control**—You can use the subversion repository on Google Code to control your source code updates. Projects are accessed in Google Code using the URL format: http://code.google.com/u/<your gmail username>. The page at this URL presents a list of your projects. You can then access any project listed to browse the files and change settings.

- **Ancillary files**—You can add existing ancillary resource files (HTML, XML, CSS, and so on) to an application in Google Mashup Editor and use the editor to edit the files.

Microsoft Popfly

Microsoft Popfly (http://www.popfly.com/) allows you to build and share mashups, gadgets, and web pages. Microsoft Popfly consists of online visual tools for building web pages and mashups and a social network where you can host, share, rate, comment, and use mashups from other Popfly users.

Popfly is based on Microsoft's Silverlight (http://www.microsoft.com/silverlight) platform and offers a web programming environment and social network so you can bring in new data sources, create new ways to display information, or create and share Visual Studio projects.

Popfly integrates JavaScript components known as "blocks." For presentation layer blocks, you can use AJAX, DHTML, or Silverlight (XAML). Blocks have defined input and output parameters and operations (methods) that are used to connect them between other blocks. Each block also has an XML metadata file that describes what the block does. You can find built-in tutorials on how to build blocks directly in Popfly.

Content supported by Popfly includes JavaScript, AJAX libraries, HTML, XHTML, CSS, WMV, WMA, MP3, Visual Studio Express projects, JPG, PNG, GIF, and EXEs.

IBM Mashup Starter Kit

IBM Mashup Starter Kit (http://www.alphaworks.ibm.com/tech/ibmmsk) is a Web 2.0-based mashup platform that enables access to web-based content and data that is then used to build mashup applications. IBM Mashup Starter Kit can combine information from databases, the web, and proprietary data sources.

IBM Mashup Starter Kit consists of two technologies: IBM Mashup Hub and QEDWiki. IBM Mashup Hub is a mashup server that stores data feeds such as in RSS and ATOM. Mashup Hub can also merge, transform, filter, annotate, or publish information in new formats. From there, QEDWiki serves as the user interface for building mashups from the published information.

Mashup Hub and QEDWiki are web applications that manage assets such as feeds, wiki pages, and user-specific and structured data. The user interfaces use the Dojo toolkit and the AreaEdit WYSIWYG editor; internally, the applications use REST, AJAX, and JSON.

DreamFace Interactive

DreamFace Interactive (http://www.dreamface-interactive.com/) is an Open Source AJAX Framework for creating Enterprise Web 2.0 applications and mashups. The DreamFace Interactive framework allows tech-savvy business-people to create, personalize, and share their own web applications through a concept known as "Web Channels." Web Channels are mini dynamic applications that incorporate DataWidgets, which use disparate data sources located on internal systems and the Internet to display information and interact with other DataWidgets.

Intel's Mash Maker

Intel's Mash Maker (http://mashmaker.intel.com/web/) is free browser extension that allows users to change web pages in place and remix them with information from different online sources. It works with Firefox and Internet Explorer.

Lotus Mashups

Lotus Mashups (http://www-306.ibm.com/software/lotus/products/mashups/) is an offering from IBM that builds on the concepts of the QEDWiki mashup tool to offer a lightweight mashup environment for building mashup applications by assembling disparate content and data. Lotus mashups uses a browser-based environment to assemble applications from widgets. You can also use

Lotus mashups to create your own reusable and shareable widgets and browse a centrally approved catalog of widget sources.

Summary

Numerous tools for building mashups are now available for nearly all popular programming languages. This appendix discussed some of the current servers, technologies, APIs, and editors available today for mashup development and deployment.

Index

Indispensable Patterns and Insights for Making Mashups Work in Production Environments

Mashup Patterns: Designs and Examples for the Modern Enterprise

by Michael Ogrinz

ISBN 978-0-321-57947-8 • © 2009

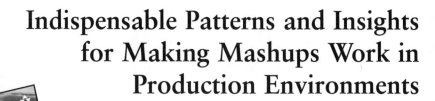

Design patterns for succeeding with enterprise mashups are one of today's fastest-growing areas of software development. This book

- Provides authoritative insights based on extensive real-world experience, from of the world's leading innovators in enterprise mashups and integration
- Covers every part of the mashup development lifecycle, from planning core functionality through integration, testing, and much more
- Includes six state-of-the-art, real-world case studies, plus a full chapter of must-avoid "anti-patterns"

With the recent explosion in mashup tools and technologies, developers can now "impose" their own APIs on everything from Web sites and RSS feeds to Excel spreadsheets and PDF documents. Rather than passively absorb content, they can transform the Web into their own private information source. However, there are right and wrong ways to build enterprise mashups. As in other areas of software development, what's needed are authoritative, reliable patterns. In this book, leading enterprise mashup expert Michael Ogrinz provides them.

Ogrinz's 50+ new patterns cover virtually every facet of enterprise mashup development, from core functionality through integration, and beyond. They address crucial issues such as data extraction and visualization, reputation management, security, accessibility, usability, content migration, load and regression testing, governance, and much more. Each pattern is documented with a practical description, specific use cases, and insights into the stability of mashups built with it.

informit.com/aw • informit.com/title/9780321579478
safari.informit.com • mashuppatterns.com

Go Beyond the Book

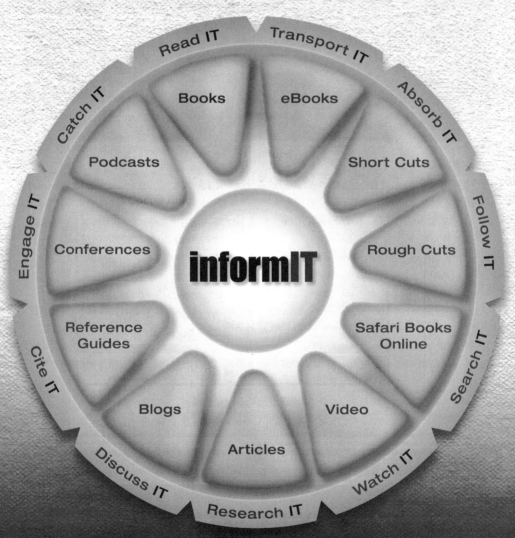

Read IT
Transport IT
Catch IT
Absorb IT
Engage IT
Follow IT
Cite IT
Search IT
Discuss IT
Watch IT
Research IT

Books
eBooks
Podcasts
Short Cuts
Conferences
informIT
Rough Cuts
Reference Guides
Safari Books Online
Blogs
Video
Articles

FREE Online Edition

Your purchase of **Mashups: Strategies for the Modern Enterprise** includes access to a free online edition for 45 days through the Safari Books Online subscription service. Nearly every Addison-Wesley Professional book is available online through Safari Books Online, along with more than 5,000 other technical books and videos from publishers such as Cisco Press, Exam Cram, IBM Press, O'Reilly, Prentice Hall, Que, and Sams.

SAFARI BOOKS ONLINE allows you to search for a specific answer, cut and paste code, download chapters, and stay current with emerging technologies.

Activate your FREE Online Edition at
www.informit.com/safarifree

> **STEP 1:** Enter the coupon code: JMCZYBI.

> **STEP 2:** New Safari users, complete the brief registration form.
> Safari subscribers, just log in.

If you have difficulty registering on Safari or accessing the online edition,
please e-mail customer-service@safaribooksonline.com